SPAIN IN AMERICA

THE NEW AMERICAN NATION SERIES

Edited by HENRY STEELE COMMAGER and
RICHARD B. MORRIS

* In preparation

SPAIN IN AMERICA

★

By CHARLES GIBSON

ILLUSTRATED

HARPER TORCHBOOKS ❧ The University Library
Harper & Row, Publishers
NEW YORK, EVANSTON, AND LONDON

SPAIN IN AMERICA

First HARPER TORCHBOOK edition published 1967 by Harper
& Row, Publishers, Incorporated, New York, N.Y. 10016.

Library of Congress Catalog Card Number: 66-21705.

Contents

Contents

Illustrations

*These illustrations, grouped in a separate section,
will be found following page 80.*

Maps

Editors' Introduction

HISTORIANS of North America have over the years debated the proposition that there is an essential unity in the Western hemisphere, that the Americans have a common history. From the days of Jefferson and the subsequent Monroe Doctrine down to the Alliance for Progress the notion that the Americas enjoy a community of interest which sets them apart from the Old World has experienced surprising vitality. While these debates have continued, historic tensions between Latin America and the United States, reaching fever point from time to time, serve to underscore basic differences. To the Latin American "colonialism" and "imperialism" too often serve as pejorative terms to explain their relationship to the people north of the Rio Grande.

These issues, so crucial to an understanding of historic trends in the Western hemisphere, are judiciously considered by Dr. Gibson. His searching, lucid, and scholarly exposition of the role of Spain in America and of developments in the Spanish lands of this hemisphere provides answers to questions long troubling North American readers. Dr. Gibson reminds us of the important elements which the Americas share in common, while not neglecting to inform us as well that their respective developments have taken distinctive and often diverse turnings. Subscribing to no mystic notion of New World unity, the author skillfully ties together many common threads. Both Latin and North America underwent a profound process of change when people from highly developed lands entered into vast and almost naked continents. The impact varied from place to place, but by one means or another the frontiers were pressed forward, the continents tamed, the aborigines subdued, removed, or exterminated, and elaborate colonial governmental structures subserving the interests of the respective mother countries introduced. Both Americas employed slavery and other forms of forced labor to run their economies. In both areas the enlightenment had a liberalizing impact. In Latin America it contributed in an indirect sense to the end of colonialism while its impact was more direct in the thirteen American colonies. Today copper, oil, sugar, coffee, bananas, among other products, bind the two continents together in tight economic bonds as powerful and pervasive at least as the cultural and political interests which have traditionally divided them.

It is not so much the common history which these areas share as it is the profound differences that one finds in their political and cultural developments that set Latin American history apart as an especially provocative field for investigation by North Americans. Dr. Gibson spells out many of these differences for us. Latin America is Spanish-Indian-Catholic, North America is Anglo-Protestant in coloration if not in statistical fact. In the United States, Indian culture has largely disappeared, smashed or buried by sledgehammer blows of "civilizing" Europeans. Not so in Latin America, where native culture has shown remarkable vigor. New Orleans, we need hardly be reminded, is more Latin than Cuzco in Peru or Otavalo in Ecuador.

In the English colonies democracy found its roots in the town meeting and the representative assembly. In Spanish America the democratic impulse was attenuated. Town councils and local governments were hardly seedbeds of democracy. In fact, communal government became weaker as the colonial period advanced, and by 1700 very little remained of municipal autonomy. Furthermore, the classic concern for individual rights which we associate with the Anglo-American tradition was notable for its absence in Latin America, where there has traditionally been more involvement with honor than with freedom, with the fulfillment of one's *dignidad,* one's *alma.*

The Spanish American Revolutions were touched off not by the American example but by the French Revolution, particularly in its Napoleonic phase, and when the revolutions did occur they were hardly mass movements but rather status revolts of *creoles* against *peninsulares,* upper class colonials seeking to oust the governing class that had been dispatched from the home country. Hence, these revolutions were neither social nor egalitarian, and, as Dr. Gibson points out, very rarely, as in Mexico after 1910 or more recently in Cuba, can one identify a revolution that transcended political bounds and transformed society. Instead of the deep-rooted respect for law and constitutionalism which we associate with the Anglo-American world, the Latin Americans have been influenced by personalism and have followed the *caudillo,* just as they had obeyed the authoritarian rulers who preceded them.

All this Dr. Gibson makes clear for us, and much else. He brings the very latest scholarship to bear in his analysis of those distinctive Latin American institutions, *encomienda* and *repartimiento,* in his description of the pervasive role of the Church and the distinctive features of its missionary activity, and, finally, of the penetration of the borderlands by presidio and mission. When Dr. Gibson completes his story we have a clearer understanding of the outlook which differentiates the Latin American world from that of the United States than we had when he began it, and this insight which he gives us is essential to Americans seeking to apply our objectives and long range goals to advance the interests of underdeveloped nations with very different backgrounds from our own and very different personal and national objectives.

This volume is one of *The New American Nation Series,* a comprehensive cooperative survey of the history of the area now embraced in the United States. Other aspects of discovery and colonization will be probed for readers of this series by David B. Quinn; the English background of colonization has already been completed for this series by Wallace Notestein; and from W. J. Eccles is forthcoming a volume on France in America.

HENRY STEELE COMMAGER
RICHARD B. MORRIS

Preface

S PAIN in America is a substantial subject. In space, time, and complexity it is a more substantial subject than England in America, and it carries the additional difficulty, for English-speaking students, that it is alien and easily misconstrued. Though impressive advances have been made, Spanish America still lags behind equivalent fields of historical investigation. In certain of its topics the overtones are such that one can hardly make any comment without sounding biased. Our ignorance of other topics is abysmal.

The subject interacts with Anglo-American history at numerous points. When the first settlers of Jamestown, refusing to work, spent their energies in a futile search for gold, they were responding not to the conditions of their own colony but to what they knew of the ways that Spaniards conducted themselves in theirs. When they planted tobacco and introduced African Negroes to cultivate it, they were adopting plantation habits developed in the Spanish colonies but still untried by their own countrymen. To patriotic Englishmen like Sir Francis Drake and James Oglethorpe, Spanish America was an immediate and hostile force. Anglo-American geography was itself a consequence of Spain in America, for Englishmen were obliged to found their colonies where Spaniards had not settled or where they had passed by.

This book is designed as an over-all summary of colonial Spanish-American history. It deals with a longer chronological period than do most other volumes of the New American Nation Series, and its treatment is more comprehensive and general. With respect to emphasis and point of view I have sought to keep in mind both the

requirements of a historical survey and the particular interests of
readers in the United States. Thus northern New Spain and the
borderlands receive some special attention, as do certain topics that
seem to offer opportunities for comparison with English colonization.

C. G.

Ann Arbor, Michigan

CHAPTER 1

Spain and the New World

FOR the origins of Spanish colonization in America we must turn back to the late medieval world of the Mediterranean, particularly to the kingdoms of the Iberian peninsula, where Christian armies had progressively recovered lands from the Moslems, and to the coasts of Africa, where the Italian cities still held the lead in exploration and trade. Venice maintained a hold upon Egyptian commerce, receiving goods from India and the Spice Islands. Genoese mariners in the late thirteenth and fourteenth centuries undertook occasional ventures of great daring, probably including sea journeys off the western shore of Africa to the Azores and Madeira Islands, and possibly including a circumnavigation of the great southern continent. Techniques of seafaring and cartography were well advanced by the end of the fourteenth century (both the compass and the astrolabe were already in use), but voyages in the Atlantic Ocean westward and southward from the Straits of Gibraltar still entailed many practical difficulties. The world outside the Mediterranean continued to be identified with regions of mystery where ancient lore had postulated Atlantis and where medieval lore postulated a limit to the finite earth and the first frontiers of Paradise.

Dominating the fifteenth-century expansion toward the south was the celebrated Prince Henry of Portugal. It was Prince Henry who was most responsible for shifting the focus of internal European maritime activity from Italy to the Iberian peninsula. It was Henry who mounted the Portuguese maritime attack (1415) upon the fortified Moslem city of Ceuta in the first act of state-directed imperialism of modern European history. Collecting, in so far as he was able, the records of earlier Asiatic and African adventures, Henry further undertook to extend Portuguese activity along the Atlantic coast of Africa. In his character and outlook he embodied a medley of motivations derived from the medieval heritage and from the contingencies of his own epoch, motivations in which nationalistic, Christian, commercial, scientific, and military purposes were united in a common effort. It is doubtful that the establishment of a sea route to India played any major role in his original design. He expressed rather a continuation of the warfare of Christians and Moors, a curiosity and eagerness for geographical discovery, and a desire to capitalize upon the trade routes of the African interior. His project for establishing contact with the supposed Christian kingdom of Prester John, and thus for surrounding Moorish Africa with Christian armies, was in the full spirit of the war against the Mohammedan invaders of the Iberian peninsula. In all, Portuguese expansion was his principal occupation and objective, and he devoted himself to this with rare singleness of purpose. Henry transformed the irregular Portuguese voyaging of the fourteenth century into a planned attack upon the imperfectly known geography to the south, and, by implication, upon the whole concept of a limited European world. At the time of his death in 1460, Portuguese maritime enterprise had extended its influence nearly to the equatorial line, a distance of some three thousand miles down the African coast.[1]

[1] Chapter VII of the work by Gomes Eannes de Azurara, the principal contemporary chronicler and authority on Prince Henry, the *Chronicle of the Discovery and Conquest of Guinea*, C. Raymond Beazley and Edgar Prestage, trans. (2 vols., London, 1896–99), is an analysis of the motives that impelled him to send out his expeditions. Azurara lists five: curiosity for knowledge, commercial opportunities, the need to discover the extent of Moorish power, the search for a Christian king with whom an alliance could be made, and the expansion of the faith. Azurara adds that all derive from one main cause, "the inclination of the heavenly wheels." For modern interpretations of Henry's motives, the two statements of Beazley have not been improved upon: "Prince Henry of Portugal and the African Crusade of the Fifteenth Century," *American Historical Review*, XVI (1910–11), 11–23, and "Prince Henry of Portugal and his Political, Commercial, and Colonizing Work," *American Historical Review*, XVII (1911–

Delays in the rate of Portuguese advance after 1460 are attributable partly to the death of the energetic Prince Henry and partly to the need for reinforcing Portuguese control over the regions already discovered. It is true that a spectacular series of voyages under Fernão Gomes substantially extended the known coast of Africa in a brief five-year period in the early 1470's; but the royal agreement with Gomes was permitted to expire, and the characteristic activity of the Portuguese for two decades after 1460 lay in the exploitation of the economic wealth of Africa, principally slaves, ivory, and gold. Only under John II, who succeeded to the Portuguese throne in 1481, did there appear a renewed impetus for systematic large-scale enterprises in the manner of Prince Henry. The voyages of the 1480's brought the Portuguese to the Congo River and finally, in the expedition of Bartholomew Diaz, to the Great Fish River, beyond the southern tip of Africa on the east coast of the continent. Contemporaneously an equally successful expedition, in an older tradition, was made by Pedro da Covilhã, who journeyed as a merchant to Cairo, Aden, and Calicut on the Malabar coast of India and returned by way of the East African coast. There can be no question of the objective of these later expeditions by land and by sea. The intention of the Portuguese in the late 1480's was to establish direct relations with India, and the immediate prospect and expectation of John II were signified in his renaming Diaz' Tempestuous Cape near the southern tip of Africa the Cape of Good Hope.[2]

Her prowess in African navigation notwithstanding, Portugal was not to be the leading nation in American affairs. In the late fifteenth century two other kingdoms of the Iberian peninsula, neighbors and traditional rivals of the Portuguese, were developing into

---

12), 252–267. For a strong statement of economic motivation, see Earl J. Hamilton, "The Role of Monopoly in the Overseas Expansion and Colonial Trade of Europe Before 1800," *American Economic Review*, XXXVIII (1948), 35–36.

[2] The standard account of these events in English, from Prince Henry to Vasco da Gama, is Edgar Prestage, *The Portuguese Pioneers* (London, 1933), which is generally accurate but which probably claims too much for the Portuguese. For the century following Henry's death, John W. Blake has edited and translated the relevant documents in *Europeans in West Africa, 1450–1560* (2 vols., London, 1942), and has written the historical commentary in *European Beginnings in West Africa, 1454–1578* (London, New York, and Toronto, 1937).

states capable of competing in the overseas world. Castile under Henry IV (1454–74) and Aragón under John II (1458–79) had been occupied in debilitating wars and internal disputes over dynastic titles. Under their successors, Isabella of Castile (1474–1504) and Ferdinand of Aragón (1479–1516), more authoritative and organized political systems came into being in both. After the marriage of Ferdinand and Isabella in 1469—a teen-age marriage, supported by a forged papal bull and negotiated in spite of opposition from Portugal, France, and the Spanish kingdoms themselves—and after Isabella had established her claim to the throne, the relation between Aragón and Castile became one of deliberate dynastic cohesion. There occurred no reconciliation or unification of institutions between the Spanish monarchies. But the royal union did make possible a final attack (1482–92) upon the emirate of Granada, the "Moorish" state at the southern tip of the peninsula, and this climactic ten-year war served to reinforce still further the royal power. The conquest of Granada may be interpreted as the final phase of the eight-hundred-year Spanish *reconquista*. It was understood at the time as a fifteenth-century crusade under the leadership of the two monarchs of Aragón and Castile. Ferdinand and Isabella further subdued the Spanish nobility, limited the authority of the towns, brought the military orders under royal control, organized the Inquisition to ensure Christian orthodoxy (Jews and Mohammedans were now forbidden to live in Spain), and enormously increased the royal revenues. By the 1480's a conspicuous transformation in the composition and strength of the Spanish kingdoms was well advanced and peninsular power relations had entered a new stage.[3]

Portuguese-Spanish rivalry in overseas activity manifested itself in mutual suspicion and open violence. The Portuguese traffic on the African coast stimulated a series of intrusive raiding actions by Spaniards, who justified their action by the claim that Africa had been a possession of the Visigothic Spanish kings. Confronted with actual and potential Spanish threats in the Atlantic, the Portuguese

---

[3] Jean Hippolyte Mariéjol, *The Spain of Ferdinand and Isabella*, Benjamin Keen, trans. and ed. (New Brunswick, 1961), pp. 115 ff.; J. H. Elliott, *Imperial Spain, 1469–1716* (London, 1963), pp. 5 ff.

constructed a series of African coastal fortresses, notably São Jorge da Mina (1482), to protect Portuguese interests. The immediate overseas world was formally divided between the two nations in the Treaty of Alcaçovas (1479), by which Castile recognized the existing Portuguese possessions and Portugal recognized Spanish dominion over the Canary Islands.[4] Spain conquered Gran Canaria and the entire Canary archipelago in the last quarter of the fifteenth century. But the price paid by the Spaniards for the Canaries was a heavy one. At Alcaçovas Spain recognized Portuguese possession of the Azores, the Cape Verde Islands, and the Madeira Islands, as well as the African coast. Thus in the 1480's Ferdinand and Isabella could boast only a limited number of foreign exploits to rival the great achievements of Diaz, Covilhã, and others in the Portuguese service. Ferdinand and Isabella furthermore were occupied with the final attack upon the Moors in southern Spain and were not to feel free to extend the *reconquista* beyond Spanish borders in any decisive way until 1492.

It was in this atmosphere of peninsular rivalry and nationalistic expansion that Columbus made his appearance on the European and especially on the Iberian scene. Columbus' project, the "enterprise of the Indies," placed its essential stress upon the westward route. The conception was not wholly new, nor was it the chimerical fancy of an impractical imagination, as has sometimes been supposed. It appears to have had the support, as early as the 1470's, of the Florentine geographical scholar Paolo Toscanelli.[5] Numerous voyagers, moreover, were familiar with at least the initial stages of Columbus' proposed route. The standard Portuguese journey to the Guinea coast and in African trade required a first course set in a southwesterly direction toward Brazil. The Portuguese monarchy had made provision for discoveries westward in the Atlantic as early

---

[4] The important parts of this treaty are translated into English in Francis Gardiner Davenport (ed.), *European Treaties Bearing on the History of the United States and Its Dependencies to 1648* (Washington, 1917), pp. 42–48; see p. 35 for relevant bibliography.

[5] Henry Vignaud, *Toscanelli and Columbus: The Letter and Chart of Toscanelli* (New York, 1902), is a skeptical account containing technical information on the famous connection between Columbus and Toscanelli. The English version is an expansion and improvement upon the French.

as the 1460's; English sailors were venturing far out from Bristol in the same period; and maps of the fifteenth century characteristically showed scattered islands—Antilia, Atlantis, Brazil—in the Atlantic Ocean. The islands were theoretical and their location depended upon the whim of individual cartographers, but they testify to a concern for oceanic geography and a confidence in the existence of unknown western lands.[6]

We may reject at once the belief, still popular in the twentieth century, that Columbus was the first to conceive of a spherical world. Pythagoreans in the fifth century B.C. already knew that the world was round, and though the notion fell sometimes into disrepute after this, it was never completely lost from view. Aristotle speculated on the distance from Spain to India by a westward route. Eratosthenes, identifying the Tropic of Cancer by observing the sun's reflection in a well, utilized the postulates of Euclidean geometry to compute the earth's circumference at 250,000 stadia, an error of approximately 15 per cent. This was in the third century B.C., and though Eratosthenes' figure was later disputed as too large, the method and the spherical hypothesis on which it depended always had adherents among learned people.

Columbus, a Genoese versed in the literature of travel and with practical experience in navigation, first offered his proposal to John II of Portugal.[7] When the proposal was refused, Columbus moved to the rival Spanish court, arguing his case there and sending his brother Bartholomew to seek the support of Henry VII of England. It should not be supposed that the delays and obstacles he encountered were due to a summary rejection of his project by the monarchies concerned. With the sphericity of the world an accepted hypothesis, the theoretical possibility of a journey to the East by sailing west was not seriously called into question. Instead the feasi-

---

[6] L. Sprague de Camp and Willy Ley, *De la Atlántida a El Dorado* (Barcelona, 1960), is a study of "imaginary geography" and its effect on exploration and discovery.

[7] The extensive literature arguing for other birthplaces for Columbus is late and unconvincing. Columbus himself said that he was Genoese, and the assertion is supported by contemporary testimony which identifies him as from Genoa or near Genoa. See on this subject Samuel E. Morison, *Admiral of the Ocean Sea: A Life of Christopher Columbus* (2 vols., Boston, 1942), I, 7 ff.

bility or practicality of Columbus' proposal and the terms demanded by Columbus himself appear to have been the decisive points debated.[8] Even this, however, may not be asserted unequivocally, nor may Columbus' "enterprise of the Indies" be strictly identified as a proposed journey to the known or fabled East. Columbus was reticent concerning his true intentions, and it was to the interest of each nation to maintain its deliberations in secret. Columbus received from Ferdinand and Isabella a letter to be presented to the Great Khan of the Far East; but the possibility of new territorial discovery in the "Ocean Sea" was expressly allowed for in his contract with the Spanish monarchs (April, 1492), and he was promised political and commercial privileges in whatever new lands he might encounter.[9]

Columbus' course on his first crossing lay toward Spain's single Atlantic colony, the Canary Islands, and thence directly west. Favored by weather, the voyage remained without incident save for strained relations between the admiral and his crew. Land was sighted in the Bahamas approximately a month after the departure from the Canaries. Columbus and his men proceeded to explore along the coasts of the Bahama Islands, Cuba, and Hispaniola (Haiti), and after an accident to one of the three ships Columbus set out on the return journey. He took with him several natives to show to Queen Isabella, leaving about forty of his own followers at La Navidad on the north shore of Hispaniola in the first European settlement planted on the American hemisphere since the days of the Norsemen.[10]

[8] Columbus, "a man of noble and lofty ambitions," according to his son Ferdinand, "would not covenant save on such terms as would bring him great honor and advantage." Ferdinand Columbus, *The Life of the Admiral Christopher Columbus,* Benjamin Keen, trans. and ed. (New Brunswick, 1959), p. 35.

[9] Columbus' powers included the hereditary titles and offices of admiral, viceroy, governor, and captain general. For a summation of the powers and the legal basis of his jurisdiction, see Mario Góngora, *El estado en el derecho indiano, época de fundación (1492–1570)* (Santiago de Chile, 1951), pp. 43–44.

[10] Detailed, firsthand data on Columbus' initial voyage are available in Columbus' own journal or log, preserved in an abstract by Bartolomé de Las Casas. Christopher Columbus, *The Journal of Christopher Columbus,* Cecil Jane and L. A. Vigneras, trans. and eds. (New York, 1960).

Having made the discovery, Columbus recorded his belief that he had tested and proved the new route to the Far East. He identified the native as Indians, and Cuba as Cipangu (Japan), or the realm of the Great Khan. That he did so attests to the authority, for a sensitive fifteenth-century mind, of that vast body of literary evidence, including travelers' tales and geographical lore, on which much of the fifteenth-century conception of the world was based. Columbus' error lay in underestimating the circumference of the earth in the Ptolemaic tradition (less accurate than the earlier tradition of Eratosthenes), and in overestimating the ratio of land to water on the earth's surface in the tradition of European geographers and travelers to the east.[11] By Columbus' computation, which was a reasonable and plausible deduction from false assumptions, the nautical distance from Palos to Cipangu was almost exactly the actual breadth of the Atlantic Ocean. Hence the islands of the West Indies lay in the supposed position of those offshore Asiatic islands with which the geographers of the period so generously sprinkled the region east and southeast of Cathay. Columbus persisted in his conviction despite all empirical evidence to the contrary. In Cuba he authorized his interpreter, Luis de Torres, to enter into negotiations with the Great Khan in a local Arawak village.

Portuguese interest lay in a rejection of Columbus' version of the famous voyage. It happened that Columbus, in an accident of weather, was compelled to seek shelter on his homeward journey first in the mouth of the Tagus, near Lisbon, and to notify the Portuguese rather than the Castilian monarch of his exploit. To John II of Portugal, who some nine years before had refused to gamble on his venture, Columbus was able in 1493 to show gold and "Indians," and to announce that he had visited the Far East in the western ocean. The rivalry between Portugal and Spain at once took on a more competitive character. Having now accelerated its own program of overseas navigation, Portugal seemed committed to the alternative, circum-Africa route. Some sentiment existed in the

---

[11] See the interesting study by George E. Nunn, *The Geographical Conceptions of Columbus: A Critical Consideration of Four Problems* (New York, 1924), pp. 1–30, on Columbus' computation of one degree and the result for his idea of the location of Asia.

Portuguese court in favor of a forcible prevention of Columbus' return to Spain. But John II chose rather to counteract Columbus' assertions by diplomatic means and in so doing depended on a more accurate estimate of the voyage than Columbus' own. In the official view of the Portuguese king, San Salvador and the other lands visited by Columbus were Atlantic islands bearing neither relation nor resemblance to Asia. Moreover, they lay sufficiently close to Portugal's own possessions in the Atlantic to justify a Portuguese claim in accordance with the terms of Alcaçovas.

In Spain as in Portugal the report of Columbus' journey was studied with interest. The report lent some popular support to the navigator's Far Eastern assertions, but it was exactly on this point that doubt was cast among the learned and the politically influential. Skepticism was expressed within a few months of Columbus' return, and in their statement to Pope Alexander VI, dispatched promptly after the return of Columbus, the Spanish monarchs avoided reference to the Far Eastern connection, speaking instead of the discovery of distant lands to the west.[12] More practically, they undertook to send a second expedition westward, again under the command of Columbus, for further colonization and exploration.

The second voyage was an impressive one in equipment, cargo, personnel, and early prospects. Columbus set sail from Cadiz in September, 1493, with a fleet of seventeen ships. From the Canaries his course lay farther south than on the former occasion and the landfall was made on the island of Dominica in the Lesser Antilles. The party turned northwest to Hispaniola, found the colony destroyed by Indians, and early in 1494 established a second settlement, Isabela, again on the northern shore of Hispaniola. Still searching for indications of India and the empire of the Great Khan, Columbus spent some months in coasting the islands of the Caribbean. Returning to the Isabela colony, he found a state of economic distress and social disorder. His brothers, Diego and Bartholomew, were involved in problems of administrative control. Illness was widespread, and Indian warfare had occupied the colonists for long

---

[12] Edmundo O'Gorman, *The Invention of America: An Inquiry into the Historical Nature of the New World and the Meaning of Its History* (Bloomington, 1961), pp. 81 ff.

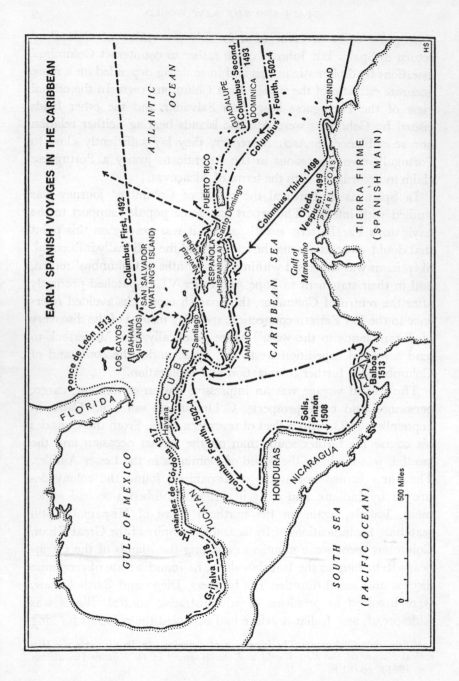

EARLY SPANISH VOYAGES IN THE CARIBBEAN

ATLANTIC
OCEAN

Columbus' Second,
1493

GUADALUPE
DOMINICA
Columbus' Fourth, 1502-4

TRINIDAD

PUERTO RICO

Santo Domingo

Isabela
ESPAÑOLA
(HISPANIOLA)
Navidad

Ponce de León 1513

Columbus' First, 1492

SAN SALVADOR
(WATLING'S ISLAND)

Columbus' Third, 1498

Ojeda,
Vespucci 1499
PEARL COAST

Gulf of
Maracaibo

CARIBBEAN
SEA

TIERRA FIRME
(SPANISH MAIN)

LOS CAYOS

(BAHAMA
ISLANDS)

Santiago

JAMAICA

CUBA

Havana

Columbus' Fourth, 1502-4

1517

PANAMA

Balboa
1513

FLORIDA

GULF OF MEXICO

Hernández de Córdoba,

Solis,
Pinzón 1508

HONDURAS

NICARAGUA

YUCATAN

Grijalva 1518

SOUTH SEA
(PACIFIC OCEAN)

500 Miles

0   500

HS

periods. In the belief that his own and the colony's welfare would be best served by his return to Spain, Columbus set sail again in March, 1496, with several hundred disheartened colonists, a number of Indians, some gold dust, an assortment of artifacts, and the information that he had located Ophir, the source of the gold, almug trees, and precious stones presented to Solomon by the Queen of Sheba.

In Spain Columbus secured a renewed expression of his rights and privileges. But the monarchs had already begun to compromise upon the earlier pledges by authorizing other voyages. The admiral's position tended now to be weakened by personal enmities, campaigns of disparagement, and sudden shortages of funds. He experienced difficulties in obtaining colonists for the proposed third voyage. In 1497 he received authority to use prisoners for this purpose, and it was not until 1498 that he was prepared to sail, in a fleet now less than half the size of the fleet of 1493. The party divided at the Canaries, and Columbus with three vessels pursued a course far to the south, landing first at the island of Trinidad and sighting the mouth of the Orinoco River. Proceeding north to Santo Domingo, a new colony on the southern coast of Hispaniola, Columbus found continued misfortune, renewed Indian war, and schism among the settlers. One of the group, Francisco Roldán, had threatened to assassinate Columbus' brothers and retired with his followers to found a separatist colony in the interior of the island. Columbus' attempts to reconcile the factions proved unavailing. Both sides complained to the Spanish monarchs, who sent a governor, Francisco de Bobadilla, to assume control. In October, 1500, Bobadilla sent Columbus and his brothers back to Spain in chains.[13]

The year 1500 marks the end of Columbus' career as a colonial administrator. He was permitted one further voyage, his fourth (1502–4). Designed as a voyage of discovery, it was appropriate to his true talents and to his now reduced position in colonial adminis-

---

[13] In his letter of 1500 to Juana de la Torre, Columbus expresses bitterness and characterizes the settlers in America as dissolute, foolish, and malicious. Cecil Jane (trans. and ed.), *Select Documents Illustrating the Four Voyages of Columbus* (London, 1930–33), II, 54 ff.

tration. In terms of American discovery it was an expedition of some importance, for the party explored the coasts of Central America in regions that had not yet been visited by Europeans. But for Columbus himself it was the most unrewarding of the four voyages, plagued by storms, Indian warfare, and a mutiny, and interrupted by a year spent marooned on the island of Jamaica. Shortly after his return to Spain what further hope he entertained for future exploration was lost with the death of Isabella. Columbus himself died two years later.

To the end of his life Columbus continued in the belief that his discoveries had been made in Far Eastern waters. His view may be regarded as an unrealistic one almost from the start, but it was consistent with the attitude of mystical determination that he characteristically adopted. Columbus did speak of an *otro mundo,* another world, and a *nuevo mundo,* a new world, but his references were imprecise and conceptually associated with references to a new heaven, *nuevo cielo,* and a terrestrial paradise situated on a large bulge of the earth up the Orinoco River.[14] The discoverer of America, an outstanding mariner even in his age of extraordinary maritime feats, never comprehended the implications of his achievement. Its full implications, of course, came to be recognized only over a long period, as the later protracted search for a western passage shows. But already during his lifetime, new voyages, new diplomatic and imperial designs, and new geographical conceptions were directing the course of events progressively farther from Columbus' interpretation, as well as from his control, of American affairs.

The new and rival expeditions were stimulated partly by Columbus' discovery, on the third voyage, of pearl fisheries off the Venezuelan mainland. In 1499 Alonso de Ojeda and Juan de la Cosa traversed some of the northern shore of South America, in the Guiana-Venezuela region, proceeding as far west as the Gulf of Maracaibo. In the same region, on an independent voyage, Pera-

---

[14] Columbus came to believe that the discovery was inspired by the Holy Ghost in time for the fulfillment of scriptural prophecies prior to the end of the world. John L. Phelan, *The Millennial Kingdom of the Franciscans in the New World: A Study of the Writings of Gerónimo de Mendieta (1525–1604)* (Berkeley and Los Angeles, 1956), pp. 19 ff., analyzes his mystical, crusading, apocalyptical, and messianic mentality.

lonso Niño gathered a profitable cargo of pearls during his voyage of 1499–1500. An expedition commanded by Vicente Yáñez Pinzón coasted north from the vicinity of Pernambuco in Brazil to the pearl fisheries, and other mariners explored further the Brazilian, Venezuelan, Colombian, and Panamanian shores.[15] In Portuguese expansion the Pedro Alvares Cabral expedition of 1500 followed immediately upon Vasco da Gama's successful voyage to India by the eastern route (1497–99).[16] Taking a long southwesterly initial course for the trip around Africa, Cabral struck the Brazilian coast before continuing eastward to India, a circumstance frequently cited to indicate the inevitability of the discovery of America under the conditions of the late fifteenth century.[17]

The most celebrated of the followers of Columbus, for the reason that his name was applied to the two continents of America, was the Florentine sailor Amerigo Vespucci (1454–1512). There is a complex and still unresolved controversy concerning his voyaging. According to his own statement, Vespucci first visited America in 1497. But it is at least possible that this was a deliberate falsification and that in reality his earliest visit occurred in 1499–1500 with the Ojeda expedition. He claimed to have made four voyages in all, the last two (1501–2 and 1503–4) designed to explore the American shores for Portugal and to reach the East Indies by the westward route.[18] Certain of Vespucci's letters, containing vivid descriptions

---

[15] Edward Gaylord Bourne, *Spain in America, 1450–1580* (New York and London, 1904), pp. 67 ff.

[16] William Brooks Greenlee (trans. and ed.), *The Voyage of Pedro Alvares Cabral to Brazil and India from Contemporary Documents and Narratives* (London, 1938).

[17] The view that Columbus was not the discoverer is developed in various ways in Rasmus B. Anderson, *America Not Discovered by Columbus: A Historical Sketch of the Discovery of America by the Norsemen, in the Tenth Century* (Chicago, 1874); Frederick J. Pohl, *Atlantic Crossings Before Columbus* (New York, 1961); Charles Michael Boland, *They All Discovered America* (New York, 1963); William Giles Nash, *America, The True History of Its Discovery* (London, 1924); and many other works. See also the argument that America was invented rather than discovered, in O'Gorman, *The Invention of America*.

[18] The Vespucci question is one of the puzzling features of scholarship on discovery and exploration. The "classic" view of historians is expressed by Clements Markham, the editor of Vespucci's letters in English: "The evidence against Vespucci is cumulative and quite conclusive. His first voyage is a fabrication. He cannot be acquitted of the intention of appropriating for himself

of the New World, received wide and repeated publication in the years following 1503, and it is on these publications that his contemporary fame chiefly depended. Although he became the official *piloto mayor* of Spain, and although he appears to have sailed in the service of both Spain and Portugal, his greatest influence was confined to the European countries north of the Pyrenees, where the support given him by the geographer Martin Waldseemüller encouraged the adoption of the name America (feminine by analogy with Europa, Africa, and Asia) for the lands of the Western Hemisphere. In Spain and its colonies the name America was not used, and the new lands continued to be known as Las Indias, The Indies.

In all, the decade and a half after 1492 witnessed a prodigious maritime expansion, and its general meaning was quickly recognized and understood at the time. In a sense the nature of this expansion was determined by the direction that Portuguese interest had been taking since the time of Prince Henry and by the necessarily competitive role occupied by Spain. Portuguese activity lay chiefly in the areas south and east of Europe. Spain, unable to operate effectively in these areas, found in America an alternative or compensatory field for exploration. Other nations, for a variety of reasons, were still only partially or intermittently concerned. Hence a division of interest between the two Hispanic nations remained for the moment sufficient.

In practice the western world of Spain and the eastern world of Portugal impinged upon each other only in the region of Brazil, which, although a part of the "New World," adjoined the normal Portuguese circum-Africa route. It was on account of the proximity or supposed proximity of America to Africa that territorial contro-

---

the glory of having first discovered the mainland. The impartial and upright Las Casas, after carefully weighing the evidence, found him guilty. This verdict has been, and will continue to be, confirmed by posterity." Amerigo Vespucci, *The Letters of Amerigo Vespucci and Other Documents Illustrative of His Career,* Clements R. Markham, trans. and ed. (London, 1894), p. xxxix. Alberto Magnaghi in *Amerigo Vespucci: studio critico, con speciale riguardo ad una nuova valutazione delle fonti* (2 vols., Rome, 1924), proposed that Vespucci made only the two voyages and that the letters describing the other two are spurious. See also Roberto Levillier, *América la bien llamada* (2 vols., Buenos Aires, 1948), and Germán Arciniegas, *Amerigo and the New World: The Life and Times of Amerigo Vespucci,* Harriet de Onís, trans. (New York, 1955).

versies similar to those of the 1470's arose in the New World. The Treaty of Alcaçovas had been predicated on a limited knowledge of overseas geography. The history of Spanish-Portuguese diplomatic relations after Alcaçovas, a history in which the Alcaçovas principle was extended over a far larger area, resulted in the earliest colonial division of American territory, that by which Brazil came to be Portuguese and the remainder of Hispanic America Spanish.

The revised Spanish-Portuguese division of empire had its basis in peninsular and papal diplomacy of the 1490's. From the mid-fifteenth century it had been customary for popes to grant to the Portuguese monarchs rights of sovereignty over lands discovered and of enslavement over non-Christian peoples in Africa. Papal authority in these matters rested on the popes' traditional role as international mediators and also upon the special papal control over relations between Christians and pagans.[19] As early as the 1450's a papal bull contained the phrase "as far as the Indies," and the papal tradition of the late fifteenth century manifestly confirmed Portuguese rights in American discovery as well as in the vague regions beyond. It was in this tradition that the Spanish sovereigns communicated with their own representatives in Rome in the spring of 1493. Their intention was to receive papal donation of Columbus' findings comparable to the donations previously received by the Portuguese in Africa and "as far as the Indies."

The donation was forthcoming in three celebrated bulls of 1493. Two authorized Spanish title to the Columbian discoveries and other non-Christian western lands still to be discovered, specifically for the propagation of the Christian faith. The third limited the donation to an area west of an Atlantic meridian drawn on a north-south axis one hundred leagues west of the Cape Verde and Azores islands. The geographical assumptions and terminology of this third bull were vague, for the line was to be distant "toward west and south" and the one-hundred-league measurement was to begin both at the Cape Verde and at the Azores islands, indefinite starting points at

[19] Luis Weckmann, *Las bulas alejandrinas de 1493 y la teoría política del papado medieval: Estudio sobre la supremacía papal sobre islas, 1091–1493* (Mexico, 1949). F. Mateos, "Bulas portugesas y españolas sobre descubrimientos geográficas," *Missionalia hispánica,* XIX (1962), 5–34, 129–168.

best. There is evidence that the Spanish monarchs may have requested a meridian farther to the east and that they were therefore not fully satisfied with the papal pronouncement. But the third bull interfered more directly with Portuguese than with Spanish expansion, for in effect it forbade Portuguese claims to land in the western Atlantic. Also, and equally important, it did not limit a Spanish claim to the Far East through a western circumnavigation of the globe.[20]

The Portuguese for their part had already taken steps to maintain the advantage in overseas discovery. The Portuguese king, within a few weeks of his interview with Columbus in 1493, had prepared a fleet with which to assert Portuguese control of the new lands, an action consistent with the monarch's official position that the Columbian territories lay within Portuguese jurisdiction. At Spanish request John II postponed the departure of this fleet pending diplomatic conferences with Spanish envoys over the question of imperial rights. Spain meanwhile held its own fleet in readiness to forestall any determined Portuguese move. A Portuguese caravel did in fact set out, but whether this was by order of John II, as the Spaniards believed, or in violation of his order, as the Portuguese insisted, remains unclear. Diplomatic negotiations between Spanish and Portuguese envoys began in August, 1493, by which time Spanish preparations for Columbus' second voyage were well advanced. In the negotiations the envoys of both nations appear to have been incompletely informed both of previous agreements and of the geographical location of Columbus' discoveries. It is certain that Ferdinand and Isabella took advantage of the negotiations to gain time, and this may have been the principal value of the diplomacy for them. In any case, they requested a revision of the papal statement, to the effect that islands or other lands lying to the east of the established meridian might now be included within the Spanish sphere.

Alexander VI, a Spanish Borgia occupying the papal throne, was thus persuaded to issue a fourth bull, *Dudum siquidem*, dated Sep-

[20] H. Vander Linden, "Alexander VI and the Demarcation of the Maritime and Colonial Domains of Spain and Portugal, 1493–1494," *American Historical Review*, XXII (1916–17), 1–20, precisely analyzes the bulls and emphasizes their pro-Spanish tendencies. The texts of the bulls are published in Davenport (ed.), *European Treaties*, pp. 9 ff.

tember 26, 1493. Its effect was to nullify the previous authorizations favoring the Portuguese and to reveal the papacy as a thoroughly pro-Spanish power. By the terms of the bull Spain became free to engage in worldwide exploration by westward or southern navigation, and the Pope specifically mentioned India as a land accessible to Spain. Only the actual possessions of Christian princes were now excluded.[21]

Thus Spain employed to advantage the earliest diplomatic negotiations with the papacy and with the Portuguese. But in the next year Spain inadvertently relinquished some of her gains by the Treaty of Tordesillas, according to which Spanish and Portuguese spheres of influence were defined by a new meridian, 370 leagues west of the Cape Verde Islands. This line, dividing the Atlantic approximately midway between the Azores and the West Indies, was intended as a peaceful compromise settlement in apparent recognition of the claims and rights of both parties and without the antecedent warfare that had attended the settlement of Alcaçovas in 1479. The Tordesillas agreement further provided for joint measurement by a naval expedition, and the contracting parties stated their intention to request papal confirmation of the new decision.[22] The treaty presented, to be sure, a number of practical difficulties, for the exact starting point in the Cape Verde Islands was not specified and the distance itself, in the geographical knowledge of the time, was subject to variant interpretation. Columbus, at this time in the West Indies on his second voyage, was invited by the Spanish monarchs to aid in the measurement, but the matter was postponed and in the end no expedition of measurement was sent. Columbus, furthermore, regarded the Treaty of Tordesillas as an unwarranted intrusion upon his own personal privileges. It later appeared that he had continued to think of a line distant only a hundred leagues from the Azores and the Cape Verde Islands. Learned opinions on the distance, drawing on Erastosthenes, Strabo, and other ancient geogra-

[21] The text is in Davenport (ed.), *European Treaties*, pp. 79 ff.

[22] For the text of the Treaty of Tordesillas, see *ibid.*, pp. 84 ff. Our interpretation follows and depends on that of Charles E. Nowell, "The Treaty of Tordesillas and the Diplomatic Background of American History," in *Greater America: Essays in Honor of Herbert Eugene Bolton* (Berkeley and Los Angeles, 1945), pp. 1–18.

phers, differed sharply from one another. In any case no dependable means were available in the fifteenth century for the accurate computation of longitudinal distances.

With the further exploration of America by Columbus and others after 1494, it became apparent that at Tordesillas the Spaniards had unknowingly granted to Portugal a substantial section of the South American coast. In appreciation of this fact King Emmanuel of Portugal requested and received from Julius II the bull *Ea quae* (1506), which endorsed the Tordesillas meridian and thus rendered it more binding upon Spain.[23] In the early years of the sixteenth century both Spanish and Portuguese geographers understood the Tordesillas line to strike the continent of South America approximately at the mouth of the Amazon. Minor discrepancies in the computed position were not of immediate or practical significance, and the tendency on the part of both nations was to pay only scant attention to the exact location. But in the second decade of the century, when the Portuguese were gaining new knowledge of the coasts to the south, the matter came to be of greater importance, and the possible claims of Spain to areas exploited by the Portuguese began to receive serious attention. The question was equally significant for its implications in the Pacific, for the assumption commonly made in Spain (though not explicitly stated in 1494) was that the Tordesillas line should be projected around the world into the Asiatic hemisphere. The relation of the extended line to the Portuguese-controlled Spice Islands in the Far East became a matter of more acute concern with the first circumnavigation of the world, by the Magellan-del Cano expedition, in 1519–21.

The plan of Ferdinand Magellan, a Portuguese with experience in the East, was similar to the original scheme of Columbus, but it was informed by a more precise knowledge of geography than any available to the discoverer of America. Not only had the southeastern coasts of South America been visited approximately as far as the Plata estuary, but the existence of the Pacific Ocean, first seen at Panama in 1513 by a Spanish expedition under Vasco Núñez de Balboa, was now well known. The size of the Pacific was

[23] Davenport (ed.), *European Treaties*, pp. 107 ff.

of course unknown, and this very uncertainty gave rise to Spanish hopes that the Spice Islands might fall within the Spanish sphere, i.e., east of an extended Tordesillas line. The Portuguese, now firmly established in the Spice Islands and deriving from them a profit far in excess of what Spain derived from the West Indies, had little interest in seeing these Spanish hopes tested or proved. The Portuguese interest lay in a status quo diplomatically undefined, and the Portuguese came to subscribe to the view that the Tordesillas line was properly confined to the Atlantic hemisphere. This view was supported by a pro-Portuguese papal bull in 1514. But Magellan, believing that a comparatively short distance separated the Molucca Islands from the western coast of South America, was proposing an expedition to disrupt the papal and Portuguese view of Pacific geography. Magellan's project lay clearly within the Spanish interest. It was supported by the Spanish royal government and it was realized in spite of determined Portuguese efforts to forestall it.

The expedition set out in September, 1519. Passing into the Pacific through the strait named for him at the southern tip of South America, Magellan turned his ships across the world's largest body of water. The voyage has commonly, and correctly, been regarded as among the most stupendous achievements in the entire history of navigation.[24] Magellan and a number of his followers were killed in a Philippine war in the spring of 1521. Juan Sebastián del Cano continued to the Spice Islands, where a profitable commerce was transacted, and thence southwestward around Africa and home to Spain, the entire journey occupying a period of three years. Although the means for verifying the exact size of the world were still not appreciably better than in the time of Eratosthenes two thousand years before, the Magellan–del Cano expedition demonstrated empirically its approximate size, and above all indicated that an enormous expanse of water separated the western coast of America from the Far East.

[24] The torments of the voyage are graphically described by its chief chronicler, Antonio Pigafetta. During the four-month open stretch in the Pacific, food was reduced to the powder of the original biscuits infested with worms and impregnated with rat urine. The crew ate the oxhide cover of the mainyard. Many died of scurvy. Charles E. Nowell (ed.), *Magellan's Voyage Around the World: Three Contemporary Accounts* (Evanston, Ill., 1962), pp. 122–123.

The true or nearly true geographical relation between America and the other land masses of the world thus came to be understood in the 1520's.[25] The knowledge stimulated a number of new Spanish-Portuguese diplomatic negotiations pertaining to the status of the Spice Islands, which were now actively claimed by both nations. In the Treaty of Victoria (1524) Portugal and Spain agreed to appoint lawyers, pilots, and astrologers to fix the overseas demarcation,[26] and these experts met in the Junta de Badajoz in the same year. But their consultation came to an end without agreement. Geographers unable to decide upon the location of the meridian in the Atlantic hemisphere were even more uncertain regarding the projected meridian in the Pacific hemisphere. The Portuguese were anxious to move the original Tordesillas meridian westward in order to gain control of a maximum territory in Brazil, but they were unwilling to do this if the consequent westward shifting of the Pacific arc would entail the loss of the Molucca Islands. In the mid-1520's clashes between Portuguese and Spaniards in the East demonstrated the effective superiority of the Portuguese forces there. Charles V, in financial difficulties, at war with France, and with ever weaker claims in the Orient, found an opportunity finally in the Treaty of Saragossa (1529) to make the best of his unfavorable situation.[27] In exchange for 350,000 ducats the emperor yielded his claim to the East Indies, and an arbitrary Pacific line was drawn seventeen degrees east of the islands, which thus fell to the Portuguese. The diplomats failed to arrive at a precise agreement for the Atlantic line (a reverse projection would have placed all of South America within Spanish jurisdiction), and the earlier positions, with their variants, remained as approximations of what was essentially an unmarked boundary. The subsequent growth of Brazil, a consequence of expansion in colonial times, belongs to another order of

[25] On the other hand one should beware of supposing that the Magellan voyage sharply changed existing geographical opinion. It was still possible to suppose that the Pacific Ocean lay principally in the southern hemisphere and that America and Asia were connected in the north as a single continent. This is the form shown on the world map of Giacomo Gastaldi. See *ibid.*, pp. 342–343.

[26] Davenport (ed.), *European Treaties*, pp. 118 ff.

[27] For the text of the Treaty of Saragossa, see *ibid.*, pp. 146 ff.

events. Only much later, with the Treaty of Madrid (1750) and the Treaty of San Ildefonso (1777), were the expanded areas of Portuguese control in America formally recognized by Spain. And the final settlement of the Brazilian boundary, like that of many other parts of Hispanic America, remained incomplete at the conclusion of the colonial period.

The outlines of the overseas area to be occupied by Spain were, however, already fixed. Save for the Philippines, Spanish interest was confined to the American hemisphere. America would be to Spain what the East Indies were to Portugal, in a disposition the essential features of which were resolved in the years immediately following 1492. Within America the particular regions to be subjected to Spanish influence were determined equally early. Columbus' landfall in the West Indies meant an immediate concentration on Caribbean and Central American territories. Spain dismissed the northern coasts, where Cabot established the English and Verrazano the French claims. To the south Spain reached ad hoc agreements with her peninsular rival Portugal, yielded Brazil, and demoted the whole Atlantic coast of Spanish South America. With a peculiar concentration Spain seemed driven precisely toward the areas that would yield the greatest and most immediate wealth, Mexico and Peru.

The reorientation in world knowledge that this whole process entailed as suggested by the series of four pictorial maps shown in illustrations 1–4 (following page 82). The first is a "world map" of about 1200 from a Psalter in the British Museum. It shows the known world in circular form, with Jerusalem as its absolute middle point.[28] The representation is confined at the periphery, fixed at the center, and wholly symmetrical in form. By contrast, the reconstructed Toscanelli map of the pre-Columbian fifteenth century (illustration 2) is in the form of a rectangle with the Atlantic coast of Europe and Africa at the extreme right and the Pacific coast of Asia at the extreme left. Its central section is one ocean, containing the islands of Cipangu and Antilia, an unobstructed waterway between Europe and Asia. The Juan de la Cosa portolan chart of 1500

[28] "Thus saith the Lord God; This is Jerusalem: I have set it in the midst of the nations and countries that are round about her." Ezekiel 5:5.

(illustration 3) shows the post-Columbian world, with Europe, Africa, the Atlantic Ocean, the West Indies, and portions of the South American coast in careful and surprisingly accurate detail. It ignores the Pacific (Columbus is reported to have censured Juan de la Cosa for depicting Cuba as an island rather than as part of Asia), and it leaves in doubt the relation of America to the Orient. The northern part of the American hemisphere is glossed as an English discovery. In an elaborate pictorial and verbal conceit, Columbus is shown as St. Christopher, the bearer of Christ to the New World.

The fourth map, by Diego Ribero (Ribeiro), reflects the Magellanic world of the late 1520's. Ribero, a Portuguese, was royal cosmographer at the court of Spain and was entrusted with the revision of the *Padrón real,* a master map for pilots. He placed Europe and Asia to the right, America at the center, and the vast Pacific in an impressive left-hand expanse. The accuracy of the American outline is remarkable. Place names and historical notes are provided in meticulous detail. Ribero's world was divided almost exactly in half by the Tordesillas line, separating Spanish and Portuguese spheres.

Thus in three cartographic centuries the world expanded, the coastline took form, the oceans were identified, and the New World, cut by a Spanish-Portuguese division, replaced Jerusalem as the focal center. The process of expansion accelerated in time. Above all, the generation that lived in the late fifteenth and early sixteenth centuries—the generation of Erasmus, Copernicus, Machiavelli, and Leonardo da Vinci—witnessed the most rapid transformation in geographical knowledge and experience that the world had ever known. When this generation was born, the frontier of Europe seemed to have been temporarily halted. Constantinople had fallen and Christian Europe had lost territory to the Ottoman Empire. Portuguese coastal voyaging in African waters was being less systematically directed than before, and mariners were still reluctant to sail out of sight of land. The southern part of the Iberian peninsula remained in non-Christian control. European travels to China and India had sharply declined in number and importance. Yet by the time that this generation died, America had been discovered, India reached, and the world circumnavigated. The "Renaissance," a period whose dimensions and limits have repeatedly defied historical investigation, is nowhere more conspicuously or measurably evident than in this sudden burgeoning of geographical movement and knowledge.

In the new geographical movement the Spanish discovery of America was a central and dominant event. The remarkable rapidity of expansion—Diaz in 1487, Columbus in 1492, da Gama in 1498, Magellan in 1519–21—emphasizes the movement's continuity and inner connections. The fact that all the leaders of expansion were employed in the service of Spain or Portugal again relates the events to a concentrated Iberian historical process. Portugal and Spain were beyond all question the leading nations in this first stage of the expansion of Europe. The Iberian peninsula formed a separate state system within Europe, with its own national rivalries and jealousies. The gross outlines of Iberian political geography were instantly and magnificently mirrored in the political divisions of the New World, where Portugal received a part and Spain a larger part, and where for a century no non-Iberian power was able to establish more than a temporary foothold.

CHAPTER 2

Conquest

IN SIXTEENTH-CENTURY terms the interval from 1506, when
Columbus died, to 1518, when Fernando Cortés set out for the
Mexican conquest, appeared as an eventful and productive period.
In included a notable voyage by Juan Díaz de Solís and Vicente
Yáñez Pinzón from Honduras to a point near or beyond the eastern
limit of Brazil in 1508–9. The Panamanian isthmus and its adjacent
territories to north and south were opened to settlement in the years
immediately following. The celebrated expedition of Juan Ponce de
León to Florida in 1513, the discovery of the Pacific Ocean by
Balboa in the same year,[1] and Solís' discovery of the Plata River in
South America in 1516 were steps in a process of steady geographical discovery. Meanwhile new colonial communities were founded,
and Spaniards established themselves in the Caribbean islands as
ranchers and slave owners, the masters of native Indian and imported Negro populations.[2]

Permanent Spanish colonization nevertheless remained confined
for a surprisingly long time to Hispaniola, Puerto Rico, Jamaica,
Cuba, and scattered points on the mainland along the southern

[1] The reader will note with what qualification the term "discovery" must be
understood. Portuguese were sailing on the Pacific at the moment when Balboa
"discovered" it and claimed it for the Spanish monarchs. See Charles E. Nowell,
"The Discovery of the Pacific: A Suggested Change of Approach," *Pacific Historical Review*, XVI (1947), 1–10.

[2] These voyages and the related events are narrated in Edward Gaylord
Bourne, *Spain in America, 1450–1580* (New York and London, 1904), pp.
104 ff.

fringes of the Caribbean. As late as 1516 nothing was officially known of Yucatan or of mainland Mexico. Only in 1517–18, after the Mexican coastal journeys of Francisco Hernández de Córdoba and Juan de Grijalva, did the colonists of the islands receive reports of wealthy native civilizations in these parts of the mainland.[3] And only with the plans to explore and exploit these further may the Age of Conquest be said to have begun. It is true that conflict character- ized relations between Spaniards and American natives from the start and that the occupation of such areas as Cuba and the south- ern Caribbean coast involved forceful invasion and subjugation. But these were conquests or attempted conquests only in a limited or preliminary sense, and many of the early activities might more ac- curately be classified as skirmishes or slave raids. The "age of con- quest" had quite a different character. It "began" in 1519, when a small band of amateur Spanish soldiers proceeded to march against and subdue the huge populations of the mainland.

The Aztecs, probably the best known of the American peoples won through conquest, were Indians of elaborate culture inhabiting the Valley of Mexico and its surrounding regions. Modern knowl- edge of the Aztecs derives from the written reports of the first Spaniards who encountered them, from the historical and ethno- logical researches of colonial Spanish friars, from archaeology, from postconquest Indian literature and arts, and from the practices of their modern descendants, many of whom still speak the Nahuatl (Aztec) language today and continue in ways of life only partially modified by four centuries of contact with Europeans. Like all American Indians, the Aztecs were Mongoloid peoples whose ances- tors migrated from Asia by a Siberian-Alaskan route some thirty thousand years ago (there exists only a remote possibility that peoples migrated in significant numbers directly across the Pacific to America).[4] The Aztec occupation of the Valley of Mexico was

[3] Henry R. Wagner (trans. and ed.), *The Discovery of Yucatan by Francisco Hernández de Córdoba* (Berkeley, 1942), and *The Discovery of New Spain in 1518 by Juan de Grijalva* (Berkeley, 1942). Richard Konetzke, *Entdecker und Eroberer Amerikas, von Christoph Kolumbus bis Hernán Cortés* (Frankfurt, 1963), has as one theme the timidity of the post-Columbian mariners and their willingness to conform to conservative plans and instructions. This pattern was sharply broken by Cortés in 1519.

[4] Not all students accept this view of the matter. See the various essays in

preceded by a series of distinct other Indian occupations, of which the Chichimec and the Toltec are the most clearly delineated.[5] The transition from the nomadic hunting and gathering stage to the sedentary agricultural and village stage occurred between about nine thousand and about three thousand years ago. The Aztecs themselves were relative latecomers. Their urban capital, Tenochtitlan, the site of modern Mexico City, was founded in the fourteenth century on an artificial island in the valley lake, to which they were driven by hostile pressures from the populous environs. Gradually conquering and subjugating their neighbors, the Aztecs developed a military state that waged aggressive warfare against surrounding tribes and brought an increasingly larger Mexican population under its sway.[6] As overlords of this expanding empire the Aztec ruling classes engaged in human sacrifice and a methodical exaction of tribute. Under the emperor Montezuma II, who succeeded to the chieftainship in 1502, the final Aztec conquest of Indian towns on the Gulf Coast of Mexico was accomplished. Thus for many native peoples in the region of Veracruz, where the first conquering Spanish landed, Aztec domination and Spanish domination were rapidly successive experiences, separated by only a few years. This fact goes far to explain the ease with which Cortés and his followers established their mainland foothold. As deliverers or apparent deliverers, here and at many other points, the Spaniards were repeatedly able to turn native political conditions to their own advantage.

Cortés, the leader and chief chronicler of the Mexican conquest, was an Estremaduran who had settled in Hispaniola in 1504 and risen to a position of local prestige in Cuba after 1512.[7] Following the return of Juan de Grijalva, he was commissioned by Diego Velázquez, the Spanish governor of Cuba, to establish full contact

Marion W. Smith (ed.), *Asia and North America: Transpacific Contacts* (Menasha, Wis., 1953).

[5] George C. Vaillant, *Early Cultures of the Valley of Mexico* (New York, 1935); Walter Krickeberg, *Altmexikanische Kulturen* (Berlin, 1956).

[6] Robert H. Barlow, *The Extent of the Empire of the Culhua Mexica* (Berkeley and Los Angeles, 1949).

[7] The classic sixteenth-century life of Cortés is Francisco López de Gómara, *Historia de la conquista de México,* Joaquín Ramírez Cabañas, ed. (2 vols., Mexico, 1943). A modern skeptical biography is Henry R. Wagner, *The Rise of Fernando Cortés* (Los Angeles, 1944).

with the empire of Montezuma. Disassociating himself from the sponsorship of Velázquez, Cortés moved by sea to the coast of Mexico and then overland to the elevated central valley that was the center of the Aztec state. At a number of points along the route, notably at the independent province of Tlaxcala, Cortés formed alliances with native peoples who were already enemies of the Aztecs or who were disaffected under their control. At Cholula, where the forces of Montezuma planned a decisive ambush, Cortés was forewarned by friendly natives, and his soldiers executed a wholesale slaughter that quickly brought this community and its dependencies to the Spanish side.

Thus the several hundred Spanish soldiers were reinforced by many thousands of Indian aides by the time that Cortés arrived at Tenochtitlan in the autumn of 1519. Here Montezuma exchanged formal greeting with the Spaniards and invited them to enter the city. While Cortés quietly held Montezuma prisoner and ruled through him as puppet emperor, the Spanish soldiers circulated throughout the area, gathering gold and other plunder. Relations between the two peoples remained superficially harmonious until the spring of 1520, when, during the temporary absence of Cortés from the city, the Aztec populace suddenly rose in rebellion. Despite Cortés' speedy return and his determined effort to halt the uprising, the Aztecs achieved their aim; on the Melancholy Night (*Noche Triste*) of June 30, 1520, the intruders were expelled and Tenochtitlan reverted to Indian control. Montezuma met his death on this occasion under circumstances that remain mysterious. The Spaniards, beaten in battle and lacking a native puppet ruler, found refuge with their Indian allies in the province of Tlaxcala. Their final attack on Tenochtitlan in the summer of 1521, accomplished partly through the use of brigantines on the lake and partly by land assault over the causeways, is one of the celebrated sieges of history. It proved wholly successful, and the Aztec defenders, now under the command of Montezuma's nephew and son-in-law Cuauhtemoc, were compelled to surrender to Cortés in August, 1521.[8]

---

[8] The two basic sources on the conquest of Mexico are the letters of Cortés and the *Historia verdadera* of Bernal Díaz. Both are available in English trans-

To the invaders Mexico City was a major prize. In Spanish hands the city served as the center of an expanding colonial territory, the character and practical limits of which came to be identified during the next two decades. Cortés retained control of affairs until 1528, when he returned to Spain to answer charges against him and to petition for royal confirmation of his authority. To his subordinates was given much of the task of completing the conquest in southern and northern Mexico, in Central America, and in Yucatan.[9] These lesser conquistadores committed acts of insubordination against Cortés, sought to control areas for themselves, and made occasional and unsuccessful efforts to usurp Cortés' power in the capital. But Cortés emerged from the confusion of Spanish rivalries by 1530 with the title of Marquis of the Valley (i.e., the Valley of Oaxaca in southern Mexico) and as the most powerful private citizen of the New World. The establishment of crown offices and especially the appointment of a viceroy in 1535 prevented him from realizing any large-scale political ambitions, but his postconquest achievements—the rebuilding of the destroyed Aztec city, the sponsoring of further expeditions, above all the control of his own soldiers, who became the first Spanish settlers in Mexico—mark him as an individual of enormous strength and capacity. Cortés, in contrast to many of the lesser figures in this drama, was far more than a military conqueror. He possessed a vision of imperial greatness. The city of Mexico, he wrote to the Emperor Charles V, "will each day grow more noble, and as it was before the Lord and Mistress of all these provinces, so will it be in the future."[10] To be sure, not all of the early Spanish achievement in Mexico may be directly attributed to its farsighted conquistador. But by the time of Cortés' last departure for Spain in 1540, the

lations: Hernando Cortés, *Five Letters, 1519–1526*, J. Bayard Morris, trans. (London, 1928); Bernal Díaz del Castillo, *The Discovery and Conquest of Mexico, 1517–1521*, A. P. Maudslay, trans.; Genaro García, ed. (London, 1928).

[9] Pedro de Alvarado, *An Account of the Conquest of Guatemala in 1524 by Pedro de Alvarado* (New York, 1924); Robert S. Chamberlain, *The Conquest and Colonization of Honduras, 1502–1550* (Washington, 1953).

[10] See Viktor Frankl, "Die Begriffe des mexikanischen Kaisertums und der Weltmonarchie in den 'Cartas de Relación' des Hernán Cortés," *Saeculum*, XIII (1962), 1–34. Frankl imaginatively analyzes Cortés' letters on the subjects of sovereignty, empire, and universal monarchy.

city that he had conquered and rebuilt had become a powerful colonial metropolis, the capital of a Spanish territory extending south into Central America and north to or beyond the Gulf of California. Cortés' example stimulated discoveries extending beyond the land that Spaniards were capable of settling or ever would settle in America. A series of expeditions far to the north, made with the object of locating the Seven Cities of Cibola, of medieval legend, culminated in the famous Vásquez de Coronado expedition which penetrated as far as modern Kansas in 1540–42.[11] The movements reveal how actively and energetically the society that Cortés founded devoted itself to the pursuit in remote regions of non-existent Indian wealth.

Although no other conquistador rivaled Cortés in military skill or in the capacity to control the conquest aftermath, all subsequent campaigns were in some measure modeled upon the conquest of the Aztec empire. In Yucatan and the adjacent parts of Guatemala, where the Maya were located, conquest was undertaken by leaders familiar with Cortés' methods and eager to win a victory as decisive and complete as his. But the conquest of Yucatan proved to be a time-consuming operation, broken by continual advances and retreats and many temporary failures. The Maya civilization was less militaristic than the Aztec, and for this very reason proved better prepared to withstand the warfare that the Spanish armies waged. Aztec society had been vulnerable to the degree that its rigid, highly organized state was vulnerable, and the whole imperial structure had fallen as one entity. In Yucatan the routes of the conquistadores closed behind them in intermittent guerrilla forays. Towns were captured and lost, and no administrative capital compared with Tenochtitlan to determine the survival or loss of the entire civilization. In 1535, eight years after the conquistador Francisco de Montejo had made his first assault, the Spanish armies were in full retreat from the peninsula. Only in 1542 was a Spanish victory clearly in sight, and not until 1545 was Yucatan assuredly in Spanish control.[12]

[11] Herbert E. Bolton, *Coronado, Knight of Pueblos and Plains* (New York, 1949).

[12] Robert S. Chamberlain, *The Conquest and Colonization of Yucatan, 1517–1550* (Washington, 1948).

Meanwhile other conquest armies extended the wars to South America, where still other rich civilizations had long been known to exist. In the Andean highlands of the western coast, Quechua (Inca) peoples had developed one of the most remarkable social and political systems of the non-European world. The Incas lacked some of the more striking traits of Aztec and early Maya cultures— their calendar, for example, was an unprepossessing and functional time count as compared with the elaborate chronological constructions of aboriginal Mexico. But the Incas were the creators of the most organized and rational society in all native America. Their paternalistic welfare government was headed by a chief (Sapa Inca) who was at once emperor and deity, and whose queen was his own sister. Dynastic succession devolved upon a male offspring who in his turn married incestuously in order to prevent the introduction of any impure strain. The court was composed of members of the imperial family, from among whom the main administrative posts were filled. The state exacted labor tribute from a population divided according to age groups. Public buildings, temples, waterworks, terraces, and fortresses were constructed under the direction of professional architects and builders who were supported by the government. A system of roads connected outlying parts of the empire to its center, with postal stations for the rapid relay of messages to and from Cuzco, the capital city.[13]

The Inca empire, like the Aztec, was still comparatively new in the early sixteenth century. At the time of the Spaniards' arrival it was undergoing a severe internal crisis, in the form of a civil war between two rival heirs for the chieftainship. The schism much facilitated the Spanish conquest. Francisco Pizarro, the principal conquistador,[14] made two early attempts to reach Peru by sea from

[13] The most reliable modern description is John Howland Rowe, "Inca Culture at the Time of the Spanish Conquest," in Julian H. Steward (ed.), *Handbook of South American Indians* (7 vols., Washington, 1946–59), II, 183–330. The famous "socialist" features of the Inca state are emphasized in Luis Baudin, *L'empire socialiste des Inka* (Paris, 1928).

[14] History has been less kind to Pizarro than to Cortés. In the traditional comparison Pizarro suffers by way of lowly birth, illegitimacy, illiteracy, cruelty, and the failure of that larger vision that is so conspicuous in the conqueror of Mexico. Contrasts between Cortés and Pizarro often obey dramatic rather than historical rules. A humble origin, which might be regarded as a point in Pizarro's favor, is frequently held against him. Circumstantial tales concerning

Panama in the 1520's. Only on his third attempt, after having visited Charles V in Spain to obtain royal support, was he able to effect a satisfactory attack. Again sailing from Panama (1531), Pizarro landed at Tumbez on the Pacific coast just south of the equator and proceeded overland south and east toward Cuzco. Along most of the way he was able to dispel suspicion and avoid conflict in the native civil war by informing each faction that he came as the enemy of the other. By the time of his arrival at Cajamarca, part way between Tumbez and Cuzco, the Inca dynastic crisis had reached a point of temporary stability. After the example of Cortés, Pizarro captured Atahualpa, the foremost claimant to the Incaship, and employed his Spanish soldiers in the collection of treasure. In intricate and underhanded diplomacy, Pizarro negotiated also with the rival faction, while Atahualpa secretly prepared a military force to expel the Spaniards. When Atahualpa's treasure was collected, the Spaniards refused to free him. Instead, in one of the most famous events of conquest history, they conducted a trial, charged him with usurpation, idolatry, polygamy, and other crimes, and executed him.[15]

Many factors complicated the history of the Peruvian conquest after 1533. Conflict developed over the disposition of the booty between Pizarro's followers and certain followers of Diego de Almagro, who had arrived with reinforcements just prior to Atahualpa's execution. An intrusion by one of the old lieutenants of Cortés, Pedro de Alvarado, was countered by the combined action of Almagro and Sebastián Belalcázar near Quito in the northern limits of the Inca empire in 1534. After 1535 Almagro spent several years in exploration and attempted conquest in Chile, and on his return rebelled against Pizarro in Peru. With this a full-scale civil war broke out in which one Spanish faction fought against another while each sought to enlist the aid of Indian parties. The opposing Spanish groups elevated rival Incas, whose

his youth are given a pejorative flavor. Pizarro was an experienced military leader, not a mere opportunistic adventurer, at the time of the conquest of Peru. See the remarks of M. M. E. in *Estudios americanos,* XVIII (1959), 173–174.

[15] See, in addition to standard older sources, George Kubler, "The Behavior of Atahualpa," *Hispanic American Historical Review,* XXV (1945), 413–427.

policies reflected a continuation of the original schism in the native
political state. Almagro was imprisoned and killed in 1538. Pizarro
was murdered in 1541. The Spanish government sent royal officers
in an attempt to establish order, and these also were drawn into
the strife. The Spanish viceroy himself was killed in battle in 1546.
Only in 1548, with the defeat of Pizarro's brother, may the period
of warfare be said to have come to an end. Thus the conquest of
Peru merged with a period of civil disorder, and the civil disorder
in turn prolonged the conquest and afforded an opportunity for a
separatist Inca faction to maintain an independent existence in a
remote Andean retreat. Relations between the Inca state and the
colonial government assumed the character of a war of attrition,
with sporadic raids and occasional diplomatic negotiations. Finally
in 1572, under the viceroy Francisco de Toledo, the last Inca heir,
or supposed heir, Tupac Amaru, was captured and killed.[16]

Despite such conflicts the Spanish colony in Peru, like its counterpart in Mexico, became a center from which further expeditions
of discovery and conquest set out. To the south, Pedro de Valdivia
undertook to continue the task begun by Almagro against the
Araucanian peoples of Chile. The line of Araucanian hostility was
pushed southward, and Spanish colonists moving from Peru in the
1540's established themselves in the regions won.[17] In the north the
native Chibcha civilization of Colombia (the most precise of many
locations of El Dorado) drew groups of Spaniards from Peru and
Ecuador, as well as from the regions of the Caribbean coast. The
foremost conquistador of the Chibcha area was Gonzalo Jiménez
de Quesada, whose ascent of the Magdalena Valley in the 1530's
is one of the renowned achievements in the history of American
exploration.[18]

[16] A firsthand and partial account is Pedro Pizarro, *Relation of the Discovery
and Conquest of the Kingdom of Peru,* Philip Ainsworth Means, trans. (New
York, 1921). The best treatment in English for most readers is still William H.
Prescott, *History of the Conquest of Peru, with a Preliminary View of the
Civilization of the Incas* (2 vols., New York, 1847, and many other editions).
Prescott reviews the standard older writers.

[17] Louis De Armond, "Frontier Warfare in Colonial Chile," *Pacific Historical
Review,* XXIII (1954), 125–132.

[18] Germán Arciniegas, *The Knight of El Dorado: The Tale of Don Gonzalo
Jiménez de Quesada and his Conquest of New Granada, now called Colombia,*
Mildred Adams, trans. (New York, 1942). For this, as well as for other con-

One may not speak in the same sense of "conquest" in other parts of South America. The term cannot be appropriately applied to the early Spanish entry into the Plata estuary, where no genuine conquistadores emerged. The Plata was explored by Sebastian Cabot in the late 1520's. Its occupation in the 1530's was encouraged by the belief that the river offered an avenue to Peru. But its chief city, Buenos Aires, was abandoned after the first foundation, and the estuary was later relinquished almost wholly to native peoples. Settlement in the interior of this southern region came later through expansion from the west, and the cities of Santiago del Estero, Tucumán, and Córdoba were all founded by colonists from Chile and Peru. In the area of Asunción in Paraguay, a thousand miles up the river from the Plata mouth, cooperating Spanish and Guaraní armies waged offensive and defensive battle against the Guaycurú and other Chaco peoples. Here, through intermarriage and military prestige, Spaniards gained the status of native chiefs, practicing polygamy and creating an ethnically mixed (mestizo) population.[19] In the Amazon basin farther north, Spanish settlement never took place at all. The great river, rising in the Andean mountains only a hundred miles from the Pacific, drained a forbidding jungle, populated by primitive and nomadic peoples. Francisco de Orellana descended the Amazon from Peru to its mouth in 1541–42, but, like Coronado in the north in the same period, he succeeded mainly in covering distance and demonstrating fortitude.[20]

Overt military conquest merged easily with other forms of domination, and there is no exact terminal date for the "age of conquest" in Spanish-American history. In some localities, as in central Mexico, where the transition from a state of war to a state of creative colonization was sharp and evident, the military con-

quests not mentioned here, see Frederick A. Kirkpatrick, *The Spanish Conquistadores* (London, 1946).

[19] Enrique de Gandía, *Historia de la conquista del Río de la Plata y del Paraguay: Los gobiernos de Don Pedro de Mendoza, Alvar Núñez y Domingo de Irala, 1535–1556* (Buenos Aires, 1932); Elman R. Service, "The Encomienda in Paraguay," *Hispanic American Historical Review,* XXXI (1951), 231–234.

[20] Gaspar de Carvajal, *The Discovery of the Amazon according to the Account of Friar Gaspar de Carvajal and Other Documents,* Bertram T. Lee, trans. (New York, 1934).

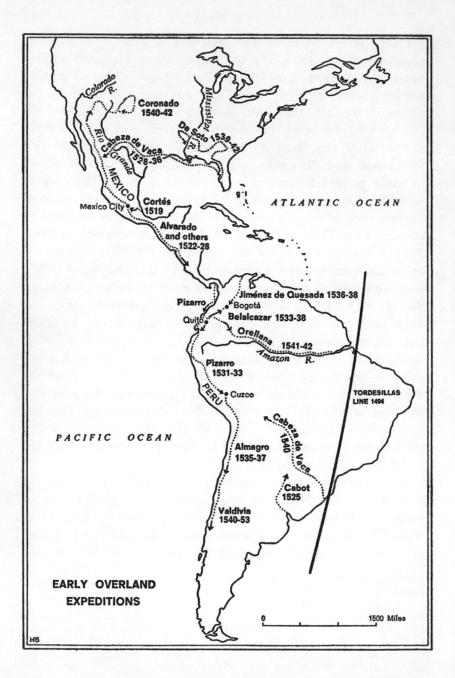

Colorado R.

Coronado
1540-42

Mississippi R.

De Soto 1539-42

Cabeza de Vaca
1528-36

Rio Grande

MEXICO

ATLANTIC OCEAN

Mexico City

Cortés
1519

Alvarado
and others
1522-28

Pizarro

Jiménez de Quesada 1536-38
Bogotá
Belalcazar 1533-38

Quito

Orellana
1541-42

Amazon R.

Pizarro
1531-33

Cuzco

TORDESILLAS
LINE 1494

PACIFIC OCEAN

PERU

Almagro
1535-37

Cabeza de Vaca
1540

Cabot
1525

Valdivia
1540-53

EARLY OVERLAND
EXPEDITIONS

0   1500 Miles

HS

quest was confined within brief chronological limits. If one thinks of the great war efforts conducted in the tradition of Cortés, conquest may be dated between 1519, when Cortés landed in Veracruz, and the mid or late 1540's, when the conquering armies had virtually completed their work. Warfare of this type took place where organized native societies offered resistance, where native population was most dense, and where Indian wealth was most conspicuously in evidence. But in other areas conditions were less clear and conquest lingered longer, only gradually losing its military character.

Why was it that Spaniards, so greatly outnumbered and with such dangerously extended supply lines, uniformly won the conquest wars? Part of the answer lies in the firearms and horses of the Spanish armies, which furnished tremendous military advantages. Indians were struck with terror at the explosions of guns, and men on horseback were so unfamiliar to them that they took them at first to be single creatures, awesome in their power. Imaginative campaigning, as in Cortés' use of brigantines on the waters of the Valley of Mexico, contributed to particular campaigns.[21] Indians were weakened psychologically through their superstitions, which sometimes foretold their defeat at the hands of strangers, even white and bearded strangers, coming from the east. The policy of Spanish alliance with Indians meant that the imbalance in numbers was not always a crucial factor. Commonly the alliances reflected pre-existing rifts within Indian society, rifts of which the Spaniards were then able to take advantage. Thus Cortés profited from the long-established hostility of Tlaxcalans toward Aztecs, and Pizarro could hardly have made his way so readily through the Inca empire without the dynastic schism that divided its people. Indian allies served to provide and carry goods as well as to fight in battle, and this meant that Spaniards were less dependent upon supply lines than would have been the case in more conventional military operations.

Though its dimensions were distinctly limited in time and place,

---

[21] On Spanish arms see the study of Albert María Salas, *Las armas de la conquista* (Buenos Aires, 1950); on Cortés' brigantines see C. Harvey Gardiner, *Naval Power in the Conquest of Mexico* (Austin, Tex., 1956).

conquest has ever since been the most celebrated of the accomplish-
ments of Spain in America. Few episodes of history can rival these
American wars for excitement and drama. They are among the
spectaculars of all time, with lush and exotic scenes, fast action, and
the full measure of derring-do. The dramatis personae include
swashbuckling Spaniards and inscrutable native kings. Cortés' destruction of his ships, Pizarro's drawing a line on the ground and
inviting all who rejected comfort and craved danger and wealth to
step across—these are evocative incidents, well known everywhere,
and they illustrate the dramatic and adventurous character of conquest.[22]

In addition conquest reveals more graphically than any other
activity of Spain in America those peculiar Hispanic traits that fasci-
nate and puzzle the outside world. In conquest Spaniards demonstrated an almost superhuman determination to overcome obstacles
and a supreme indifference to difficulties. Spanish fatalism, the
obsession with death, and the mockery of life recur under ever-
changing conditions. Material and spiritual goals mingle in fascinating patterns. Combinations of lust and sentimentality, of honorable
and base conduct, of altruism and selfishness occur and reoccur.
The Spaniard appears as a man of epic qualities who descends to the
depths of inhumanity. Valiant, cruel, indefatigable, ferocious,
courageous, and villainous—Spanish character alternates among
extremes and displays that "coexistence of contrary tendencies" for
which it is so celebrated.

The Indian response to conquest is recorded in a literature that
was written down by Spaniards at Indian dictation, or in some
instances written directly by literate Indians themselves, after the
conquests were over. In the native commentary on the Spanish
penetration of Mexico we can observe as standard themes eyewitness
descriptions of the warfare and mournful lamentations relating to
defeat. Some revealing accounts of Spanish military behavior are

[22] The ideology of conquest is closely linked with the European tradition of
exotic myth. See Enrique de Gandía, *Historia crítica de los mitos de la conquista americana* (Buenos Aires and Madrid, 1929), and Irving A. Leonard,
*Books of the Brave, Being an Account of Books and Men in the Spanish Con-
quest and Settlement of the Sixteenth-Century New World* (Cambridge, Mass.,
1949).

to be found in the colonial Aztec record. When Cortés first met Montezuma's envoys, the Indian leaders carried gold ornaments and precious objects as gifts, and an Indian witness of the scene reported:

When they were given these presents, the Spaniards burst into smiles; their eyes shone with pleasure. . . . They picked up the gold and fingered it like monkeys; they seemed to be transported by joy, as if their hearts were illumined and made new. . . . Their bodies swelled with greed, and their hunger was ravenous. They hungered like pigs for that gold. They snatched at the golden ensigns, waved them from side to side and examined every inch.[23]

The Indian literature further contains detailed first impressions of Spanish soldiers, their arms, their horses, and their other equipment. What may appear in a Spanish chronicle as a simple statement of victory takes on in the Indian account a special poignancy and sense of doom. The native language expresses a certain innocence in the face of destruction, and the Indian memory is of unexpected detail that in a few words or sentences adds new dimensions to the historical event. The lamentations in defeat sometimes achieve a literary power that can be appreciated even in translation:

> Broken spears lie in the roads;
> We have torn our hair in our grief.
> The houses are roofless now. . . .
> And the walls are splattered with gore. . . .
> We have pounded our hands in despair
> Against the adobe walls.[24]

But it should be borne in mind that Indian, like Spanish, character was complex and various. In still other instances Indians expressed attitudes far removed from either resentment or remorse. Paradoxically, they associated themselves with the conquerors and adopted conquistador points of view. Vast numbers of Indians were able to recount truthfully that they had assisted the Spanish armies in the conquest wars, and after peace came they petitioned the king

[23] Miguel León-Portilla (ed.), *The Broken Spears: The Aztec Account of the Conquest of Mexico,* Angel María Garibay K. and Lysander Kemp, trans. (Boston, 1962), p. 51.
[24] *Ibid.,* p. 137.

for favors and rewards due their status as native conquistadores. Both Charles V and Philip II took the appeals seriously and granted coats of arms to Indians. Indian delegations traveled to Spain to request favors in audience with the king, and countless such favors were granted. Illustration 5 shows a drawing by the Indians of Tlaxcala about 1550 for presentation to the king. It illustrates Tlaxcalan soldiers joining with Spanish soldiers in the conquest of Cholula. Marina, Cortés' Indian interpreter and companion, stands at the right. A Spanish rider tramples on dismembered Indian bodies. Tlaxcalan and Spanish soldiers together lay siege to the temple of Cholula. Here the Indians' purpose is to deny the unity of Indian society and to argue that selected Indian peoples, having befriended the Spanish soldiers, were deserving of recognition and reward.

Among Spaniards the response to conquest underwent a number of changes. In Spain itself, following the excitement of the first news, questions relating particularly to the ethic of conquest made their appearance in speech and writing. Both in the mother country and in the New World, Spaniards found their consciences disturbed by the course that Christian warfare was taking in America. The slaughter of masses of non-Christian peoples, however precedented in European history, seemed inconsistent with professed Christian aims. The papacy had confirmed, and the Spanish monarchy had accepted, the duty of American Christianization, but the extent to which this duty required or permitted conquest was specifically called into question and remained a subject of debate. The debate was to bring forth denunciations of the conquerors' conduct and of the entire conquistador philosophy, as well as counterarguments and official justification on the other side.

The earliest document issued by the royal government on the ethical issues of Spanish-Indian warfare was the Requerimiento (Requirement), a copy of which was to be carried by every conquistador. Its probable author, Juan López de Palacios Rubios, was a Spanish juridical expert on the doctrine of just war. He appears to have drafted the Requerimiento at royal order shortly before 1514, during the time when slave raiders were active in the Antilles. Its message, a summary of Christian history from the creation of the

world to the Alexandrine bulls, was to be read to Indians, by interpreters if possible, at the beginning of every battle. It required
the Indian hearers to recognize the authority of church, pope, and
monarch, and it further detailed, in graphic phrases, the consequences should they refuse to acknowledge proper allegiance. The
consequences were coercive subjugation, alienation of property, and
punishment appropriate to traitors. On each occasion the record
was to be notarized and signed by witnesses. The reading of the
proclamation was held to absolve the conquistadores from responsibility and to free them from suspicion of aggressive war.[25]

Even at the time the Requerimiento was condemned as ludicrously
and tragically naïve. It served as a justification for conquest mainly
among persons already prepared to adopt apologist positions. But it
was seriously defended by Palacios Rubios and others, and there can
be no question that it was formally and repeatedly pronounced by
Spanish conquistadores prior to battle—commonly, however, in the
Spanish language and at a distance that made it inaudible to the
Indian enemy. The central point of Requerimiento philosophy was
its insistence that Indians were to blame for the Spanish conquest.
"The resultant deaths and damages shall be your fault," it read,
"and not the monarch's or mine or the soldiers'."

At best the Requerimiento assumed a rapid native comprehension
of unfamiliar subjects. Even granting that Indians were rational
beings—a point on which additional debate ensued—a number of
practical questions arose over Requerimiento procedure. Palacios
Rubios, enunciating a doctrine of Indian rationality, argued that
the Requirement and the whole Spanish dominion in America were
justified by papal grant. Others attacked this view and expressed
themselves as opposed both to the Requerimiento and to the assumptions on which it was based. Philosophical controversy came to
embrace a variety of topics: the true nature of the grants, the original authority of the pope, the definition of "just war," the capacity
and rationality of Indians, the superiority of Spaniards, and the
very nature of man.[26] Erudite scholastic arguments were brought to

[25] Lewis Hanke, "The 'Requerimiento' and Its Interpreters," *Revista de
historia de América,* I (1938), 25–34.
[26] Paul III declared the Indians of America to be rational beings in a bull of

bear on all these subjects, and the debate was followed attentively in the learned circles of Spain during the whole period from the drafting of the Requerimiento through the age of conquest.

In America the most outspoken critic of conquest was Bartolomé de Las Casas, the famous "Protector" of the American Indians. In his earlier life Las Casas had observed, and had even participated in, the uncontrolled Spanish exploitation of native peoples in the Antilles. Thereafter, as an advocate of colonial reform, Las Casas entered the Dominican order, promoted a number of humanitarian projects, became bishop of Chiapas in southern Mexico, and devoted himself to the writing of tracts condemning the cruelty of the conquests and the whole of Spanish behavior in America. The papal donation, in Las Casas' view, authorized and obligated the Spanish monarchs to convert Indians and to exercise spiritual authority over them. But neither the papal donation nor any other ordinance or rule entitled Spain to undertake the American conquests. Las Casas dismissed much of the traditional medieval and Renaissance literature on relations between Christians and non-Christians in the assumption that American Indians constituted a special class of non-Christians. Moslems in the Old World had attacked Christendom, but American Indians had no previous knowledge of Christianity at all. As rational beings Indians were entitled to retain their properties, and the Spanish monarch was duty bound to return America to its rightful Indian owners. The whole of Spanish action in America, Las Casas asserted, was contrary to justice and to law. With respect to the Requerimiento, Las Casas said that he did not know whether to laugh or to weep.[27]

The Las Casas criticism was itself denounced in the 1540's by

---

1537, and the matter was thereupon officially resolved. Lewis Hanke, "Pope Paul III and the American Indians," *Harvard Theological Review*, XXX (1937), 65–102. See also Edmundo O'Gorman, "Sobre la naturaleza bestial del indio americano," *Filosofía y letras*, No. 1 (1941), pp. 141–158; No. 2 (1941), pp. 305–315.

[27] For a systematic modern summary of Las Casas' position, see Lewis Hanke, *The Spanish Struggle for Justice in the Conquest of America* (Philadelphia, 1949), pp. 54 ff. For further materials on the life and controversies, see Lewis Hanke and Manuel Giménez Fernández, *Bartolomé de Las Casas, 1474–1566: Bibliografía crítica y cuerpo de materiales para el estudio de su vida, escritos, actuación y polémicas que suscitaron durante cuatro siglos* (Santiago de Chile, 1954), listing some 850 titles.

Juan Ginés de Sepúlveda, who defended, more energetically and more learnedly than any other individual in Spain, the doctrine of just conquest. The Biblical text, "Go out into the highways and hedges, and compel them to come in" (Luke 14:23), Sepúlveda interpreted as divine authorization for the use of force. His position was that the Christian end, the conversion of the natives to Christianity, provided absolute justification for the American wars. The papacy *had* authorized conquest in the Alexandrine bulls. The Indians, moreover, were guilty of tyranny, human sacrifice, cannibalism, idolatry, and other sins. The conquests were just and right, for the reason that they brought an end to the barbaric civilizations that countenanced such practices. Moreover, through introducing Indians to Spanish ways of life, conquest prepared the way for the adoption of civilized customs. Sepúlveda argued that Spaniards were naturally superior to Indians. They came as deliverers, for countless Indians were the victims of illegitimate local masters.[28] Even the failure of Indians to withstand the conquest warfare was cited by Sepúlveda as evidence of their inferiority. "How can we doubt," he asked, "that these people—so uncivilized, so barbaric, contaminated with so many impieties and obscenities—have been justly conquered by such an excellent, pious, and most just king?"[29]

Sepúlveda's interpretation of interracial relations was Aristotelian and theoretical. He depended on a scholastic tradition, and he had no direct experience with America. Las Casas, on the other hand, was long familiar with colonial life and pursued the advantage with which this knowledge provided him. Each was sincerely convinced of the justice of his own view. But Las Casas, wanting further verification, undertook to prove through direct demonstration that his argument was in conformity with the realities of colonization. Those who defended conquest made much of the point that conquest served as an unavoidable preliminary to Christian conversion. Las

[28] The notion that Spaniards came as deliverers was frequently expressed. It appears to have been justified in the case of the conquest of Quito by Belalcázar. See, among other treatments, Kirkpatrick, *Spanish Conquistadores,* pp. 172, 218 ff.

[29] Hanke, *Spanish Struggle for Justice,* p. 123. Sepúlveda's argument is developed in Juan Ginés de Sepúlveda, *Democrates segundo o de las justas causas de la guerra contra loss indios,* Angel Losada, ed. (Madrid, 1951).

Casas offered to select an unconquered region in America and to Christianize it without the use of force. The region selected was known as Tierra de Guerra, or Land of War, a province that had successfully resisted Spanish military conquest in Guatemala. Here in the late 1530's Las Casas and other Dominican friars introduced Christian doctrine and propitiated the natives through peaceful trade. Once the chiefs had been won to Christianity, the most difficult part of the task was over. An effective conversion was accomplished in a period of a few months. The name of the region was changed to Vera Paz, or True Peace. The demonstration appeared to be successful, and the Spanish monarch was impressed. The remarkable achievement lost only a portion of its effect later, when the province rebelled, reverted to paganism, sacrificed one of the friars, and had to be punished at royal order.[30]

In Spain the Las Casas campaigns had direct consequences in stimulating official caution toward the question of conquest. The monarchy, increasingly sensitive on the subject, did not adopt the full Las Casas position. To have done so would have meant the relinquishment of the American empire. But the monarchy did come to adopt a moderate position, one that reconciled some of the differences between Las Casas and his opponents. In 1550, the king ordered all conquests halted while a royal court heard testimony on the question. Later, regulations were issued designed to control the course of conquest: all penetrations into new territories were to be duly licensed; licenses were to be granted only to persons of "good conscience," persons who were "zealous for the honor of God" and "lovers of peace." All was to be done in accordance with Christian doctrine, in a spirit of "love and moderation." The word conquest was no longer to be used; Spanish occupation was to be known as "pacification" and "settlement," lest continued talk of conquest encourage the further use of force.[31] It is true that these regulations

---

[30] Marcel Bataillon, "La Vera Paz, roman et histoire," *Bulletin hispanique*, LIII (1951), 235–299; Karl T. Sapper, *Die Verapaz im 16. und 17. Jahrhundert* (Munich, 1936); Benno Biermann, "Missionsgeschichte der Verapaz in Guatemala," in *Jahrbuch für Geschichte von Staat, Wirtschaft und Gesellschaft Lateinamerikas*, I (1964), 117–156; Hanke, *Spanish Struggle for Justice*, pp. 77 ff.

[31] *Colección de documentos inéditos relativos al descubrimiento, conquista y*

appeared at a time when the real "age of conquest" was already past in America. They represent a late moral response to an accomplished fact. And the restrictions placed on the word conquest suggest a kind of official nominalism, as if evil might be exorcised through euphemism and deliberate imperial taboo.

The seventeenth and eighteenth centuries, in contrast to the sixteenth, witnessed a gradual mutation, a selective process, and a quantitative reduction among the reactions to conquest. Indian literature, on this and other subjects, tended to disappear. In Europe, the Las Casas type of criticism shifted from a domestic to an international basis. Las Casas' works, convincingly authenticated by the Spanish citizenship and episcopal rank of their author, and seized upon by the national rivals of Spain, were reprinted in many translations. The result was the Black Legend of condemnation of Spain. The process began in the sixteeneth century, but it gained a cumulative power later, when Spanish decline could be more clearly seen. The translated texts were enriched with eloquent titles and horrifying illustrations. Their sense and purpose pointed to a conclusion that Las Casas had never intended. The late reprintings of Las Casas' works were not designed to induce any reform in the Spanish program. Their objectives were the denigration and abuse of Spanish character for national and patriotic ends.[32]

Thus there continued to develop, out of the new balance of power in Europe, that preoccupation with Spanish character of which conquest historians are still prone to speak. Additional meaning was given to the Spanish character in the philosophical speculations of the eighteenth century. Marmontel's *Les Incas,* De Pauw's *Recherches philosophiques,* Voltaire's *Alzire,* and many other works extended and elaborated the theme of conquest evil. The writers were less concerned with the historical reality of conquest than with its symbolic content. Conquest was a preferred item in their cata-

---

organización de las antiguas posesiones españolas de América y Oceanía, sacados de los archivos del reino, y muy especialmente del de Indias (title varies; 42 vols., Madrid, 1864–84), XVI, 142–153, 181–187.

[32] Rómulo D. Carbia, *Historia de la leyenda negra hispanoamericana* (Madrid, 1944); Sverker Arnoldsson, *La leyenda negra: Estudios sobre sus orígenes* (Stockholm, 1960); Sverker Arnoldsson, *La conquista española de América según el juicio de la posteridad: Vestigios de la leyenda negra* (Madrid, 1960).

logue of anti-Spanish themes. They postulated a Spanish character unchanged by the intervening two centuries and spoke of conquest in universal terms, together with the oppression and fanaticism with which it was associated. The Las Casas legacy was reactivated in the light of reason. Those earlier tendencies to understand conquest as an epitome of Spanish behavior in the New World were reinforced by the simple nobility now attributed to the Indian. Was not the unspoiled, idealized native a secular version of the Indian of Las Casas? He had been oppressed by two additional centuries of Spanish cruelty in the conquest tradition. His spiritual salvation, which had been the objective of the Spanish missionaries, had been frustrated and could be viewed only with irony.

The *"neolascasista"* argument of the eighteenth century encountered a response in Spain that may be regarded in turn as a secularized counterpart of Sepúlveda. Its spokesmen were such figures as Benito Feijóo and Juan de Escoiquiz. Arguments inapposite to the conquest period were now advanced. In contrast to the character or "spirit" of Spain these Spaniards offered an equally characteristic eighteenth-century concept, the "spirit" of the age. The conquistadores had lived in an "age" of conquest, an age to which they had involuntarily submitted. To live in an unenlightened age might be a misfortune, but no private guilt could be attached to individual failure to rise above the standards of one's time. Nor were Spaniards now averse to justifying the conquistadores by means of the general nature of imperialism or to relating this behavior with that of mankind as a whole. "It is no wonder that there were certain cruelties," wrote Escoiquiz at the end of the eighteenth century. "But consider the atrocities of other nations, the barbarisms and tyrannies that have been committed not just by a small number of individuals but by whole governments, and not against cruel and barbaric Indians but against cultured and peaceful people who never did them the least harm."[33]

The eighteenth century rounded out the moral argument and cast it in terms that still carry meaning today. Our history still confronts, or evades, the moral question of conquest at some compro-

[33] Juan de Escoiquiz, *México conquistada: Poema heroyco* (3 vols., Madrid, 1798), I, xix ff.

mise position between the character of Spain and the spirit of the age. If we readily admit that Spain has been disproportionately criticized, we do not find in that a reason for total exculpation. Nor did the eighteenth century modify, above all for our own legacy in English, the interpretation of postconquest history as "conquest aftermath" or that original absence of concern for conquest antecedents. The scientific historiography of modern times, which sets aside the moral question as an unrelated issue, has not escaped these factual derivatives of a period when right and wrong were as important as truth and falsehood.

Morality is only one component of conquest interpretation. To the attitudes toward conquest already mentioned we should add the contribution of the Age of Romanticism, when the dramatic, exotic, and emotional features of the conquest narratives received an almost exclusive attention. Romantic writers of the eighteenth and nineteenth centuries could attach readymade decorative details to conquest without any limitations of reality. In the tales, plays, poems, operas, and painting of the Romantic Age, the conquest theme was reiterated and its romantic changes rung. Authenticity became subordinated to atmosphere and picturesque accouterment. Atahualpa wore a jeweled crown, his courtiers wore togas, and their habitations appeared as moated, turreted castles. Conquistadores fell on their knees before Indian maidens on ottomans. Treasure chests lay open under palm trees. Moorish, classical, medieval, and Indian elements made a medley of romantic symbol. The conquest of Mexico as a romantic love story is shown in illustration 6. Here the female figure is Marina, and the male figure is Cortés himself. The poem may be translated as follows:

> Within a tent of silk,
> Whose red banner
> Waves freely in the breeze
> With a hundred capricious turns,
> Hernán Cortés and the Indian girl,
> She beautiful and he genteel,
> With passionate tenderness
> Contemplate each other.[34]

[34] The reproduction is from the "Romancero de Hernán Cortés" of Antonio

The most recent period of conquest interpretation has seen the
development of scientific historiography, marked by the effort to
arrive at as exact a statement as possible of what happened, usually
with a minimum of interpretation beyond the events themselves.
The American historian William H. Prescott was a romantic writer,
but he also gave strict attention to fact and to problems of historical
criticism. The names of Manuel Orozco y Berra, José Fernando
Ramírez, Henry Wagner, Ramón Iglesia, Raúl Porras Barrenechea,
and Robert S. Chamberlain will be remembered for their contributions to recent conquest research. Modern scholarship is less dis-
posed to render categorical judgments upon the conquistadores than
to see them as products of their time and of their surroundings. The
cruelties of our own time have probably blunted some of their impact on modern audiences. Apologists for Spain have observed that
Anglo-Americans also killed Indians, and that if they did so in
lesser numbers than Spaniards, this was because they had lesser
numbers to kill. Serious modern interpretations have paid a reduced
attention to Spanish heroism, while in historical fiction and in
Hollywood the conquests continue to be romanticized. Indian
peoples in particular areas remember the conquests in pageants and
folk dances, frequently with modernized or anachronistic texts. In
one pageant Cortés is referred to as *tejano,* a Texan, and in others
the battle scenes are confused with wars of Christians against Moslems and include portrayals of European kings and popes.

That the issues brought into being by conquest remain alive in
Spanish America is demonstrated by the Mexican Cuauhtemoc cult
of the twentieth century. The outstanding event in the recent history
of the cult is the discovery of the supposed bones of Cuauhtemoc at
Ichcateopan in Guerrero in 1949. The Spanish world ordinarily
pays far more attention to actual remains of deceased heroes than
is the case in the United States, where graves are honored but where
bones tend to be kept discreetly below ground. In Spanish America
the remains of Columbus and Cortés and many others evoke an
emotional response. Adulation, publicity, and imaginative reporting
attend the surprisingly frequent acts of exhumation and transfer. In

---

Hurtado. See Jaime Delgado, "Hernán Cortés en la poesía española de los siglos
XVIII y XIX," *Revista de Indias,* VIII (1948), 394–469.

the case of Cuauhtemoc there is evidence that the popular need for adulation exceeded what could be accommodated by the meager facts of the case. We know that Cuauhtemoc was executed by Cortés during the march to Honduras in 1525. Ichcateopan is not, however, the most probable of many possible burial places, and expert opinion after 1949 raised many doubts concerning the authenticity of the Ichcateopan find. One suspicious circumstance was that the bones of Cortés, after having been lost for a century, had been rediscovered, exhumed, and reported with much journalistic fanfare in 1946. For a period of three years, then, supporters of the conquest and the conquistador tradition, with its corollaries of white supremacy and aristocratic Hispanic lineage, had been able to point without opposition to a venerated cult object. Descendants of the defeated Indian masses, now chiefly mestizo, had no comparable cult object, and it has frequently been suggested that the supposed bones of Cuauhtemoc were contrived to fill the need. In the 1950's, when academic experts declared the Cuauhtemoc find to be false, or at least unauthenticated, public excitement in Mexico rose to a high pitch. Defenders of the discovery thought of themselves as the only Mexican patriots, and the academic critics were denounced in the press as traitors to the nation. Thus four and a half centuries later the two principal protagonists of the conquest (in Mexico, Cuauhtemoc is regarded as superior to Montezuma) symbolize the two continuous strains of Spanish-American ethnic and cultural history.[35]

[35] Literature on the Cuauhtemoc find is summarized by Wigberto Jiménez Moreno, "Los hallazgos de Ichcateopan," *Historia mexicana,* XII (1962–63), 161–181.

CHAPTER 3

Encomienda

IN THE aftermath of conquest a variety of persons, classes, and interests became rivals for control of what had been won. The Indian had now been excluded as a significant competitive element and would ever afterward be held subordinate. The early settlers' fear of Indian revolt proved for the most part groundless, and no Indian uprising was ever more than temporarily successful. The conquest did resolve the question of racial mastery. The postconquest conflicts were not between Spaniards and Indians but among factions of Spaniards, who vied for domination over Indians and over one another.

Divisive forces that had already appeared within the conquest armies continued or reappeared in the postconquest years. Indeed conquest had been a cohesive influence, uniting Spaniards against Indians, and the disputes among Spaniards during the wars arose in spite of the danger of the common enemy. The subsequent period now offered more ample opportunities for factionalism, and the political history of every Spanish-American region in the sixteenth century may be read as a local contest for power. The quarrels tended everywhere to take a personalized form, for loyalty to the leaders served as party bonds, providing groups both with their names (thus the Almagrists and the Pizarrists in Peru) and with their raisons d'être. Moreover they remained always within relatively narrow geographical bounds. They never expanded to pan-colonial dimensions. The Spanish settlers of Mexico recognized few competitions in their relations with the Spanish settlers of the West Indies or of Peru or of New Granada. The intervening distances were too extensive, contact was too infrequent, and local affairs were too demanding for disputes between region and region.

In each postconquest area we may identify three conflicting elements, to which we now devote three successive chapters. The first is the *encomendero* class, consisting of former conquistadores, leading civilian colonists, and other privileged Spaniards. These formed an early colonial aristocracy exercising its power in the institution known as encomienda. The second is the colonial church, dedicated to the tasks of converting Indians, preventing Indian exploitation by *encomenderos,* and establishing a Christian society. And the third is the Spanish secular state with its expanding colonial officialdom and its monarchical insistence on state control over all persons and parties in America.

Through a formal grant of encomienda, designated Indian families, usually the inhabitants of a town or of a cluster of towns, were entrusted to the charge of a Spanish colonist, who thus became the *encomendero.* In the characteristic phrase, he "held" these Indians "in encomienda." The first *encomenderos* were permitted to exact both commodity tribute and labor service from the Indians whom they "held." In this way they derived an income and were able to control labor groups without risk or effort. In return they were expected to render military service (a traditional obligation for the privileged as well as a consequence of the fear of Indian uprisings) and to provide for the Christianization of the Indians committed to their charge. Technically the term encomienda referred to the conditions of trust under which Indian peoples were granted; they were *entrusted* to an *encomendero's* care as a responsibility and favor, in return for military and religious obligations on his part.[1]

An analogy may be made between Spanish encomienda and the later institutions by which other imperial nations compensated the

---

[1] Definitions of encomienda are all after the event. As with many other historical institutions, the development occurred before any need to define was recognized. As will be seen, the early encomienda was frequently called *repartimiento* (distribution or allotment). On terminology, see F. A. Kirkpatrick, "Repartimiento-Encomienda," *Hispanic American Historical Review,* XIX (1939), 372–379.

private agents of their expansion: the proprietorship of the British, the patroonship of the Dutch, the seigneury of the French, and the captaincy of the Portuguese. Each of these differed from the others in important ways. What they had in common was an official award of authority issued to a private individual in return for specified contributions to an imperial end. In no case was a monarchy prepared to undertake imperial projects of its own. In all, the initial efforts were to be made by individuals licensed by the crown. The British, Dutch, French, and Portuguese institutions required the transportation of colonists. The Spanish did not, for the territories of Spanish settlement were already populated by Indians, and the problem was one of controlling an existing population and rewarding colonists already on the scene.

In Spain, Christian knights had acquired jurisdiction over lands and people captured from the Moors in a form sometimes known as encomienda.[2] In America, occupation took place under conditions similar to those of the Spanish *reconquista* and it yielded a comparable solution. The process required a degree of reversion or recapitulation, and this also has an analogy with the later practice of other imperial nations, as in the history of the English proprietorship. But in both the Spanish and the British empires the colonial solutions came to be more significant and more controversial than the prototype of the parent countries. With respect to encomienda, the differences are to be explained by the tradition of African enslavement, by the availability of large numbers of American natives, by their extreme vulnerability to Spanish demands, and by the need for creating, provisioning, and housing a society in a new environment.

Encomienda in an irregular, uncontrolled, and highly exploitative form appeared in America at an early date. Its initial unregulated phase preceded the "age of conquest," for it was widely established in the West Indies during the early years. In the first Spanish settlements encomienda represented a simple solution to a labor problem. Frontier life—the West Indies at this time were the western frontier

    [2] Robert S. Chamberlain, "Castilian Backgrounds of the Repartimiento-Encomienda," in *Carnegie Institution of Washington Publication* No. 509 (Washington, 1939), pp. 19–66.

of European civilization—implied a condition of labor demand. The settlers were few, and the tasks of constructing the colonial community great. White settlers, in the Iberian hidalgo tradition, performed manual labor only with reluctance and distaste. Native labor was the result. Indians were assigned as workers to Spanish employers and the encomienda system was inaugurated.[3]

The West Indian experience from the time of Columbus' first voyage was one of Indian labor for Spanish masters. When this labor was not given "voluntarily" it was extracted by force. As Spaniards arrived in increasing numbers, the need for labor became more pressing, and the burden upon Indian manpower progressively more severe. Spaniards raided Indian communities, took captives, and, in order to prevent escape or to ensure the full measure of work, practiced large-scale enslavement. Columbus, at first, appears to have made some attempt to regulate this forced labor, but without appreciable success.[4] In general the first Spanish contacts with the natives of America followed the precedent of European contact with the natives of Africa, and the practicality and legitimacy of enslavement were everywhere assumed.

The problem for Queen Isabella lay in reconciling economic needs with the professed Christian purposes of Spanish imperialism. There can be no question that the obligation to Christianize the Indians, as originally enunciated by the papacy, was taken seriously by the queen. On the other hand, her condemnation of Indian slavery—a condemnation frequently cited by her modern admirers—was neither uncompromising nor disinterested. On a number of occasions the queen countenanced, and even demanded a share in, the trade of Indian captives as slaves.[5] It is true that formal enslavement, in the

[3] Our general remarks on the history of encomienda derive mainly from the following: Silvio Zavala, *La encomienda indiana* (Madrid, 1935), and *De encomiendas y propiedad territorial en algunas regiones de la América española* (Mexico, 1940); Lesley Byrd Simpson, *The Encomienda in New Spain: The Beginning of Spanish Mexico* (Berkeley and Los Angeles, 1950); Mario Góngora, *El estado en el derecho indiano: Época de fundación, 1492–1570* (Santiago de Chile, 1951), pp. 105–132; Manuel Belaúnde Guinassi, *La encomienda en el Perú* (Lima, 1945).

[4] See Columbus' Memorial of January 30, 1494, in Martín Fernández de Navarrete (ed.), *Colección de viajes y descubrimientos, que hicieron por mar los españoles desde fines del siglo XV* (5 vols., Madrid, 1825–37), I, 232 ff.

[5] *Colección de documentos inéditos relativos al descubrimiento, conquista y*

queen's view, was not to affect the entire native population. It was rather a punishment meted to resisting, rebellious, or cannibalistic individuals and tribes. The queen explicitly took the position that Indians innocent of punishable crimes were "free" crown subjects. But, like other such subjects, they were liable to tribute exaction, and in the conditions of the West Indies colony they might be compelled to work. Thus "free" Indians became available for encomienda assignments.[6]

The monarchy, notably inconsistent in many aspects of its imperial administration, never deviated from its position that the indigenous population was technically free. The encomienda regulations, as encomienda developed in the West Indies under the first royal governors, paid strict, formal recognition to this freedom. Indians under the system were not to be chattels. They could not be bought or sold. They were to be assigned for stated purposes, and *encomenderos* were to treat them with humane respect and with regard for the principles of Christian social intercourse. The object of encomienda was to Christianize pagan peoples through the ministrations of the *encomenderos* and to civilize them by encouraging orderly habits of industry.

But royal declarations of Indian freedom had little connection with the manner in which Indians continued to be treated in America. To the *encomenderos* the encouragement of orderly habits of industry meant only that permission was given for forced labor. In Hispaniola, natives were formally distributed to Spanish colonists who used them in placer mining, agriculture, and stock raising, and who reduced their Christianization to baptism en masse. Encomienda Indians were overworked, abused, bought and sold, and otherwise treated in ways that did not distinguish them from non-encomienda Indians. And even in law those who escaped might be recaptured and condemned to outright slavery, as punishment for neglecting their obligation to "voluntary" work.

---

organización de las antiguas posesiones españolas de América y Oceanía, sacados de los archivos del reino, y muy especialmente del de Indias (title varies; 42 vols., Madrid, 1864–84), XXXI, 187–193. In this contract Indian slaves were to be taken "without doing injury to them" and "so far as possible with their volition."

[6] *Ibid.*, pp. 196–200, 209–212.

After the death of Isabella in 1504, Ferdinand further indulged the *encomendero* class and profited from the encomienda system himself. He ensured a revenue from the islands by employing Indians as gold miners directly in the royal service and by taxing the *encomenderos* proportionately to the number of Indians held.[7] Only when missionaries of the Dominican order made strong humanitarian protests against the actual conduct of *encomenderos* was Ferdinand's attention brought back to the ethical and Christian aspects of the problem. He answered the Dominican accusations with the Laws of Burgos (1512–13), a code of Spanish-Indian relations that expressed the royal government's first considered and official position on the question of encomienda.[8]

The Laws of Burgos sanctioned the encomiendas, but sought to surround them with specific directives: that Indians should not be mistreated; that *encomenderos* should earnestly provide for Indian Christianization; that encomienda Indians were not to be enslaved; that encomiendas should be limited in size. The laws were carefully drafted, copied, and sent to America for promulgation. But what was lacking was a means of enforcement. Governors in the West Indies functioned without power and were at the mercy of the *encomenderos*.[9] It may be doubted whether any West Indian *encomendero* modified his conduct as a result of the Burgos legislation. Thus the royal government's initial effort to establish control was frustrated, and the Laws of Burgos stand as one of many instances in Spanish colonial history of the ineffectiveness of law.

The years 1515–20 witnessed a number of events of importance

[7] The foremost modern student of royal legislation on Indians in this period concludes: "So far as can be judged from the royal correspondence, Ferdinand would have been in favor of enslaving the whole Indian population—which, indeed, is virtually what happened in any case." Simpson, *Encomienda in New Spain,* p. 17.

[8] Lewis Hanke, *The Spanish Struggle for Justice in the Conquest of America* (Philadelphia, 1949), pp. 23–25. For the text, and for commentary on the Laws of Burgos, see Rafael Altamira, "El texto de las Leyes de Burgos de 1512," *Revista de historia de América,* No. 4 (1938), pp. 5–79; Roland D. Hussey, "Text of the Laws of Burgos (1512–1513) concerning the Treatment of the Indians," *Hispanic American Historical Review,* XII (1932), 301–326.

[9] Ursula Lamb, *Frey Nicolás de Ovando, gobernador de las Indias, 1501–1509* (Madrid, 1956), is an excellent study of the governorship. There is no comparable study of Ovando's successor, Diego Columbus.

in encomienda history. One was the death of Ferdinand and the accession of his grandson Charles I (1516). Another was the rise to favor of Las Casas, who advocated not simply peaceful Christianization but also the total abolition of encomienda. Under Las Casas' urging the colonial government was temporarily placed in the hands of three Jeronymite friars, who, after conducting their inquiry, reported that encomienda could not be eradicated without grave damage to the whole colonial fabric.[10] An official position of reluctant compromise appeared to be called for. But Charles I—he remained Charles I of Spain while becoming the emperor Charles V in 1519—adopted the opposite, or Las Casas, position. In 1520, while Cortés was subduing new populations that would be coveted by *encomenderos* in Mexico, the royal government ruled that the entire institution of encomienda was to come to an end.[11]

The situation appeared to be a critical one. The future of privately controlled labor and tribute in the Indies hung momentarily in the balance. If the royal order were to be obeyed, encomienda would terminate in the islands. It would never be carried to the centers of mainland colonization and would be remembered simply as an introductory and temporary phase of Spanish-Indian relations. But the order was not obeyed. Encomienda was carried to Mexico, and from Mexico to other parts of the American empire. It proceeded to follow all the routes of the conquistadores. Because Cortés was the one who first permitted encomienda in Mexico, the entire mainland development has sometimes been charged to him. But it is obvious that encomienda was stronger than any single individual. As Cortés insisted in his explanatory letter to Charles V, its prevention or abolition at this juncture would have been impossible. The soldiers of the Mexican conquest, familiar as they were with life in the West Indies, demanded encomiendas as rewards for conquest services. Moreover the opportunities for encomienda in Mexico, where Indians were available in immense numbers, were

---

[10] The Jeronymite government is summarized in Simpson, *Encomienda in New Spain,* pp. 38 ff.

[11] Existing encomiendas were not necessarily to be abolished immediately. But those vacated through death or other cause were not to be reassigned. See the royal letter of May 18, 1520, in Manuel Serrano y Sanz, *Orígenes de la dominación española en América* (Madrid, 1918), p. DCVI.

much more extensive than in the islands.[12] The king yielded under the pressure of petitions from the new Mexican *encomenderos*. Charles V, like Ferdinand and Isabella before him, came to the official position that "free" Indians might be placed in encomienda without any compromise of freedom.[13]

From the time of the conquest of Mexico through the "age of conquest" and after, encomienda flourished openly in the Spanish colonies of America. Everywhere the soldiers of the conquest armies repeated the demands of the soldiers of Cortés. It was everywhere accepted that the largest and most remunerative grants were to be assigned to those whose military services had been most substantial.[14] Cortés became the foremost *encomendero* of all, with his holdings in the Valley of Oaxaca and scattered additional grants elsewhere. His tremendous riches—it is likely that he was at one time the wealthiest person in the entire Spanish world—depended chiefly on encomienda, which furnished him a large annual tribute income and labor for his various enterprises. It is of course highly probable that Cortés' refusal to halt encomienda was based not only on his soldiers' demands but also on his own opportunism and anticipation of personal gain.

The original connection between an *encomendero* class and a conquistador class could not persist for long. As royal governors

---

[12] Fernando Cortés, *Cartas y relaciones de Hernán Cortés al emperador Carlos V,* Pascual de Gayangos, ed. (Paris, 1866), p. 271. Cortés' letter to the king of October 15, 1524, is his full justification. See Joaquín García Icazbalceta (ed.), *Colección de documentos para la historia de México* (2 vols., Mexico, 1858–66), I, 472 ff.

[13] The king's initial position was that encomiendas already granted by Cortés in Mexico should be abolished. See the instructions to Cortés of June 26, 1523, in *Colección de documentos inéditos relativos al descubrimiento, conquista y organización de las antiguas posesiones españolas de ultramar* (25 vols., Madrid, 1885–1932), IX, 171. But encomienda was permitted in a royal order to the *audiencia* in 1528 and frequently thereafter to 1542. See Vasco de Puga, *Provisiones cedulas instrucciones para el gobierno de la Nueva España . . . Obra impresa en Mexico, por Pedro Ocharte, en 1563 y ahora editada en facsimil* (Madrid, 1945), fol. 9.

[14] See Puga, *Provisiones,* fol. 9. By royal laws of 1568 and 1595 the preferred recipients of encomiendas were "those of the foremost merits and services, and of these the descendants of the first discoverers, pacifiers, settlers, and oldest citizens who have best and most faithfully served in the royal service." *Recopilación de leyes de los reynos de las Indias: Edición facsimilar de la cuarta impresión hecha en Madrid el año 1791* (3 vols., Madrid, 1943), Lib. VI, tít. VIII, ley V.

were appointed, the assignment of new encomiendas passed from the control of conquest leaders to the control of crown representatives. In the rapidly changing postconquest society, new *encomenderos* arose who had never fought in conquest wars. The distinction between conquistadores and postconquest arrivals tended everywhere to become blurred. In the transitional period, with the influx of new settlers, an individual could pass as a conquistador for having engaged in some frontier raid or for having helped to suppress some local Indian uprising. Membership in the *encomendero* class was rapidly increasing in the 1530's and 1540's, and there presently remained no additional native societies worth conquering. Thus encomienda came to be regarded as a reward for generalized imperial service, whether or not rendered in a war of conquest, and a number of the most powerful *encomenderos* were simultaneously civil officers or ecclesiastics in the royal service.

In all conquered lands encomienda was the institution that provided most effectively for the transition from a state of war to a state of peace. Everywhere encomienda ensured the continued subordination of conquered people and their utilization by new white masters. In all Indian areas a lower class was available for exploitation. The existence of Indian communities of different sizes allowed for the accommodation of differing degrees of wealth and authority. Minor awards to relatively undistinguished colonists took the form of individual assignments of small towns. At the other extreme the wealthiest, most deserving, or most powerful colonists controlled grants consisting of clusters of towns or held scattered towns in various localities. Many single *encomenderos* were entrusted with a dozen or more communities and with thousands of laborers and tribute payers.[15]

An economical administration of encomienda required much

---

[15] Distribution in accordance with rank was a continuous policy from the beginning. See Ferdinand's stipulation of numbers to Diego Columbus, August 14, 1509, in *Colección de documentos . . . de Indias,* XXXI, 449–452. The names and possessions of the *encomenderos* of Mexico in the mid-sixteenth century are summarized in Sherburne F. Cook and Lesley Byrd Simpson, *The Population of Central Mexico in the Sixteenth Century* (Berkeley and Los Angeles, 1948), pp. 166 ff. The tabulation identifies some individuals with numerous large encomiendas, and others holding only a small encomienda per person.

managerial skill and careful record-keeping on the part of the *encomendero*. But economical administrations were rare. Encomienda was a large-scale operation in a period of cheap labor, and *encomenderos* preferred less meticulous methods of coercion. The developed Indian societies were already sufficiently organized to allow a management through overseers and puppet rulers. *Encomenderos* operated through existing Indian leaders and engaged in relatively little direct contact with mass populations. Procedures of labor control and tribute exaction ordinarily followed the original Indian procedures themselves, now turned to the profit of the *encomendero*. Many circumstances, not the least of which was the huge number of Indians available, conduced to set *encomenderos* apart and to render them a distinct and intolerant ruling class.

Encomienda Indians were made to perform many new tasks. Spanish agriculture required plows, draft animals, and new crops. Sugar milling, a standard *encomendero* operation in the tropical zones, involved methods of work previously unknown to American natives. The prodigious construction labors likewise followed Spanish rather than native techniques. But it would be idealistic to suppose that Indians in encomienda developed private skills or otherwise derived personal benefit from their training. Most labor remained routine, unskilled, mass labor. Abundant records of the early post-conquest period testify to the abuses—the punishments, tortures, exorbitant tribute demands, labor cruelties, enslavement, and other excesses—committed by *encomenderos* and their overseers.[16] Indian leaders were the accomplices and agents of white bosses in these practices, and native society frequently found itself substituting one form of submission for another. In Aztec, Inca, and many other societies of America, exploitation of the masses was not an inno-

---

[16] Thus Motolinía, writing about 1540: "The Spaniards began to exact heavy tributes from them, and the Indians, terrified of the Spaniards ever since the war, gave everything they had. As the tributes, however, were so continuous that they had scarcely paid one when they were obliged to pay another, they sold their children and their lands to the money lenders in order to meet their obligations; and when they were unable to do so many died because of it, some under torture and some in cruel prisons, for the Spaniards treated them brutally and considered them less than beasts." Motolinía (Toribio de Benavente), *Motolinía's History of the Indians of New Spain,* Elizabeth Andros Foster, trans. and ed. (Berkeley, 1950), p. 41.

vation of the colonial period. This fact, sometimes cited in extenuation of the *encomenderos'* conduct, may be cited also in partial explanation of it, for the *encomenderos'* techniques were much facilitated by the Indians' previous experience.

Encomenderos made repeated efforts to reinforce and further legalize their status. Their acknowledged aim was to transform encomienda into an instrument for complete and lasting control not only of Indians but of the colonies as a whole. To this end they sought to make encomienda an inheritable possession and to make of themselves a perpetual colonial nobility. It had been insisted at first that the grants were to be limited to a tenure of a few years, or to a single lifetime, or to the pleasure of the crown. But the first *encomenderos* proceeded to bequeath their holdings to their widows and children, and the legacies were not denied by royal officers. From the practical monarchical point of view, the question of succession in encomienda—a question that received lengthy and impassioned attention in the official correspondence of the 1530's and early 1540's—could be regarded as one of rivalry for power between the monarchy and the incipient colonial aristocracy. If the *encomenderos* could perpetuate encomienda through inheritance, a nobility might be created in the New World comparable to that of fifteenth-century Spain prior to the centralizing measures of Ferdinand and Isabella.[17] It became the task of Charles V to establish royal authority in America equal to that already secured at home. The task was beset by many difficulties and could not be accomplished immediately or without compromise. The foremost effort to achieve it was the legislation known as the New Laws, promulgated suddenly in 1542–43.

The New Laws, to be sure, were expressed not in terms of the struggle for royal power but in terms of the humanitarian policy toward native peoples, a policy to which the crown repeatedly gave

---

[17] Serious demands for rights of inheritance began with Cortés in 1524. *Colección de documentos . . . de Indias*, XII, 275–285. It should be pointed out that although *encomenderos* were frequently landholders, land was not a part of encomienda possession. See F. A. Kirkpatrick, "The Landless Encomienda," *Hispanic American Historical Review*, XXII (1942), 765–774. This applies at least to the main encomienda regions of Mexico and Peru. There is still some doubt on this point concerning certain marginal zones.

theoretical priority. The New Laws prohibited Indian enslavement, even as punishment. They forbade the granting of new encomiendas. They ordered ecclesiastics and royal officers to relinquish immediately any encomienda holdings they might possess, officially separating the agents of both arms of the state from implication in the system and defining the terms of the contest more closely. Other *encomenderos* were to retain their grants but were not to bequeath them to their heirs, a regulation calculated to destroy encomienda utterly within a generation. Tributes taken from Indians were to be fixed and regulated and were not to be exorbitant. The New Laws were far less ambiguous and far more extreme than the Laws of Burgos thirty years before. The difference in mood between 1512 and 1542 is to be attributed to the more confident authority of Charles V and to the influence of his humanitarian advisers, including Las Casas, at the court.[18]

At the most the New Laws could be termed only partially successful. The outcry of the *encomendero* class against them was general throughout the Spanish colonies. Rebellion, which threatened everywhere, erupted seriously in Peru, where it added one further element of disorder to the continuing civil war. In Mexico a cautious viceroy refrained from announcing the offending legislation. Recognizing the New Laws to be unenforceable, the monarchical government now repealed the prohibition of inheritance and allowed most encomiendas then in force to continue. The repeal, in 1545–46, was hailed everywhere in the colonies as a signal victory for the encomienda interests.

Encomienda was thus given a certain reinforcement and a renewed sanction in the 1540's despite the New Laws. But though abolition could not be made effective, much restrictive legislation remained in effect, and the strength of the monarchy was everywhere more visible. Royal enactments after the mid-1540's aban-

---

[18] *Las leyes nuevas de 1542–1543: Ordenanzas para la gobernación de las Indias y buen tratamiento y conservación de los indios* (Seville, 1961); Francisco Morales Padrón, "Las leyes nuevas de 1542–1543: Ordenanzas para la gobernación de las Indias y buen tratamiento y conservación de los indios." *Anuario de estudios americanos,* XVI (1959), 561–619. Simpson, *Encomienda in New Spain,* pp. 123–144, and Hanke, *Spanish Struggle for Justice,* pp. 91 ff., are valuable modern discussions of the New Laws.

doned the effort to terminate encomienda in any immediate or over-all way. Crown policy was now dedicated instead to more attainable goals: control over existing encomiendas, the limitation of *encomendero* behavior, and the gradual reduction of encomienda so that it might no longer threaten monarchical rule.[19] In law, and to a large extent in practice, the mid-1540's represent the highest point of encomienda influence.

A series of restrictive acts beginning in the mid-sixteenth century related particularly to the *encomenderos'* manipulation of labor and tribute.[20] In the conception of the time, labor (*servicio personal*) was held to be a form of tribute, the payment of commodities, including money, and the payment of services both being understood as due the *encomenderos* by the Indians entrusted to them. Royal regulations of 1549 and after began to disrupt this connection. Henceforth commodity tribute alone was to be paid, and *servicio personal* was not to be considered a part of tribute. This distinction between tribute and labor service, though not easily or quickly enforced, came to be accepted in the centers of Indian population and colonial rule. The dual powers of *encomenderos* over Indians were separated in the latter part of the sixteenth century, and efforts were made to bring Indian labor under the state through other means.[21] With respect to tribute, the royal administrators now dedicated themselves to the drafting and enforcement of *tasaciones*, or statements of legal amounts that *encomenderos* could demand. Each encomienda was assigned a separate *tasación*, and all were based upon a principle of equality in Indian payment. Each Indian was to give an equal amount of tribute, and *encomenderos* were not to

[19] A representative selection of later encomienda enactments will be found in *Recopilación de leyes*, Lib. VI, títs. VIII and IX.

[20] José Miranda, *El tributo indígena en la Nueva España durante el siglo XVI* (Mexico, 1952), pp. 103 ff.

[21] This is the interpretation commonly placed on the matter by modern historians as well as by colonial lawyers. Solórzano Pereyra cites the order of 1549 and subsequent orders applying to various regions. The orders continued to be issued in the seventeenth century. The legal and historical ramifications of this subject are exceedingly complex. But the general intention of the legislation of 1549 and after was to separate labor and tribute, "so that if any Indians serve the Spaniards in labor, it is to be of their own free will and not in any other way." Juan de Solórzano y Pereyra, *Política indiana* (5 vols., Madrid and Buenos Aires, 1930), I, 142 ff.

charge in excess of the *tasación* limits. Viceroys and other royal officers undertook to enforce these regulations, and each *encomendero*'s income was accordingly limited to a fixed quota, a multiple of the number of Indians held.[22]

In responding to the *encomenderos*' demands for privileges of inheritance, the crown of the later sixteenth century avoided the drastic prohibitions of the New Laws. But the crown also refrained from any approval of inheritance in perpetuity. Royal legislation concerned itself with definitions of the term *vida* (life or generation) and with the number of *vidas* that were to comprise an encomienda's legal duration prior to reversion to the crown. If the first holder of an encomienda bequeathed it to his son, that encomienda was said to be in the second *vida*. The grandson of the first holder accounted for the third *vida*, and the great-grandson for the fourth. But few encomiendas were so simple as this, and complicating questions arose. In the absence of sons, could a daughter inherit? If so, in a society dominated by males, what was the status of a daughter's husband, or, to introduce additional difficulties, of her second husband after the death of the first? Meanwhile was any share of the income to be reserved for the widow of the first holder, or for the widow's second husband? Was an encomienda always to go to the eldest son? Could it be subdivided among several sons, and if so would these parts later revert to the eldest son or to the widows or sons of the cadet sons?[23]

A labyrinth of legalism surrounded these uncertainties, all taken very seriously by the crown and by the individuals concerned. *Encomenderos* sought to evade the restrictions and to argue their cases as best they could. Elderly *encomenderos* on their death beds married young girls so that the single life might be prolonged. The complications of law and action supported a class of colonial lawyers, and disputes proceeded interminably in the courts. Royal prosecutors studied personal case histories, seeking to revise the number of legal lives in ways that would force escheatment. For New Spain the

[22] Walter V. Scholes, *The Diego Ramírez Visita* (Columbia, Mo., 1946); Simpson, *Encomienda in New Spain,* pp. 146 ff.

[23] Solórzano, who relished complex legal questions, devotes a number of chapters to problems of this kind. Solórzano y Pereyra, *Política indiana,* II, 145 ff.

crown allowed a third *vida* in 1555 and a fourth in 1607. In Peru, the third *vida* was legalized in 1629. But these dates are deceptive. Special privileges were granted in particular instances, and despite the general rules, there were always numerous exceptions. In many cases encomiendas that had reverted were reassigned and the new recipients were understood to be possessors in the first *vida*. Hence, although only two or three generations might be permitted in legal generalization, the real history of encomienda lasted for a much longer time.[24]

With the escheatment of each encomienda the crown registered a gain and the encomienda interests suffered a loss. Tribute that had formerly been directed to a private recipient was redirected to the royal treasury. The crown introduced royal officers as collectors of tribute from Indians who were no longer in encomienda, and the private beneficiaries of the system were progressively reduced in number. Individuals who suffered hardships were sometimes compensated by other royal grants. No single instance of escheatment was in itself consequential, but the succession of many instances through the sixteenth and seventeenth centuries meant a cumulative change from private to monarchical authority.

Royal legislation relating to encomienda has often been accused of inconsistency, and the accusation is not without substance. Even perpetual, nonrevocable encomiendas were permitted in a few instances. The inconsistent enactments on the subject of inheritance illustrate Spanish legalism in a revealing form. But in a larger sense the crown did succeed in its campaign against the incipient American aristocracy. Again this success may be likened to that of other and later imperial nations, as when Portugal brought the *donatários* under royal administration and when England royalized its corporate and proprietary colonies. The vacillations of the Spanish crown, particularly in the later stages, should be understood in a context of growing domination. The crown could afford to make isolated and strategic exceptions to its encomienda policy precisely because the independent encomienda power had been so thoroughly reduced.

[24] See the various encomienda histories of the Valley of Mexico summarized in Charles Gibson, *The Aztecs under Spanish Rule: A History of the Indians of the Valley of Mexico, 1519–1810* (Stanford, 1964), pp. 413 ff.

The progressive limitation of encomienda, however, was not due exclusively to the astuteness and strength of the crown. An additional and unexpected factor was the continuous decrease in Indian population. The history of encomienda is closely linked with native American demography. A large Indian population was essential for the continued well-being of an *encomendero* class. But from their first contact with Spaniards the Indian peoples of America started to melt away. The numbers killed in the conquests were small in comparison with the tremendous numbers who died during the post-conquest decades. Indians were all but extinct in the West Indies by the 1540's. Severe losses occurred on the tropical coasts and highland areas of New Spain, where native peoples had been exceptionally dense. In many tropical areas of the mainland Indians were sparse or wholly nonexistent by 1600, and in the highland areas population losses up to 90 per cent were not uncommon by the early seventeenth century. The most painstaking of modern studies records a decline in New Spain from about 25 million in 1519 to slightly over one million in 1605.[25] Depopulation in South America has not been computed so precisely, but it is at least possible that it was equally severe.[26]

The crown had nothing to do with this appalling depopulation. To have deliberately undercut the *encomenderos'* powers through a policy of Indian extermination would have been unthinkable in the responsible, Christian courts of Charles V and Philip II, where the Indians of America were still regarded as free crown vassals. Far from encouraging any lethal conduct on the part of the colonists, the Spanish kings in general were unaware of the magnitude of the loss, and in so far as they comprehended it they sought to offset it

[25] Woodrow Borah and Sherburne F. Cook, *The Aboriginal Population of Central Mexico on the Eve of the Spanish Conquest* (Berkeley and Los Angeles, 1963); Woodrow Borah and Sherburne F. Cook, *The Population of Central Mexico in 1548: An Analysis of the Suma de visitas de pueblos* (Berkeley and Los Angeles, 1960); Sherburne F. Cook and Woodrow Borah, *The Indian Population of Central Mexico, 1531–1610* (Berkeley and Los Angeles, 1960).

[26] Henry F. Dobyns, "An Outline of Andean Epidemic History to 1720," *Bulletin of the History of Medicine,* XXXVII (1963), 493–515. Borah has shown, with reference to Australia, the Pacific islands, Africa, and other parts of the world, that the critical correlation is between depopulation and isolation. Woodrow Borah, "¿América como modelo? El impacto demográfico de la expansión europea sobre el mundo no europeo," *Cuadernos americanos,* Año XXI, No. 6 (nov.-dic., 1962), pp. 176–185.

and ameliorate its consequences. A common interpretation attributed the Indian deaths to the cruelties and exploitative measures of the *encomenderos,* and the crown was thus persuaded to see the campaign against encomienda and the halting of depopulation as aspects of a single policy undertaken on behalf of Indian welfare.

We know now that Indian depopulation was an ecological phenomenon, uncontrollable in sixteenth- and seventeenth-century terms. Humanitarian enactments were powerless against it, and it therefore reduced encomienda in a process quite unrelated to royal legislation. Even casual contacts between Spaniards and Indians meant that Indians died, for they immediately became victims of the diseases that Spaniards carried. Disease traveled rapidly in America, more rapidly than encomienda and more rapidly than the particular individuals who were carriers of disease. It is possible that the population of the Inca empire had already been reduced by half or more by the early 1530's, when Pizarro reached the coast and began the conquest.[27] Because Indian and European civilizations had been maintained in isolation, diseases against which Europeans had developed effective, if partial, immunities became destructive epidemics when Indians were exposed to them. Smallpox, typhoid, and measles were wholesale killers in Indian society, and no one could halt the devastation once it had begun. The balance was heavily on the side of the white population. The only possible compensating infection offered by the Indians was syphilis, which seems to have occurred in mild forms in native America and which raged in virulent plagues in Europe after 1493. The effects of syphilis in Europe were severe, but they were far less severe than the diseases with which Spaniards infected Indians. Moreover the history of syphilis is complex and incompletely resolved, so that we cannot be fully certain that it originated in Indian America or was carried by Spaniards to Europe.[28]

Encomienda was the first institution of the Spanish colonial world to depend on large numbers of Indians. The power of the first *encomenderos* resulted from their manipulation of great labor forces

---

[27] Dobyns, "Andean Epidemic History," p. 494.
[28] Hubert U. Williams, "The Origins and Antiquity of Syphilis," *Archives of Pathology,* XIII (1932), 779–814, 931–983.

or their receipt of tribute from the Indian masses. When these human resources were depleted, encomienda necessarily declined. *Encomenderos* could make certain practical adjustments by revising the tributary system or modifying the rules of tribute exemption to their own advantage. But finally all such devices were exhausted, the population continued to decline, and encomienda could no longer be relied upon to produce a satisfactory income for an aristocratic white class.

The result in the late sixteenth century was a pattern of institutional decay unmistakable in its tendency and implications. *Encomenderos'* incomes dropped year by year. Expenses remained steady or increased. Most *encomenderos* met the obligation to provide for the spiritual welfare of their Indians by paying the salaries and some other expenses (such as those for wine and oil) of resident or visiting clerics, and this standard item of cost persisted. Necessary operating funds were spent on administrators' salaries, transport of tribute goods, legal fees, inspections, sales taxes, and other taxes. Net profits were squeezed to ever lower figures. *Encomenderos* responded psychologically by banding together, issuing petitions to the crown, intensifying the campaign for perpetuity in encomienda inheritance, and arguing the dignity and social utility of the encomienda institution. None of the efforts was successful.[29]

Encomienda persisted in the late colonial period, but its force was spent and it could no longer be regarded as a meaningful colonial institution. Many individual grants came to an end through the failure of succession in the encomienda families. The intricate inheritance laws took effect, and the absence of legal heirs in one generation or another resulted in reversions to the crown. Partial reversions took place when, in various critical years, the crown demanded a fraction of each *encomendero*'s annual income.[30] Compensating short-term awards were sometimes made to unsuccessful legatees, and these were also known as encomiendas in late colonial terminology. Other grants of funds directly from the royal treasury

[29] See the record of expenses and income in Lesley Byrd Simpson, "A Seventeenth-Century Encomienda: Chimaltenango, Guatemala," *The Americas*, XV (1958–59), 393–402.

[30] *Recopilación de leyes*, Lib. VI, tít. VIII, leyes XXXVIII–XXXIX; Zavala, *Encomienda indiana*, pp. 332–335.

were likewise sometimes referred to as encomiendas, particularly if the moneys derived originally from Indian tribute payments. Repeatedly the crown allocated annuities to members of the titled nobility in Spain, who might in their turn be called *encomenderos*. But these late meanings of encomienda had little relation to the usages of the early colonial period. The funds assigned were minuscule in comparison with the huge incomes of the sixteenth century. A late colonial *encomendero* might never see or be aware of the Indians of his encomienda, and exploitation would be impossible for him. He would receive a pension equal to the annual tribute that they paid, while all the procedures of collection and disbursement were handled by officials of the treasury.[31] The arrangement was similar to many other financial grants depending on other sources of royal income, and in effect it signified full royal control.

Thus in various areas of the colony encomienda was prolonged in modified form or with a sense and meaning quite different from that of an earlier time. The decline developed later in South America than in central New Spain. Where Indian populations were smaller or where the shock of depopulation was less decisive or where administrative controls were ineffective, the changes were less far-reaching. In the Platine region and in Paraguay the Indian population continued to provide labor as well as tribute to the *encomenderos* in the seventeenth and eighteenth centuries. It is probable that the transformations were most substantial and the decline most evident in the regions where encomienda had once been most powerful, i.e., the central areas of the two major colonies, Mexico and Peru.[32]

The laws of the eighteenth century ultimately abolishing encomienda are deceptive, especially for the areas of sharpest decline. They evoked no cataclysmic colonial opposition, for they implied

[31] Examples from the Valley of Mexico may be found in Gibson, *Aztecs under Spanish Rule,* pp. 413 ff.

[32] Elman R. Service, "The *Encomienda* in Paraguay," *Hispanic American Historical Review,* XXXI (1951), 230–252; Eduardo Arcila Farías, *El régimen de la encomienda en Venezuela* (Seville, 1957). See the report of the Marqués de Avilés, in 1803, to the effect that there had been no reduction in Indians in encomienda in Paraguay: *Documentos para la historia argentina* (29 vols., Buenos Aires, 1913–61), III, 28.

the cessation of a system of limited incomes or of fixed royal pensions rather than an instrument of private power, and many of the recipients were peninsular Spaniards rather than colonials. Ambitious colonists had long since turned from encomienda to other avenues of wealth and authority. The new colonial aristocracy would be based on land, commerce, or mineral wealth, rather than upon native tribute payments, and the labor necessary for these new enterprises would be secured in ways quite unrelated to encomienda.

The original encomienda nevertheless was an institution of importance for Spanish America. Upon it many of the first power conflicts were concentrated. It was a transitional device, between conquest and a settled society. Its crudity was appropriate to an era dominated by conquistadores and by others who would have been conquistadores if there had remained Indian peoples still worth conquering. The progressive legalization of encomienda reflects the complexities of American Hispanization, with the crown in control and a host of lawyers ready to exploit the subtleties of law. Encomienda allowed a thin surface of dominant, class-conscious Spaniards to spread over Spanish America. Its history is revealing for the discrepancies between intentions and achievement, and between word and deed. Economically encomienda performed the very real function of transferring Indian wealth to Spanish hands, in a procedure that was more orderly than outright looting of spoils.[33] Encomienda was less dramatic than conquest, and it has achieved a lesser renown, but it was the dominant institution of its period and through it the first work of the colony was done.

[33] José Miranda, *Tributo indígena,* pp. 186 ff.

CHAPTER 4

Church

IT IS paradoxical that Spain, the nation that performed the conquests and established encomienda, was the same Spain that occupied itself so determinedly with the Christian conversion of native peoples. The paradox has sometimes been commented upon in a critical and hostile spirit. It gives rise to the belief that the true Spanish objective was exploitation, and that Christianization was only a hypocritical justification, or a means to an end. "It is not Christianity that leads them on," Lope de Vega had the devil say in his play *El Nuevo Mundo* (ca. 1600), "but rather gold and greed," and the accusation has echoed through history to our own time.[1]

But it is clear that at least for a select group of Spanish missionary friars Christianity did lead them on. To doubt their motive is to carry skepticism to unreasonable and unnecessary lengths. For the early friars the propagation of the faith was an objective as compelling as gold to the conquistadores or tribute to the *encomenderos,* and no one who reads their record can seriously think that it was not. It is true that for other clergy, including

---

[1] The idea appears in contexts far removed from Lope de Vega's devil. "The pious purpose of converting them to Christianity sanctified the injustice of the project. But the hope of finding treasures of gold there, was the sole motive which prompted [them] to undertake it. . . . The subsequent Spanish enterprises [after Columbus] were all prompted by the same motive." Adam Smith, *An Inquiry into the Nature and Causes of the Wealth of Nations,* Edwin Cannan, ed. (2 vols., London, 1904), II, 63–64.

some missionary clergy, the objectives were less clear. Competing spiritual and material goals were always present. Historians, aware of the complexities of human psychology, are naturally reluctant to ascribe single motives in an unqualified way. But to judge from the evidence it would be as foolish to deny missionaries a religious motive as it would to deny conquistadores a material one.

Behind the movement for converting Indians lay some important influences in Spain. The Spanish church of the earlier fifteenth century had been an institution of privilege and corruption, with standards of conduct that responsible Christians could view only with shame. This was then modified—it would be an error to state that it was more than modified—in the time of Ferdinand and Isabella. The "Catholic monarchs" established new royal controls over the ecclesiastical benefices and over the immense wealth of the church. In suppressing the non-Christian state in Granada and in forcibly expelling Jews—both acts occurring, with an exaggerated historical coincidence, in the year of Columbus' discovery of America—Ferdinand and Isabella sought to purify Spanish society in a spirit of Christian unity. The acts were militant expressions of religious statehood at the moment of the beginning of American colonization.

Religious nationalization was attended by a new sense of Christian purpose. A principal leader was Isabella's royal confessor, Francisco Jiménez de Cisneros, Cardinal of Toledo, who dedicated himself to the reform of the Observant branch of the Spanish Franciscan order. Cisneros used suasion, force, expulsion, and excommunication in a vigorous campaign against laxity. The Conventual (non-Observant) Franciscans progressively lost prestige and authority.[2] The innovations were most far-reaching among Franciscans, but a reforming mood affected other orders also, with the result that by the 1520's the Mendicant clergy as a whole was prepared as it had not been before for the missionary labors on the mainland of Spanish America.

A crucial feature of the reforms was humanistic learning. Moving easily from Italy to the Iberian peninsula, Humanism affected the established Spanish universities of Salamanca and Valladolid, and,

[2] J. H. Elliott, *Imperial Spain, 1469–1716* (London, 1963), p. 93.

still more, the new university of Alcalá de Henares, founded by Cisneros in 1508. Isabella mastered Latin and encouraged its use, and her daughter, Juana la Loca, wrote and spoke Latin with facility. The Spanish Renaissance scholar par excellence was Antonio de Nebrija (Lebrija), who spent ten years in humanist studies in Italy, returned to teach at Salamanca and Alcalá, prepared a Latin grammar and a Latin-Spanish dictionary, and published the first modern Spanish grammar, the *Gramática sobre la lengua castellana*. At Alcalá, Cisneros directed the editing of the Complutensian Polyglot Bible (1514–17) in Latin, Greek, and Hebrew, a project on which many scholars, including Nebrija, labored for some fifteen years.[3] The friars who later studied Nahuatl in Mexico and Quechua in Peru were to owe a particular debt to these humanistic language studies. ("Language has always been the companion of empire," Nebrija wrote in his dedicatory preface to Isabella.) The missionaries' formal knowledge of American languages would be expressed in the declensions and conjugations and other paradigms of humanistic Latin, which served as their model for all foreign languages.[4]

Finally, in the second and third decades of the sixteenth century, when Spaniards in the New World were turning from the limited West Indies to the more ample field of Mexico, a special humanistic influence reached Spain from northern Europe. Christian Humanism had only a few years in which to gain currency in the Spanish church and to affect the conversion programs of the American mainland, and it spread at a rapid rate. Erasmus himself, while he

[3] Alcalá was Roman Complutum. The Bible appears to have been completed in 1517 but issued only in 1522.

[4] "The Maya grammars, or *artes,* composed by some of the best Franciscan linguists for the instruction of newly arrived missionaries, have been severely criticized by modern scholars. They contain translations of the paradigms from a Latin grammar into Maya. For verbs four regular conjugations were compiled, which include the subjunctive mood, pluperfect and future perfect tenses, gerunds, supines, and participles, but the aspects of the verbs seem to be little recognized. Naturally these writers missed the spirit of the language in their treatises, although a number of them are known to have spoken it idiomatically. Coronel, San Buenaventura, and Beltrán de Santa Rosa, I think, were aware of this failure, for they sought to remedy the deficiency by numerous explanations." Ralph Roys, "The Vienna Dictionary," in Carnegie Institution of Washington, Division of Historical Research, *Notes on Middle American Archaeology and Ethnology* No. 41 (November 1, 1944), pp. 98–99.

never visited Spain, was an influential figure. Erasmus spoke of the general social and moral corruption of Europe and of the European failure to achieve Christian goals. He compared sixteenth-century Europe unfavorably with the civilizations of classical antiquity. If classical antiquity could achieve greatness without Christianity, he argued, the achievement of contemporary Europe, invigorated and favored by Christianity, should be still greater. The Erasmian vogue in Spain, brief but intense, provides one of the most striking illustrations of Spanish receptivity to reforming ideas prior to the Reformation.[5]

European Humanism, even in its original terms, was not entirely unrelated to America. Erasmus, while he did not speak directly of American Indians, addressed himself to Christians and pagans and all mankind. Erasmus' friend and fellow humanist Thomas More located Utopia in the American hemisphere as a foil and challenge to Europe. But it remained for Spanish ecclesiastics to make the practical humanist application to the colonial scene. The message of Christian Humanism to the missionary friars was that the pagan peoples of the New World too were capable of greatness and that the most effective instrument for civilizing them would be this same purified Christianity.

The new religious stimulus, the sense of purification, the campaign of reform, and an Erasmian concern for the true or primitive Christianity were all carried to the New World by missionary friars. To them America offered a larger and more challenging stage than Europe. The non-Christian peoples of America were not simply to be converted. They were to be civilized, taught, humanized, puri-

---

[5] Marcel Bataillon, *Erasme et l'Espagne; recherches sur l'histoire spirituelle du XVIᵉ siècle* (Paris, 1937). The Spanish edition, *Erasmo y España, estudios sobre la historia espiritual del siglo XVI,* Antonio Alatorre, trans. (Mexico, 1950), contains an appendix on Erasmus and the New World. The aspects of Erasmian philosophy mentioned are most clearly expressed in the *Institutio principis christiani.* See also Fritz Caspari, "Erasmus on the Social Functions of Christian Humanism," *Journal of the History of Ideas,* VIII (1947), 84 ff.: "The key to Erasmus' position is his ideal of humanity. . . . He was convinced . . . that Roman humanism contained nothing alien or opposed to Christianity, but that the two elements formed an organic unity—both as regards their historical growth and the way in which they complement each other systematically. . . . He insisted that only the aid of *humanitas* could save Christian civilization."

fied, and reformed. To the humanist friars, America appeared as
Christian obligation writ large. Its vast populations were to be
set on new paths of Christian virtue and godliness. The Erasmian
Philosophia Christi was to be applied. Utopia was to be realized.

The task of course presented enormous difficulties. The Indians
to be converted were strangers speaking many unfamiliar tongues.
In most cases, when friars first encountered them, they had been
only recently conquered and subjugated, and even if not actively
hostile they were likely to retain covert antagonisms. In their experience all Spaniards were exploitative. Indians were unprepared
to identify the missionary friars or any other group as peacefully
intentioned. For the friars the problem of personal reconciliation
had to precede the problem of Christian communication.[6]

Because Indian religions were complexes of ceremonies and attitudes of the most diverse sort, no single or simple technique of
conversion could be employed. Each group possessed its set of
beliefs and rites, and within the larger groups many local differences
appeared. Native American religions included certain practices—
such as cannibalism, or attributions of divinity to material objects,
or the sacrifice of human beings—that horrified the friars and had
to be eliminated. Practices that suggested a similarity with Christianity posed special difficulties. Creator myths and cult heroes
seemed to indicate some pre-existing Indian awareness of the
supreme deity of Christendom. Fasting and confession of sins suggested analogous Christian duties. The cross was noted with amaze-
ment whenever Spaniards encountered it.[7] Such parallels gave rise
to a number of fanciful theories respecting a supposed earlier
Indian contact with one or another of the church fathers. But ultimately all such features of the American religions had to be rejected
as ingenious works of the devil, for they were mockeries and parodies
of the true faith.

The friars' common procedure in converting any area was to
divide into groups of two or three and to go out into the Indian

---

[6] Las Casas' effort in Vera Paz provides a striking example. He began by
sending in Indian merchants with Spanish goods.

[7] The most famous native American cross is at the Maya Temple of the Cross
in Palenque, Chiapas.

communities to preach. They went barefoot and unarmed, in deliberate contrast to lay Spanish colonists. At first they spoke through interpreters. After some experience and study they spoke directly in Indian languages. Immediately they performed individual and mass baptisms, for the rapid saving of souls.[8] In each community they sought to convert the chief and the members of the governing class, for Indians tended to follow the example of their leaders in religion as in other matters. Idols, temples, and other material evidences of paganism were destroyed. At an early stage a temporary church or chapel was built, and after this the permanent church and the monastery (convento) to house the friars. When possible, Christian buildings were constructed on the sites of destroyed native temples, in order to symbolize and emphasize the substitution of one religion by the other.[9] In the successful conversions, Indians supplied construction labor on the churches without recompense, voluntarily, or at the command of their newly Christianized chiefs. In a converted community, services and fiestas were regularly held in the church building and atrio. The friars then proceeded to expand the Christianized area, moving out into surrounding towns, where subordinate chapels were built. Cooperating Indians were brought into the conversion work as lay aides.[10] Other sacraments than baptism were gradually introduced.[11] Indians who refused to accept Christianity were punished, sometimes by death.

A remarkable feature was the direct application of Christian-humanist doctrine to the missionary enterprise. The Franciscan Juan de Zumárraga, a leader in Erasmian thought, was appointed first bishop of Mexico in 1527, and became a dominant figure in

[8] A controversy over the practice of mass baptism resulted in its gradual elimination. The crucial point concerned the converts' lack of preparation for the sacrament.

[9] Johann Specker, Die Missionsmethode in Spanisch-Amerika im 16. Jahrhundert, mit besonderer Berücksichtigung der Konzilien und Synoden (Schöneck-Beckenreid, 1953); Ursula Lamb, "Religious Conflicts in the Conquest of Mexico," Journal of the History of Ideas, XVII (1956), 526–539.

[10] But not as clergy. On this question, an important one in the early period of conversion, see Juan Alvarez Mejía, "La cuestión del clero indígena en la época colonial," Revista javeriana, XLV (1956), 57–67, 209–219.

[11] Lamb, "Religious Conflicts," pp. 526–539; Constantino Bayle, "La comunión entre los indios americanos," Revista de Indias, IV (1943), 197–254.

the early church of New Spain. In his *Doctrina breve,* a Christian manual for the use of the Mexican clergy, and in his *Doctrina cristiana,* a catechism for Christianized Indians, Zumárraga provided published texts and gave currency to Christian-humanist thought among missionaries and their pupils.[12] The Colegio de Santa Cruz at Tlatelolco (a part of Mexico City) was founded to teach rhetoric, logic, music, and philosophy, and in the mid-sixteenth century its Indian pupils were conversing in Latin. One of the college's functions was the translation of Scripture into native languages, a program supported by Zumárraga in the Cisneros and Erasmian tradition of Biblical study.[13] Zumárraga's associate and fellow humanist Vasco de Quiroga undertook to create actual communities in New Spain modeled on Thomas More's *Utopia,* with communally owned property, communally performed labor, representative government, and a variety of other features of More's ideal society.[14] It would not be an exaggeration to say that America in the second quarter of the sixteenth century exhibited a phase of the European Renaissance that transcended European terms, one in which Christian-humanist programs, inapplicable and "utopian" in European society, came to be realities.

In summary, an elaborate missionary preparation in Spain was followed by a substantial achievement in the New World. But to perceptive clerics the results were nevertheless disappointing. Spaniards were not completely successful in converting the American Indians to Christianity. Conversion required both the introduction of Catholic Christianity and the extirpation of existing native religions, and of the two tasks the latter was the more difficult. Modern anthropology demonstrates conclusively that the elimination of pagan traits was only partial. In Indian society of the twentieth century, even in the areas of most active Christian labor,

[12] On Zumárraga as an Erasmist, see Richard E. Greenleaf, *Zumárraga and the Mexican Inquisition, 1536–1543* (Washington, 1961), pp. 37 ff.

[13] Francis Borgia Steck, *El primer colegio de América, Santa Cruz de Tlaltelolco* (Mexico, 1944).

[14] Silvio Zavala, *La "Utopía" de Tomás Moro en la Nueva España y otros estudios* (Mexico, 1937); Silvio Zavala, *Ideario de Vasco de Quiroga* (Mexico, 1941); Fintan B. Warren, *Vasco de Quiroga and His Pueblo-Hospitals of Santa Fe* (Washington, 1963).

residual pagan forms survive. The result of the mission programs was a "syncretic" Indian religion, Catholic-Christian in its externals but non-Christian in some of its basic postulates or in its enveloping world view. Indians might respond enthusiastically to the new teaching, but they tended to interpret Christianity as a doctrine compatible with their own tolerant pagan religions, and they allowed Christianity and paganism to exist simultaneously as alternative or complementary faiths. Indians predisposed to polytheism almost necessarily reached a distorted understanding of the Christian trinity. A common Indian view held that one religious form was to be resorted to when another failed to bring a desired result, and the elements of diverse doctrines came to be fused in such a way that the worshipers possessed neither the historical nor the ecclesiastical knowledge to distinguish them.[15]

The Christian-humanist movement itself was short-lived. In Spain, Erasmianism became tainted and confused with Protestantism, and Erasmus' writings were officially condemned. Spain embarked upon its role as the European leader of the Catholic Counter Reformation. In America the early enthusiasm of the friars gradually fell away. Even in Mexico, where proselytization had been most vigorous, nothing like the Quirogan communities or the Colegio de Santa Cruz came into being after the midcentury. There is perhaps a natural limit to the continuing zeal of any missionary program, for success implies a slackening of ardor, and with it the initial challenge no longer exists. In Spanish America, as conversions were accomplished, there remained, or seemed to remain, correspondingly less to do.[16]

The labor of Christianization was impeded further by conflicts between friars and other branches of the society. Church and encomienda became rival institutions, each in its way seeking control over native populations. The issue between them erupted openly in 1511, when the Dominican friar Antonio de Montesinos first condemned the colonists' treatment of Indians in Hispaniola. There-

---

[15] On missionary labor, see especially Robert Ricard, La "Conquête spirituelle" du Mexique (Paris, 1933). For Peru, see Antonine Tibesar, Franciscan Beginnings in Colonial Peru (Washington, 1953), and Fernando de Armas Medina, Cristianización del Perú (1532–1600) (Seville, 1953).

[16] Ricard, "Conquête spirituelle," pp. 285–331.

after, under the leadership of Las Casas and others, ecclesiastical criticism of encomienda became frequent and outspoken. *Encomenderos* for their part saw the friars as officious meddlers whose object was to pry into the livelihood of encomienda Indians, criticize the *encomenderos'* use of Indian labor, and denounce encomienda in letters to the king.

In terms of pure power the monarch could for a time regard both *encomenderos* and friars as threats to royal rule. Ferdinand forbade the Dominican controversies and unsuccessfully proposed the Laws of Burgos to reconcile encomienda with the Christian spirit. Missionary labor had to be encouraged, but the missionaries could not be permitted to dominate the colony at the cost of royal rule. Having granted the friars authority to convert Indians, the Spanish state confronted the task of limiting that authority in the royal interest. Parallels with the history of the crown's relations with Columbus and with the *encomenderos* are obvious.

Ferdinand had long since taken steps to legalize and guarantee his authority over the church. By papal bulls of 1501 and 1508, under the comprehensive title Patronato Real (Royal Patronage), he had secured a full corpus of ecclesiastical controls. Patronato Real implied the basic power to appoint churchmen in the colonies, and the additional power to administer ecclesiastical jurisdictions and revenues and to veto papal bulls. With this the crown could decide which clerics would be appointed, where they should go, what the limits of their jurisdictions were to be, and what they should be paid. During the entire period of Spanish imperialism in America the crown possessed these powers over the church.[17] For the missionaries Patronato Real seemed to provide security and privilege as well as authority. In any case the missionaries sided with

---

[17] Patronato Real had both a peninsular and a colonial aspect, but it was more extensive and powerful in America, which contained millions of pagans to be converted, than in Spain, which was already Christian. Only over Granada, likewise a recently conquered area, did the Spanish monarchy receive powers comparable to those of the colonies. A full modern study, with texts of relevant documents, is William E. Shiels, *King and Church: The Rise and Fall of the Patronato Real* (Chicago, 1961). See also appropriate parts of John Lloyd Mecham, *Church and State in Latin America: A History of Politico-Ecclesiastical Relations* (Chapel Hill, N.C., 1934).

the monarchy against the *encomenderos* and never sought to create an independent organization in defiance of royal government.[18]

They were prevented from doing so, and royal controls were further strengthened, by internal divisions within the church.[19] The principal conflict between "regulars" and "seculars" was one of long standing in ecclesiastical history, but it acquired a special meaning and intensity in Spanish America. The missionary friars were "regulars"—Franciscans, Dominicans, Augustinians, and members of other orders—so-called because they lived by *regula* or rule. "Seculars" were the parish priests and other clergy not bound by vows or rules, so-called because they lived in the world (*saeculum*). In America, though the terms continued to be used, the regulars also lived in the world, as missionaries to Indians. They were privileged and obligated by Pope and king to administer sacraments and to perform parochial tasks in the conversion program. From the viewpoint of the seculars the assignment of this work to the regulars represented a disruption of the traditional parochial structure. The seculars, with some exceptions, found their own ministration limited to white society.[20] So long as the Indian missionary program remained important, the regulars preserved their initial advantage. But like so many other early solutions of Spanish-Indian relations, the priority of the regulars was destined to fail with the drastic native depopulations and other changes of the middle sixteenth century and after.

In brief, in the second half of the sixteenth century, the monarch came to favor the seculars against the regulars. The preference was expressed formally in the Ordenanza del Patronazgo (1574), designed to limit the regulars' work and to effect their replacement by seculars. From the royal point of view the regulars had accom-

---

[18] The statement requires qualification. Ecclesiastics under certain conditions defended encomienda as an institution necessary for the preservation of colonial society. And an argument against the Jesuits in the eighteenth century was that they were seeking to create an independent organization against the crown.

[19] Encomienda was at once more integral and more fragmented than the church. *Encomenderos* were rivals of one another as individuals, but they were not factionally divided as was the church.

[20] For the nonregular contribution to the missionary movement, see Constantino Bayle, *El clero secular y la evangelización de América* (Madrid, 1950).

plished their purpose and the time had come to establish the orderly, traditional, episcopal hierarchy everywhere. By the rule of the Council of Trent, all clerics with parochial powers were subject to episcopal control. Bishops in the late sixteenth and seventeenth centuries insisted on the enforcement of this provision, while the regular orders resisted it. But the resistance could not be successfully maintained and the regular orders progressively lost out. It is true that in some areas regulars preserved parochial functions on into the eighteenth century. But as in the long late history of encomienda, the royal position was secured and the last stages of the struggle were anticlimactic.[21]

A privileged episcopal hierarchy and a continuing, partially displaced body of regular clergy created frequent situations of petty strife. Franciscans, Dominicans, and other orders competed among themselves, and all competed with the seculars. In the central areas of the colony, where the conversion labors were regarded as completed, any innovation, any change in jurisdiction, any observance of ceremony, could occasion conflict. Two branches of the church might take opposite positions on any issue, each insisting not only that its own view was legal and proper but that it was divinely inspired. In individual parishes one order might forcibly eject another, only in its turn to be ejected by the seculars. Clergymen born or ordained in Spain conflicted with those born or ordained in the colonies. The familiar notion of a controlled, monolithic Spanish colonial church is inaccurate. Church history in colonial Spanish America is a history of constant internal squabbles.

Ecclesiastical disputation and the shifting focus from Indian conversion by regulars to the maintenance of white society by seculars are additionally reflected in the history of the colonial Inquisition. The Inquisition in Spain, established by Ferdinand and Isabella, was a royal instrument designed to purge the Christian nation of its alien elements, especially Jews. Transferred formally to America in the late sixteenth century, the Inquisition set up tribunals in Mexico

[21] A list of bishoprics and archbishoprics, with dates of foundation and a dated list of colonial bishops and archbishops to 1700, will be found in Ernesto Schäfer, *El Consejo real y supremo de las Indias: Su historia, organización y labor administrativa hasta la terminación de la casa de Austria* (2 vols., Seville, 1935–47), II, 565 ff.

City, Lima, and Cartagena. Significantly, the tribunals were denied jurisdiction over Indians. Their function was to discover and eradicate from non-Indian society all heresy, heterodoxy, and sins against God. The American inquisitorial tradition from the early 1570's on thus resembled not the early period of evangelization in America but the conditions of Christian Spain under Ferdinand and Isabella. The American inquisitors became zealous, ruthless defenders of ecclesiastical purity. In Spanish America surviving Indian superstition fused with the occult lore of Europe to create a rich, necromantic, lower-class tradition, marginal to Christianity, and the task of the inquisitors, faced with this, was to separate the orthodox from the unorthodox. Their record is one of frequent accusation against bigamists, Judaizing "New Christians," blasphemers, witches and sorcerers, and priests who used their spiritual authority to seduce or rape women parishioners. Before the Inquisition marched the psychopaths of the colony. As in Spain the Inquisition employed torture, encouraged spying and talebearing, confiscated property, sowed distrust, and destroyed reputations through "guilt by association."[22]

Between the Inquisition and other branches of the colonial church relations became insecure or openly hostile. Inquisitors were outspoken critics of regular and secular clergy, on both of whom their authority tended to encroach. The earlier episcopal jurisdiction over heresy was given up only with reluctance and resistance, and to the other conflicts of the church was added that between episcopate and Inquisition. Inquisitors displayed arrogance in their formal and in-

[22] José Toribio Medina, *Historia del tribunal del Santo oficio de la inquisición de Cartagena de las Indias* (Santiago de Chile, 1899); José Toribio Medina, *Historia del tribunal del Santo oficio de la inquisición de Lima (1569–1820)* (2 vols., Santiago de Chile, 1887); José Toribio Medina, *Historia del tribunal del Santo oficio de la Inquisición en Chile* (2 vols., Santiago de Chile, 1890); José Toribio Medina, *Historia del tribunal del Santo oficio de la inquisición en México* (Santiago de Chile, 1905); Henry C. Lea, *The Inquisition in the Spanish Dependencies; Sicily—Naples—Sardinia—Milan—the Canaries—Mexico—Peru—New Granada* (New York and London, 1908). Much work remains to be done in Inquisition studies, which always prove revealing not only for ecclesiastical history but also for social and cultural history. Greenleaf, *Zumárraga and the Mexican Inquisition*, demonstrates the rewarding possibilities of modern Inquisition research. Medina and Lea relied chiefly on *relaciones de fe* rather than on the inquisitorial trial records themselves.

formal relations with noninquisitorial clerics. Evidence is unmistakable that they and their agents in a surprisingly large number of cases lived secretly, and sometimes not so secretly, in sin and crime. Even the most responsible inquisitors yielded to the sadism with which the Holy Office conducted its interrogations.

Patronato Real implied state domination over the church, but it simultaneously allowed for ecclesiastical intrusion into civil and political affairs. In the complexities of law and precedent it was impossible to say where church authority ceased and state authority began. Civil law frequently carried explicit religious justifications and sanctions. Ecclesiastics were often appointed to high political posts. The whole of imperial government, and hence any aspect of imperial control, could be justified as propagation of the faith, and if this served as authorization to the crown to legislate on ecclesiastical matters, it served equally as authorization to ecclesiastics to extend their activities to government. Few viceroys in Spanish America were able consistently to remain on cordial terms with the high-ranking churchmen of their viceroyalties. Disputes between viceroys and bishops, often ostensibly over matters of protocol, interpretation, external symbol, or personal preference, reflect real struggles between church and state.

Only on the frontiers did something akin to the original enthusiasm for Christian conversion endure. On the margins of the colony the Mendicant orders continued to operate with their original authority, and a strong new influence for Christianization was added by the Jesuits. The advancing clerics were agents for the expansion of the colonial area in North and South America, and the missions emerged as characteristic features of the peripheral societies where Spanish and Indian cultures met. The mission ordinarily took a village form, with Indian inhabitants performing both civil and ecclesiastical duties. Nomadic Indians were taught sedentary ways of life; hostile Indians were pacified; hunting and gathering economies were transformed into agricultural economies; polygamous peoples were induced to adopt monogamy; and a variety of pagan religious practices yielded to Christianity. In confronting new hostile peoples the ecclesiastics of the seventeenth and eighteenth centuries

1. The medieval world, in circular form with Jerusalem as its central point.
(Courtesy, The British Museum)

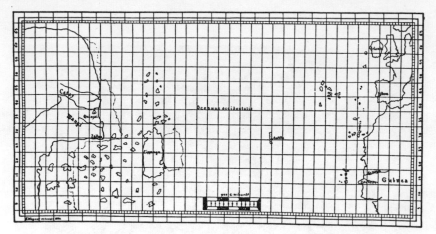

2. Reconstruction of the Toscanelli map (1474): Europe, Africa, and the Orient, without America.

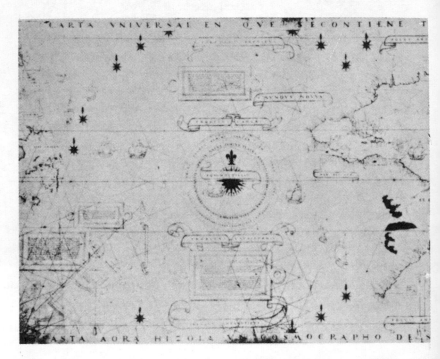

4. Diego Ribero map (1527):

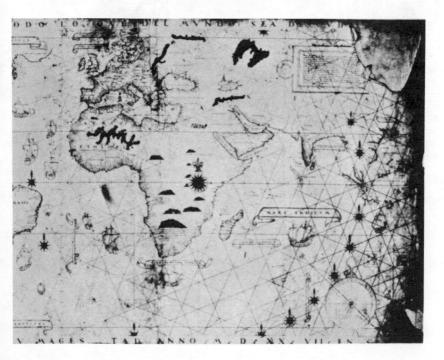

3. Juan de la Cosa map (1500) showing the first American discoveries
in relation to the Old World.

The New World between East and West.

5. Attack on Cholula. Spaniards and their Indian allies conquer a native town. Indian drawing from the *Lienzo de Tlaxcala*, ca. 1550.

ROMANCE XIV

HERNÁN Y MARINA

Bajo una tienda de seda,
cuyo pendoncillo rojo
libremente al viento ondula
con cien giros caprichosos,
Hernán Cortés y la Indiana,
ella hermosa y él airoso,
con ternura apasionada
se contemplan uno y otro.

6. Romanticization of conquest, a publication of the 19th Century
by Antonio Hurtado

7. Charles V
Portrait by Amberger
Staatliche Museum, Berlin (*Marburg-Art Reference Bureau*)

8. Charles II
Portrait by Carreño
Kunsthistorisches Museum, Vienna (*Bruckman-Art Reference Bureau*)

BVENGOBIERNO
DONLVIS·DEVELAS

9. Viceroy Luis de Velasco
as seen by a native American subject.
Drawing by Guaman Poma

10. An American Priest
Biblioteca del Palacio, Madrid

11. Man on horseback in Peru
by Baltasar Compañon,
Biblioteca del Palacio, Madrid

12. Sor Juana Inés de la Cruz
Museo Nacional, Mexico City

13. Young Mexican Lady
Chapultepec Museum, Mexico City

14. Mexican Indian
Museo de America, Madrid

15. Lady and Gentleman
of Chile
Museo de America, Madrid

16. A Spaniard mistreats
an Indian bearer
Drawing by Guaman Poma

17. A friar beats
a native Peruvian weaver
Drawing by Guaman Poma

18. The Black Legend: the Amsterdam edition of Las Casas (1620)

19. Plaza of the city of Panama, 1748
Archivo de Indias, Seville

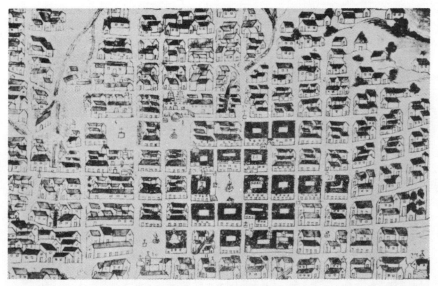

20. Central portion of Quito, 1734
Archivo de Indias, Seville

21. Lima Cathedral
M. Gonzales Salazar, Lima

22. Central portion of Lima, 1687
Archivo de Indias, Seville

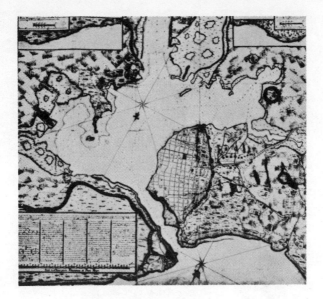

23. Port and city of Havana, 1733
Archivo de Indias, Seville

24. Fortification at Cartagena, 1594
Archivo de Indias, Seville

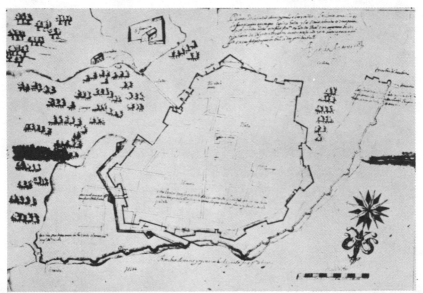

25. Sanctuary of Nuestra Señora de Ocotlan, Tlaxcala, Mexico
(Photograph courtesy The Museum of Modern Art, New York)

characteristically advanced in conjunction with soldiers. The nature of the "spiritual conquest" had now altered, and the presidio or frontier fort balanced and reinforced the church as an agency of strategic control and defense. In time Spanish settlement filled in, the normal civil government and secular clergy supplanted the mission clergy, and the latter moved beyond to found new frontiers.[23]

From the point of view of the royal government this procedure was an effective one through the remainder of colonial times. The successive displacement of Franciscans, Jesuits, and other frontier missionaries by royal officers and members of the secular ecclesiastical hierarchy implied an economical expenditure of resources, an expanding imperial territory, and a minimum of risk. Christianization made slow but continuous advances in new regions, as in northern New Spain and on the Chilean and Argentine frontiers. Crown government was ready to assume control after the Indian hostility had passed and before the missionaries could assume positions of significant local power. In each frontier locality diminishing Indian strife and expanding missionary organization approached an equilibrium that was carefully watched by royal and ecclesiastical authorities. A term of ten years was commonly designated for the transition to settled Christian society, after which the secular clergy would take charge. But in practice the period was often longer than ten years, and on the far frontiers the regular orders were allowed to continue to the end of colonial times.

When secularization was postponed, the problem for the crown tended to become more acute, as the expulsion of the Jesuits in 1767 shows. By the eighteenth century Jesuits were established in many parts of America, in selected parishes, as teachers in schools and universities, and as missionaries on the frontiers. In northern Mexico and especially in the Paraguay region of South America the Jesuits had developed the mission into an efficient and prosperous enterprise. In southern South America, because of slave raids from Portu-

[23] Herbert E. Bolton, "The Mission as a Frontier Institution in the Spanish-American Colonies," *American Historical Review,* XXIII (1917–18), 42–61, is principally concerned with the northern frontier of New Spain. Constantino Bayle, "Las misiones, defensa de las fronteras," *Missionalia hispánica,* VIII (1951), 417–503, emphasizes the Spanish-Portuguese frontier in South America.

guese Brazil, they had retrenched and concentrated their attention upon the Guaraní peoples in the Uruguay and Paraná valleys. This was the location of the best-known Jesuit "reductions,"[24] and here as elsewhere the Jesuits imposed a discipline of Christian duties, with manual labor, partially common property, and strict daily schedules. Contact with the world outside the reductions was limited, and for a long time the Indian subjects were organized, as in an army, for internal discipline and for defense against outside intrusions. The Jesuits regulated all aspects of native life in the missions: food and clothing, living habits, prayer, and schedules of work and rest. They reluctantly permitted occasional visits from episcopal and political authorities. Their tendency was to close off the mission compound, forbid access to it or egress from it, and govern the reductions as paternalistic and isolated enclave states. The Jesuits' regime was severely criticized by political officials and other colonists, who accused them of enslaving the Guaraní, profiting from the economy of the missions, and defying the royal government.[25]

In 1767, in a sudden and devastating move, the crown expelled all members of the Society of Jesus from the colonies. In explanation the monarchy cited the need to bring local Jesuit powers to an end and to assert royal powers in their stead. The expulsion was related to the general Bourbon attack upon Jesuit society in Europe, the result of Enlightenment ideas, religious nationalism, and resistance to papal authority. In America one consequence of the expulsion was the decay of the large number of Jesuit educational institutions. Indians in Paraguay, dependent on Jesuit tutelage, were unprepared for a non-Jesuit world and underwent a process of "deculturation." Exploitation, desertion, crime, and disorder were the immediate consequences of the expulsion. In many formerly Jesuit areas the crown made efforts to introduce other branches of the church to

[24] "Reduction" implies the congregating of neophytes into a community form. The location of the Paraguayan reductions, in the Alto Paraná basin, was quite different, and distant, from the Asunción region which forms the heart of historic non-Jesuit Paraguay.

[25] The abundant materials on the Jesuit missions in Paraguay are surveyed in the foremost modern work on the subject, Magnus Mörner, *The Political and Economic Activities of the Jesuits in the La Plata Region: The Hapsburg Era* (Stockholm, 1953), pp. 6–21.

take their place, but no other branches were prepared for such substitutions and they were at best only partially successful.[26]

The main branches of the late colonial church were not dedicated to missionary work, and Indian society played almost no role in their operations or their plans. From an original missionary institution the church as a whole became, most spectacularly, an institution of wealth, a holder of mortgages, and a proprietor of real estate.[27] In general the transformation corresponded to the demographic and social changes of the sixteenth and early seventeenth centuries, for as Indian populations declined Christianization became less important and unoccupied lands became available for ecclesiastical possession. By 1700 the church had emerged as the foremost landholding body of the colonies, with a huge investment in buildings, ranches, cattle, mills, agricultural supplies, and all else that accompanied property ownership. In addition to properties owned outright, the church controlled many other properties through rental, money lending, and devices of credit.[28]

In the early period the church had been dependent for its income mainly on royal disbursements, tithes, and private bequests. Even in the late period these remained important sources of church revenue. But they progressively yielded to ecclesiastical investment in urban lands and buildings, rural estates, and mines. By 1600, the first scruples had been overcome, royal laws forbidding property ownership by religious bodies had been set aside, and the long process of

---

[26] On the efforts of the civil government to control the missions and late colonial consequences for the mission areas, see John Lynch, *Spanish Colonial Administration, 1782–1810: The Intendant System in the Viceroyalty of the Río de la Plata* (London, 1958), pp. 186 ff. On the expulsion, see Pablo Hernández, *El extrañamiento de los jesuitas del Río de la Plata y de las misiones del Paraguay por decreto de Carlos III* (Madrid, 1908). José M. Mariluz Urquijo, "Los guaraníes después de la expulsión de los jesuítas," *Estudios americanos*, VI (1953), 323–330, cautions against too sweeping a generalization on Guaraní deterioration. The Indians of the missions found refuge in cities and on farms, and did not revert to a primitive migrant state.

[27] Ecclesiastical landholding has received only a small fraction of the scholarly attention the subject merits. François Chevalier, *La Formation des grands domaines au Mexique: Terre et société aux XVIᵉ–XVIIᵉ siècles* (Paris, 1952), pp. 301 ff., provides an indication of the possibilities.

[28] Jesuit properties, which were extensive and profitable, were confiscated by the crown after the Jesuit expulsion. How far this served as a motive for the expulsion we do not know.

acquisition was under way. We do not know how much of the usable land of the colony finally came under ecclesiastical domination, but estimates on the order of half or more do not appear excessive.

A consequence of wealth was ostentation. The prodigality with which religious bodies garbed their ministers, conducted their ceremonies, and decorated their buildings is a striking feature of a society that allowed most of its members to live in poverty. A particularly nice distinction between material and nonmaterial values was now required, for while the poverty of the lower classes was often commented upon by ecclesiastics, the ultimate goal of the religious life continued to be expressed in spiritual terms. The visible evidence of the colonial church meanwhile was quite real. Mexico City had over eight thousand ecclesiastics in a total white population of about sixty thousand in the late eighteenth century.[29] Cathedrals and churches, impressive for sheer numbers, were everywhere the largest and most ornate structures of the colony.[30] The most pretentious were those of the cities, as one would expect. But it is important to recognize that behind them, in the hinterlands of Spanish America, were the church-owned haciendas that made them possible.

It is not sufficient of course to say that as lands became available they were taken by the church, for many nonecclesiastics were successful also in obtaining landed property. We must explain the peculiar achievement of the church in an economic operation that attracted many competitors. Here an advantage lay in the church's spiritual prestige, for it was above ordinary criticism and in a sense even piety could be measured in material terms. Wealthy individuals bestowed donations and bequests on the church. Though church lands were former Indian lands, most of them came into ecclesiastical possession not through direct seizure but through lay intermediaries. Further, such properties were held in legal mortmain. They could

[29] "Noticias de Nueva-España en 1805," *Boletín del Instituto nacional de geografía y estadística de la república mexicana,* época 1, II (1864, ed. 3), 8.
[30] Two Spanish visitors to Lima in the eighteenth century described in awe the silver altars, gold-fringed tapestries, huge silver candlesticks, gold vessels covered with diamonds and pearls, and divine service "performed with a magnificence scarce to be imagined." Jorge Juan and Antonio de Ulloa, *A Voyage to South America,* John Adams, trans.; Irving A. Leonard, ed. (New York, 1964), p. 181.

not be sold or subdivided, and the process of ecclesiastical acquisition was thus one of steady accretion. The total accumulation and the entire economic role of the church extended beyond what had originally been contemplated, for recurrent crises weakened the economic position of competitors. As one of the few enduring institutions of the colony, the church readily capitalized on the failure of lay property owners. Its presence was universal. Its personnel included many astute financiers. Its wealth allowed it to hire the most capable lawyers in defense of its interests. It stood to gain in any situation involving a developing economy, and in times of recession it alone possessed the means and the stamina to succeed.

Accusations to the effect that clerical landholders were conducting themselves in improper ways could be countered by a number of arguments. The church's spiritual and cultural contributions to the society could be emphasized. Its schools, colleges, and universities were everywhere respected. Missionaries in the frontier regions could be identified as dedicated persons preserving the traditions of Indian Christianization under extreme and difficult conditions. The wealth of the church could be represented as the product not of active acquisition but of passive receipt. If the church surpassed other institutions in its material substance, this was to be explained not by the cupidity of the clerics but by the devotion and faith of the whole society and its generosity to an organization dependent on charitable contributions. It was the clerical institution, not the individual clerics, that profited, a conception that permitted clergy to deny material motives as individuals and to represent wealth as a manifestation of religiosity.

The church of the later colonial period frankly abandoned "reform." The record tells of ecclesiastics who abused their parishioners, kept mistresses, conducted orgies, exploited the confessionals, profiteered in business negotiations, and behaved in other ways unbecoming to their calling.[31] The rule of clerical celibacy, recognized in principle, was widely violated throughout the colonies. A revealing

---

[31] Archival material on this subject is abundant, but no historian has dealt with it in detail. Jorge Juan and Antonio de Ulloa, *Noticias secretas de América* (London, 1826), is a celebrated colonial exposé. See especially pp. 489–542.

feature is that clerical conduct received so little criticism from political authorities or from the public at large. The fact suggests an
indifference to existing conditions and a reluctance to interfere. A
possible explanation is to be found in royal policy, which was still
committed to church support, and which consistently refrained from
calling public attention to clerical transgressions. In addition the
tradition of inquisitorial and other church courts was to deal harshly
with criticism, and public complaint was surely restrained by fear.
A church so institutionalized and so wealthy, a total theocratic
system so hostile toward expressions of unorthodoxy, may have been
above popular attack for these reasons alone.

Moreover Christianity pervaded all aspects of late colonial society.
Christian concepts, often in a vulgarized form, remained strong.
Among the most enduring aspects of Christian doctrine in Spanish
America were those relating to divine judgments—this may have
been connected with the public's indifference toward corruption—
and to the impotency of human action. God's will, frequently understood as punitive, was the universal explanation for plague and
famine, for public disasters, and for private misfortunes. Selected
religious symbols were everywhere respected. The Christian fatalism
of white society was matched by the pagan fatalism, Christianized
in various degrees, of Indian society. The church encouraged lay
participation in confraternities, which instilled security and loyalty
in exchange for labor and dues; in fiestas, which provided opportunities for emotional release; and in autos-da-fé, which were spec-
tacles of macabre punishment for society's and Christianity's good.
Religion was accommodated to the social order, to the roles of men
and women (as in many other Christian societies, piety was more
evident among women than among men), and to rank. Religion
furnished a justification for white authority and a solace for Indian
pain. In New Spain, through the whole colonial period, the Virgin
of Guadalupe served as the protectress of Indians, in intermittent
rivalry with the Virgin of Los Remedios to whom whites paid
homage. At the end of the colonial period, in the time of independence, the one Virgin was adopted by the revolutionists and the other
by the royalists, as if to demonstrate again the adaptability of Christianity to the divisions of the society.

In Spanish America as in Europe, the historic failures of the church should be measured against its historic achievements. Spanish Christianity, like Spanish government and Spanish culture generally, was transplanted to a new area twenty times the size of Spain. The competing religions of Europe were excluded. Millions of American pagans were introduced to Christian thought. Religious art and architecture displayed an unexpected florescence. A case could be made for the proposition that in Spanish America the religious forms of one major civilization were replaced by those of another as successfully and as rapidly as anywhere else in the world.

Most of the monumental building of colonial Spanish America was religious in character, and the emphasis tells us something of the status of religion in colonial society. Only infrequently did the church builders of Spanish America deliberately depart from European traditions—indeed, one of the conspicuous features of all Spanish American colonial art was its imitation of Spanish models. Building plans themselves might be sent directly from Spain or from Rome. But imitation was often indirect, as when selected details or the over-all mood of a particular prototype were re-created from a distant memory. The range of styles available was immense. The modifications of peninsular styles and the developing regional varieties gave colonial architecture a unique quality.

The earliest church buildings in Mexico and Peru were those of the period of missionary vigor, when a large labor force was available and when the direction of the labor fell to the Mendicant orders. Immediate need brought into being one of Spanish America's most effective and simplest architectural designs, the "open chapel" where Mass was celebrated for a large congregation assembled out of doors.[32] Only in a few places did the open chapel survive the sixteenth century. In the principal regions of the colony great Mendicant constructions were under way by the 1550's. Under the direction of the friars, Indian laborers became conversant with rib vaulting and the entire repertory of contemporary Spanish technique.[33] Varieties of church and *convento* construction reflected dif-

[32] John McAndrew, *The Open-Air Churches of Sixteenth-Century Mexico: Atrios, Posas, Open Chapels, and Other Studies* (Cambridge, Mass., 1965).
[33] George Kubler, *Mexican Architecture of the Sixteenth Century* (2 vols., New Haven, 1948), I, 134–186.

ferences in physical environment and in Mendicant conception of the
need. The Franciscan order outdistanced others in sheer quantity of
building. The Augustinians were celebrated for the magnitude of
single undertakings. Mendicant churches in the sixteenth century
were like fortresses, with massive walls and crenelations, as if the
doctrine of "spiritual conquest" were to be taken in a literal sense.
The outstanding constructions of this period are represented at
Acolman (Augustinian) in central Mexico, at Quito (Franciscan)
in Ecuador, and by hundreds of other surviving buildings throughout Spanish America.

As the proselytization program waned, attention shifted to religious building in the cities. The late sixteenth and seventeenth
centuries witnessed prolonged labors on cathedrals and other urban
ecclesiastical buildings. The great Mexico City Cathedral was under
construction for a full century, from the 1560's to the 1660's. Imitation of peninsular prototypes was now more deliberate, as between
the cathedrals of Puebla and Valladolid, or those of Lima and Jaén.
A particular solution in the seismic zones of southern Mexico and
Central America was the development of massive foundations and
walls, for which a rich external and internal decoration was made
to compensate. In Lima, walls of plaster on wooden frames survived
the earth tremors and remained intact in the dry climate. After
1650, elaborate surface ornament appeared in Baroque and Rococo
styles, becoming progressively more lavish and ornate. Variations
developed between capital and provincial schools, between northern
and southern Mexico, and between coastal and highland Peru.
Some of the finest examples of seventeenth- and eighteenth-century
building are to be found in unexpected places in Spanish America,
such as Ocotlan near Tlaxcala in Mexico, or Zapita on the southern
shore of Lake Titicaca in Peru.[34] Indian traditions were almost
totally absent, even in the areas of the most developed Indian civilizations. This was true of architecture, a public art form under the

[34] George Kubler and Martin Soria, *Art and Architecture in Spain and
Portugal and Their American Dominions, 1500 to 1800* (Baltimore, 1959); Pál
Kelemen, *Baroque and Rococo in Latin America* (New York, 1951); Harold
E. Wethey, *Colonial Architecture and Sculpture in Peru* (Cambridge, Mass.,
1949).

direction of the church, more than of painting or sculpture or folk art.

Ecclesiastical history remains one of the most difficult branches of colonial Spanish America's past to evaluate accurately. Much depends upon one's conception of the proper role of religion in any society, a matter on which historians, no less than others, disagree. Students have paid chief attention to the early period, to the missionary labors on the frontiers, and to the architectural record. The institutional history of the church in the central colonial areas, especially after the sixteenth century, has been a much less attractive subject, and the reasons surely relate to a fundamental ambivalence concerning the points of view that may reasonably be expressed. No one knows whether to interpret "laxity" in a puritanical spirit or to treat it with the tolerance that colonial society itself was able to achieve. With respect to the wealth of the church, everyone recognizes that a spiritual institution must have a practical economic base; but the extent of this base in colonial Spanish America raises questions of limit, and again the problem is one of the reasonable role of a religious institution in society. Similar problems of course intrude upon an assessment of religious institutions elsewhere. But the controversial features of the question are especially acute in those areas—outstandingly exemplified by Spanish America—where dispute over the position of the church extends into recent history and to the present.

CHAPTER 5

State

THE establishment of a patrimonial and centralized Spanish monarchy was the great achievement of Ferdinand and Isabella. With the extension of Spanish dominion overseas there occurred some diminution in this new royal authority, diminution of a type common to many imperial undertakings in the early stages of their history. The Spanish monarchy at first delegated powers in order that an empire might be founded. It then faced the problem of regaining control from its own delegated agents. The powers granted to Columbus were revoked after the monarchy began to glimpse the potentialities of American imperialism. (Columbus' son Diego spent some twenty years in vain petition for the privileges inherited from his father.) Those granted to the conquistadores were brought to an end before extreme degrees of political influence could be involved. The powers granted to *encomenderos* proved more difficult to recapture, but the monarchy made a vigorous statement in the New Laws and thereafter proceeded to impede, wear down, and limit encomienda at every opportunity. The missionary friars, to whom powers and privileges of another kind had been granted, were denied their original parochial controls after the late sixteenth century. All this meant that during the first hundred years following the discovery, an expanding royal state was dismissing its earliest imperial representatives and introducing the instruments of thoroughgoing, meticulous, Hispanic absolutism.

The royal understanding was that this state might exert its influence over every phase of colonial life. No detail of imperial administration was to be too minute for attention; no aspect of colonial existence was to be left without regulation. The Spanish imperial ideal lay in the formulation of a great centralized scheme, to which colonial history would conform. The monarchical system was to be imposed upon the New World with a thoroughness never achieved in Europe. Thus a nationalistic counterpart to the missionary philosophy envisaged America as a vast new territory inviting Hispanic organization.

Spain as a nation was institutionally diverse at the outset. It was a region of local sectionalism and local patriotism, where men were identified as Castilian or Aragonese or Galician, rather than as Spaniards. Ferdinand and Isabella declared themselves to be not monarchs of Spain but monarchs of Castile, León, Aragón, Granada, Toledo, Valencia, Galicia, Sevilla, Córdoba, and Gibraltar. They knew of course that Castile and Aragón were the most powerful and the most important of the Spanish "kingdoms," and Isabella, at least, knew that Castile alone was responsible for Spanish expansion to the west. Isabella's will denied to Ferdinand the title of king of Castile, providing instead for the succession of their daughter Juana. From the beginning the Indies were regarded as properties of the Castilian crown. Isabella understood this matter clearly: the New World had been discovered and acquired through the agency of Castile; accordingly all settlers should be Castilian, all benefits should accrue to Castile, and the laws of America should be Castilian laws. To be sure, the successors of Isabella did not totally endorse this view. The Spanish monarchs, beginning with Ferdinand even before the death of Isabella in 1504, were loath to limit American settlement and profit to Castilians. But the selection of the kingdom of Castile as the essential parent country for the American colonies was never seriously called into question until the eighteenth century.[1]

Had it been otherwise, Spanish-American history would have been very different. The Aragonese monarchy was and continued to

---

[1] Juan Manzano Manzano, *La incorporación de las Indias a la corona de Castilla* (Madrid, 1948); Mario Góngora, *El estado en el derecho indiano: Epoca de fundación (1492–1570)* (Santiago de Chile, 1951), pp. 36 ff.

be circumscribed by restrictions. In every way the crown of Castile was more free to exercise royal jurisdiction. In Aragón, all major royal decisions still required the approval of the *cortes*. In Castile, the Council was not an administrative obstacle to royal action.[2] With the application of the Castilian system to America, the way was opened for direct royal-conciliar government, and the massive authority of the monarch—"I the King," as he signed his official orders—was to pervade all American law.

In their historical derivation the governing bodies for America developed directly from the Council of Castile. An important member of this council, Juan Rodríguez de Fonseca, had been selected by Isabella immediately on Columbus' return to advise the crown in matters relating to the new discoveries. With the addition of other Castilian officers to Fonseca's staff, an administrative body came into being, and for several decades the Council of Castile as a whole retained supreme judicial authority over the American possessions. Thus in 1524, when Fonseca's staff was granted administrative and judicial jurisdiction as the Council of the Indies (Consejo de Indias), the influential councilors were persons whose experience and training had been in the Castilian royal council.[3]

Of the governing institutions for the American colonies, the Council of the Indies remained the most important during the sixteenth and seventeenth centuries. Like the Council of Castile, it was directly subordinate to the monarch, and it moved with the court from place to place, never taking up residence in America. Technically the American dominions were themselves related to Spain only through the common royal sovereignty, and they were understood to be "kingdoms," like the several kingdoms of Spain.[4] The Council drafted and issued American laws and served as the appellate judicial court for civil cases arising in the colonies. In the matter

[2] J. H. Elliott, *Imperial Spain, 1469–1716* (London, 1963), pp. 22 ff., 78 ff., *et seq.*

[3] Ernesto Schäfer, *El Consejo real y supremo de las Indias: Su historia, organización y labor administrativa hasta la terminación de la casa de Austria* (2 vols., Seville, 1935–47), I, 43 ff.

[4] This has induced some modern writers to argue that the American possessions were not true colonies. See Ricardo Levene, "Las Indias no eran colonias," *Boletín de la Academia nacional de la historia* (Buenos Aires), XXV (1951), 596–626.

of appointment to American religious and secular offices, the Council exercised the royal power of nomination. Supervision of appointees involved it in constant investigation, hearing of testimony, auditing of accounts, and reviewing of conduct.

The composition of the Council of the Indies underwent numerous changes. The councilors themselves were appointed and subject to removal by the crown. Subordinate officers came to include an attorney, a treasurer, a cosmographer, a mathematician, a historian, and a number of other officials and aides. Such changes in the Council's size and in its formal functioning did not on the whole operate to speed its work or to simplify its handling of affairs. Its tendency was meticulous and bureaucratic. It operated through lengthy, deliberative sessions surrounded by massive quantities of reports, laws, opinions, briefs, and other types of contemporary record. Especially in the seventeenth century, after the colonial administrative machinery had been created and as the internal and international position of Spain deteriorated, the Council reflected the progressive weakening of Spanish monarchy and government. In general it mirrored the characters, attitudes, and beliefs of the ruling kings: it was self-confident, vigorous, and precise under Philip II in the latter part of the sixteenth century; it was phlegmatic, dilatory, and in bad repute under Charles II a hundred years later.[5]

In America the highest ranking representatives of royal government were the viceroys, who occupied positions of great prestige and influence, and who ruled in the king's name as deputies of the crown. Viceroys were almost without exception Spaniards, born in the mother country. Their appointment was by the king and Council, and in spite of laws restricting their tenure to specific terms, their period of service was dependent on the king's pleasure. Viceroys were entrusted with the execution of colonial law and with the maintenance of civil and military order within their jurisdictions. They were responsible for revenues, justice, Indian welfare, subordinate appointments, labor regulation—indeed, every

[5] Volume I of the major work on the Council of the Indies, Schäfer, *Consejo real y supremo,* analyzes its activities in the successive reigns of the sixteenth and seventeenth centuries.

department of Spanish rule in the colonies came within the viceregal province. In the total operation of imperial government the viceroys' primary functions may be described as executive and interpretive, for in the viceregal office the royal legislation of the Council of the Indies was translated into political reality. Hence the viceroys' discretionary powers amounted at times to a de facto veto, and numerous instances are known in which viceroys substantially altered the meaning of laws in adapting them to real or supposed colonial needs. The great distance separating the colonies from Spain tended to increase the viceroy's authority as it reduced the Council's. The difference between enacted legislation at a distance and interpreted legislation on the scene was manifested again and again. *Obedezco pero no cumplo*—I obey but I do not fulfill—was the viceregal response to legislation that would not be enforced.[6]

Viceroys were assisted by advisory and judicial bodies known as *audiencias,* which ruled also in the king's name, sometimes in harmony and sometimes in conflict with the viceroys. *Audiencias* formed the appellate courts of their areas, being subordinate judicially only to the Council of the Indies in Spain. Provisional local legislation, again in a subordinate capacity to the king and to the Council of the Indies, was permitted to these *audiencias* as it was to the viceroys. *Audiencias* assumed full viceregal powers when absence or incapacity prevented viceroys from governing in person, and at other times they shared and even usurped viceregal prerogatives. *Audiencias* differed from one another both in size and in power, and their operation at any given point in time depended upon a variety of local circumstances. Their members ordinarily served longer terms than viceroys, and as corporate entities the *audiencias* provided administrative continuity from one

---

[6] Góngora, *El estado en el derecho indiano,* pp. 63 ff., provides a succinct political analysis of the viceregal office. Schäfer, *Consejo real y supremo,* II, 439 ff., tabulates the viceregal succession for New Spain and Peru through the seventeenth century. Outstanding biographies of individual viceroys include Arthur S. Aiton, *Antonio de Mendoza, First Viceroy of New Spain* (Durham, N.C., 1927); Roberto Levillier, *Don Francisco de Toledo, supremo organizador del Perú: Su vida, su obra (1515–1582)* (2 vols., Buenos Aires, 1935–40); and Bernard E. Bobb, *The Viceregency of Antonio María Bucareli in New Spain, 1771–1779* (Austin, Tex., 1962).

viceregal regime to another. At the upper levels of government in the colonies *audiencias* were the most durable and stable of the several branches of government.[7]

Spanish America was initially divided into two viceroyalties and a number of subordinate *audiencias*. The viceroyalties were Mexico (New Spain), created in 1535 with its capital at Mexico City, and Peru (New Castile), created in 1542 with its capital at Lima. *Audiencias* were established at Santo Domingo (1511), Mexico City (1528), Panama (1538), Lima (1542), Los Confines or Guatemala (1542), New Galicia (1548), and Bogotá (1549). Others were created after this, and changes in jurisdiction, status, and location continued to be made through colonial times. The *audiencias* of New Galicia, Mexico, Guatemala, and Santo Domingo were subordinate to the viceroy of Mexico; those of Panama, Lima, and Bogotá to the viceroy of Peru. The Lima and Mexico City *audiencias* were presided over by the viceroys resident in those two cities. Other *audiencias* normally recognized separate presiding officers, with differing degrees of independence from or subordination to the viceroys. The presiding officers (*presidentes*) of lesser *audiencias* might at the same time hold the offices of governor and captain general for their areas, as viceroys also did for theirs. Local traditions, formal alterations, and multiple officeholding by single individuals made for a number of practical variations, such that two officeholders of the same rank might possess quite different degrees of authority.

Subdivisions within the jurisdiction of the *audiencias* took the form of local areas over which *alcaldes mayores, corregidores,* and *gobernadores* presided. No appreciable functional distinction among these officials has yet been perceived for the Spanish American colonies.[8] Appointment to the posts was irregular, although the

---

[7] Góngora, *El estado en el derecho indiano,* pp. 56 ff., summarizes the legal-political status of *audiencias.* One of the major contributions of Schäfer, *Consejo real y supremo,* is the Appendix (II, 443 ff.), listing the *oidores* of the twelve *audiencias* of the sixteenth and seventeenth centuries. The outstanding study of a single *audiencia* is John H. Parry, *The Audiencia of New Galicia in the Sixteenth Century: A Study in Spanish Colonial Government* (Cambridge, Eng., 1948).

[8] On the peninsular origin of *corregimiento,* see Robert S. Chamberlain, "The

DISPUTED BY ENGLAND, RUSSIA, AND SPAIN

EFFECTIVE FRONTIER OF SPANISH SETTLEMENT

NEW FRANCE

ENGLISH COLONIES

Mississippi R.

ATLANTIC OCEAN

VICEROYALTY OF NEW SPAIN

FLORIDA Ceded to England, 1763-83

Guadalajara •

Mexico City •

JAMAICA Conquered by England, 1655

HAITI (SAINT DOMINGUE) Ceded to France, 1697

Santo Domingo

Guatemala •

Caracas

BOUNDARY BETWEEN THE TWO ORIGINAL VICEROYALTIES OF NEW SPAIN AND PERU

VICEROYALTY OF NEW GRANADA

Bogotá •

Separated from Viceroyalty of Peru, 1717, 1739

GUIANA

Quito •

VICEROYALTY OF PERU

Lima • — Cuzco •

BRAZIL (Portuguese)

PACIFIC OCEAN

• Chuquisaca (La Plata; Sucre)

VICEROYALTY OF LA PLATA Separated from Viceroyalty of Peru, 1776

Santiago •

AUDIENCIA OF CHILE Retained by Viceroyalty of Peru 1776

Buenos Aires

CLAIMED BUT NOT SETTLED BY SPAIN

SPAIN IN AMERICA

● Viceregal Capital

• Audiencia Seat

0 _____ 1500 Miles

HS

early tendency to appointment by viceroy and *audiencia* was later reversed so that appointment directly by the crown became a more common practice. Appointments were for an official tenure of three or five years, but in fact varied more widely than this statement would suggest. The local officers possessed judicial, administrative, and to some extent legislative functions within their areas, and each was subordinate to the viceroy and *audiencia* of the region within which his jurisdiction lay.

The *corregidores* and their equivalents were normally associated with municipal councils (*ayuntamientos* or *cabildos*). Between *corregidores* and their councils the relationship was roughly similar to that between viceroys and *audiencias,* or between the Council of the Indies and the king. The municipal councils consisted principally of officials of the rank of *alcalde* and *regidor. Alcaldes* were judges for minor crimes in addition to being councilors, and in prestige and authority they were superior to *regidores.* (*Alcalde* is frequently translated as mayor in Spanish textbooks in the United States, but this is quite meaningless for the ordinary Spanish American colonial town, which had a council but no mayor.)[9] The bodies varied considerably in size and tended to be larger in the more important towns. In addition to the *alcaldes* and *regidores* they might include a number of special officers, such as police chiefs, inspectors of weights and measures, guardians of public property, and collectors of fines, with or without the power to vote.[10] The

---

Corregidor in Castile in the Sixteenth Century and the Residencia as Applied to the *Corregidor," Hispanic American Historical Review,* XXIII (1943), 222–257.

[9] One might imagine this peculiar translation to result from a confusion with *alcalde mayor.* But a more likely explanation is that the equation between *alcalde* and mayor derives from the particular case of California, where several civil-community governments were under the control of *alcaldes,* both before and after the Anglo-American occupation. *Alcaldes* such as Alfred Geary in San Francisco and Stephen Clark Foster in Los Angeles became mayors in the 1850's. See Theodore Grivas, "Alcalde Rule: The Nature of Local Government in Spanish and Mexican California," *California Historical Society Quarterly,* XL (1961), 11–32.

[10] On *cabildos* see Constantino Bayle, *Los cabildos seculares en la América española* (Madrid, 1952); John Preston Moore, *The Cabildo in Peru under the Hapsburgs: A Study in the Origins and Powers of the Town Council in the Viceroyalty of Peru, 1530–1700* (Durham, N.C., 1954); and Frederick B. Pike, "Aspects of Cabildo Economic Regulations in Spanish America under the Haps-

minutes of their meetings, generally under the title Actas de Cabildo, are available in print or in manuscript for a huge number of communities and they constitute, as one would expect, one of the richest sources of information for local affairs.[11]

Liberal-minded students have sometimes looked optimistically to the Spanish American town councils in the hope of identifying some democratic impulse in local government and some exception to the series of authoritarian institutions by which the Spanish colonies were governed. The hope has some justification, for at the time of the outbreak of the wars for independence, bodies called open councils (*cabildos abiertos*) were developed to take control in revolutionary areas. From a certain external point of view it would be satisfying to show that some measure of anti-authoritarianism had been present from the beginning and that this gradually gained strength in opposition to royal controls, after the manner of the colonial assemblies of the English. An occasional record can be found giving support to the analogy with English institutions—thus royal orders for new settlements in the 1520's allowed for election of local conciliar officers by the citizens of the town—but the common result of such inquiries is to impress upon the student even more emphatically that democracy was not practiced in Spanish America at any political level.[12]

In reality community governments became weaker in the colonial period, and the tendency if any was toward less rather than more popular participation. Royal authority progressively limited the original wide powers of the *cabildos*. The characteristic town council became a closed body, filled by nonelective officers. *Alcaldes* and *regidores* secured their posts through appointment by superior

---

burgs," *Inter-American Economic Affairs,* XIII (1959–60), 67–80. Pike comments on the *cabildos'* preference for landowners at the expense of middlemen, artisans, and processors.

[11] Agustín Millares Carlo, *Notas bibliográficas acerca de archivos municipales, ediciones de libros de acuerdo y colecciones de documentos concejiles* (Madrid, 1952).

[12] There was some prerevolutionary precedent for the *cabildos abiertos.* No *cortes* ever met in America. Representatives of the towns never came together. The Spanish equivalent of an assembly or parliament was forbidden by the crown. See Lesley Byrd Simpson, Gordon Griffiths, and Woodrow Borah, "Representative Institutions in the Spanish Empire in the Sixteenth Century," *The Americas,* XII (1955–56), 223–257.

authority, and often as honorific dispensations by the king himself. Town councils were self-perpetuating, their members holding office for life. Their offices were sold by the crown, or were regarded as private possessions that could be sold by their holders, a portion of the price paid accruing to the royal treasury as tax. In other cases the offices were hereditary, again at a price, or were rented out to persons who were willing to pay the fee. Whereas in the early period positions in local councils were respected and sought after by leading citizens of the community, by late colonial times it frequently happened that no responsible citizen could be found who was willing to serve. In such instances arbitrary appointments and compulsory payments might be enforced. These tendencies were most pronounced in the main areas of Spanish administration, in and near the viceregal centers. *Cabildo* power and popular participation survived, where it survived at all, in marginal areas at a distance and through neglect.

The Actas de Cabildo, also, are more informative for the early history of colonial Spanish America than for the late. In the seventeenth and eighteenth centuries, community governments less often considered the kinds of topic that are of interest to historians, such as regulation of markets or administration of local finances, and in some towns they ceased to function entirely. A major source of trouble was economic. Councils of the later period rarely controlled sufficient funds to administer an effective municipal government. Their meager incomes depended on license fees and petty rents for common land, and the members themselves were apt to profit privately at the expense of community treasuries. But even with these common practices such local offices could not compete, as remunerative possessions, with other forms of colonial officeholding, and the result was absenteeism, vacancy, abrogation of authority, and loss of political power. Late colonial towns managed their affairs less in conciliar form and more through direct viceregal authority. In America, by 1700, very little remained of the municipal autonomy that was traditional in the earlier Hispanic world.[13]

---

[13] John Lynch, *Spanish Colonial Administration, 1782–1810: The Intendant System in the Viceroyalty of the Río de la Plata* (London, 1958), pp. 201 ff., gives details on relations between intendants and *cabildos,* with comment on the late stimulus to *cabildo* rule that the intendants provided.

The principal offices in the imperial hierarchy, and many of the lesser ones as well, were subjected to a controlling device called *residencia,* which further served to integrate the structure of government. *Residencia* was a formal hearing held at the conclusion of an incumbent's term in office. Witnesses testified concerning the officeholder's conduct of affairs: that he had performed his functions well or that he had abused his office. The presiding officer at a *residencia* might be a judge specially chosen, or he might be the successor in the same office who had been granted judicial powers for the purpose. Legally no incumbent could leave his position without submitting to the *residencia.* In cases of unfavorable judgment, an officeholder was required to make restitution to the persons whom he had mistreated, or in serious cases to undergo more severe kinds of punishment.[14]

The *visita* was a second device utilized by the royal government for conducting inquiries into the operation of colonial affairs. Inspectors *(visitadores)* might be sent to America to examine the enforcement procedures relating to particular laws, to report on the political situation in a given area, to circulate throughout the colonies and render a general or specific account, or to perform any similar task required by the monarchy. For the crown or any royal authority the *visita* was a means of circumventing the ordinary procedures of organized government and of securing necessary information, or corrective action, without the prolonged delays that customarily impeded political operations.[15]

All officials of the hierarchy possessed authority over economic, as over other, affairs. But because so crucial a part of the imperial organization depended on direct monetary income, a separate branch of the structure was devoted to finance, taxation, and the maritime operations between Spain and America. This centered in the Casa de Contratación, or House of Trade, founded by royal order in 1503 and located in the Castilian city of Seville. The Casa served as an administrative focal point for commercial traffic in-

[14] José María Mariluz Urquijo, *Ensayo sobre los juicios de residencia indianos* (Seville, 1952).

[15] Walter V. Scholes, *The Diego Ramírez Visita* (Columbia, Mo., 1946); Guillermo Céspedes del Castillo, "La visita como institución indiana," *Anuario de estudios americanos,* III (1946), 984–1025.

volving the Spanish colonies. Its personnel came to include a treasurer, a secretary, a chief pilot, a postmaster, a prosecutor, and a professor of cosmography. In the seventeenth century the expansion of its organization continued with the addition of departments for ordnance testing and naval tribute (*avería*). The mechanism of the Casa became increasingly complex and its sphere of operation more pervasive with the progressive expansion of the American area and the internal development of the colonies.[16]

In broad terms the Casa was created to control commerce, shipping, and finance relating to the Indies. In a sense it represented an extension to America of a monopolistic system of control already established for other purposes, as in the *consulado* of Burgos, which governed Spanish exports of wool to the north. But the Casa became a larger and more influential institution than any of its prototypes. Royal funds from the New World were channeled through it, and it served as the collecting agency for a variety of maritime taxes. Hence simply as a royal treasury and revenue office its powers were extensive. Its judicial department had jurisdiction over civil and criminal cases relating to trade and navigation. Its navigational bureau trained the pilots for American commerce, regulated their activities, recorded the progress of geographical discovery, and maintained the master map or *Padrón real*. In commercial regulation the Casa never became an institution of private royal monopoly. Instead it gave official sanction to the establishment of the mercantile guild (*consulado*) of Seville, and together the two institutions proceeded to govern commercial relations between the American colonies and Spain.

The Casa and the merchant guild of Seville were closely allied institutions. A natural co-operation existed between royal and guild interests. The concentration of royal power over America was simultaneous with the establishment of guild monopoly. The monarch, through the Casa, provided national protection to the *consulado* and excluded competitors; the guild merchants furnished capital for commercial enterprise and reinforced the administration. Seville merchants alone were granted the privilege of trade with

---

[16] Clarence H. Haring, *Trade and Navigation between Spain and the Indies in the Time of the Hapsburgs* (Cambridge, Mass., 1918), pp. 21–45.

America, and only these were admitted to the *consulado*. Merchants from other parts of Spain and merchants from foreign nations, in so far as their commercial relationship with the American colonies was legitimately conducted (much was not), necessarily dealt with the *consulado* of Seville. The result was a practicing monopoly of influential merchants, limited in number and enjoying exclusive and far-reaching privileges. Although the Casa and the Seville *consulado* did not invariably operate in harmony, their common purpose so far as the American market was concerned was a closed economic rule. Economic theory decreed that limited quantities of goods at high prices yielded the most lucrative returns. Profit rather than the satisfaction of the market was the *consulado's* principal objective. The monopoly was favored, in turn, by merchant interests in the New World, and these came also to be organized into *consulados,* primarily in Mexico City and Lima.[17]

Efforts to control ocean transportation were legalized in the *flota* system, whereby ships were to sail between Spain and America in fleets or convoys at regular intervals. This also had precedents in the Spanish wool commerce with northern Europe. Special licenses were required of single vessels on solitary runs. The fleets were to carry arms for defense, and it came to be the practice that military vessels accompanied the commercial convoys for the return of precious metals and for the protection of the trade against foreign attack. An impressive security was thus achieved. The institutionalized procedure involved two annual fleets, each numbering fifty or more ships, one sailing for Veracruz on the Gulf coast of Mexico, and the other for Panama and Cartagena. The two fleets were to rendezvous at Havana and to return to Seville together the following year, bearing American products in huge naval concentrations. One effect was to focus American trade at a few key harbors where the flow of goods could be regulated. Veracruz, Portobello, and Cartagena were the American focal

[17] Robert Sidney Smith, *The Spanish Guild Merchant, A History of the Consulado, 1250–1700* (Durham, N.C., 1940); Robert Sidney Smith, "The Institution of the Consulado in New Spain," *Hispanic American Historical Review,* XXIV (1944), 61–83; Germán O. E. Tjarks, *El consulado de Buenos Aires, y sus proyecciones en la historia del Río de la Plata* (2 vols., Buenos Aires, 1962).

points, equivalent to Seville and Cadiz in Spain. Veracruz supplied Mexico and the larger part of Central America. Portobello goods were carried across the isthmus and shipped to Lima. Conversely, a number of New World harbors—especially those of southern South America and the Pacific coast—were seriously retarded in their development as a consequence of these restrictions. Buenos Aires on the Atlantic coast actually received its *flota* import via Portobello and Lima. The Seville interests were further able to stifle trans-Pacific trade between the American colonies and the Philippines, a trade that had at first appeared to offer promising opportunities. The Pacific coast settlements of Spanish America thus found themselves dependent, so far as legal trade was concerned, on transshipment from Panama or Acapulco in a coastwise navigation. But in general the colonies found themselves more closely drawn to Spain than to one another.

A major feature of the commercial monopoly was the position of Seville as a depot for the gold and silver returned from America to Spain. Gold at first was the more important metal, and a popular view still current today is that Spanish America furnished vast quantities of gold for Spain. But with the discovery of new mines in Mexico and Peru, silver far outdistanced gold. The century from 1550 to 1650 was the great period of silver, and the prodigious import, far in excess of anything previously known in Europe, made Seville for a time the most prosperous and flourishing city of the entire continent. Approximately two-fifths of the precious metals received in Spain constituted direct royal income, derived from the *quinto,* or 20 per cent tax on mine yields, and from other royal taxes. The remainder passed to private hands, principally in commodity exchanges.

As is well known, this influx of precious metals did not result in any permanent enrichment of the Spanish crown. The government was stimulated by its wealth to embark on new ventures, particularly foreign wars and the defense of Catholic positions in Europe, and in general its expenses increased more rapidly than its income. The colonial period was a time of rapidly rising prices—the index rose 100 per cent in the first half of the sixteenth century—and the government was characteristically unable to introduce economies or

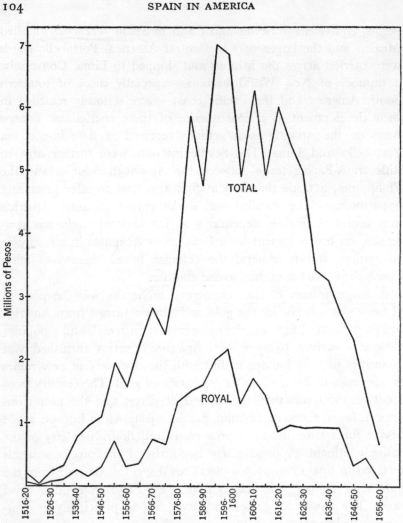

Spanish imports of gold and silver from Spanish America, yearly averages for five-year periods, 1516–1660. The royal share and the total both rose sharply to the 1590's and dropped sharply in the seventeenth century. After Hamilton, *American Treasure and the Price Revolution in Spain.*

otherwise cut costs. In critical years the monarchy summarily seized the incoming precious metals belonging to the merchants. Charles V borrowed heavily from foreign and domestic bankers, who saw the annual receipt of treasure as immediate security, and an ever larger share of royal income came to be obligated in advance and paid out on arrival. Interest rates rose, and additional funds had to be borrowed to pay the interest on existing debts. Charles V managed to maintain his government's fiscal position through deficit financing (his government was 20 million ducats in debt at the end of his reign), but his son Philip II could no longer do this, and through the seventeenth and eighteenth centuries Spanish America existed as the colonial possession of a bankrupt parent country.[18]

Precious metals, which were the major American products from the imperial point of view and the key commodities of mercantilist theory, thus only partially fulfilled their anticipated role. In many other respects also Spanish legislation failed to accomplish mercantilist objectives. The intrusion of foreigners became common after the late sixteenth century, and through the seventeenth century monopoly was maintained in name only. Royal legislation was powerless against foreign intrusions. At the same time Spanish production proved insufficient to satisfy colonial market needs. The fleets were regularly provided and financed by British, Dutch, and French merchants in defiance of imperial law, and foreign goods and foreign investment frequently exceeded the Spanish. The foreign merchants introduced their wares into Spain passing them as "Spanish" goods for export to America, or they established dummy offices in Seville to give their operations a guise of legality. The foreigners' motive of course was profit, and one result of Spain's failure to maintain the commercial monopoly was a further diversion of profit into foreign hands.[19]

New World economy came progressively to match and compete with the economy of the parent country. A key tenet of mercantilist imperialism was that the colony should provide the raw or finished

---

[18] Ramón Carande Thobar, *Carlos V y sus banqueros* (2 vols., Madrid, 1943–49); Earl J. Hamilton, *American Treasure and the Price Revolution in Spain, 1501–1650* (Cambridge, Mass., 1934); see also Earl J. Hamilton, "The Decline of Spain," *Economic History Review*, VIII (1938), 168–179.

[19] Haring, *Trade and Navigation;* Huguette and Pierre Chaunu, *Séville et l'Atlantique (1504–1650)* (8 vols., Paris, 1955–59); Clarence H. Haring, "Trade and Navigation between Spain and the Indies: A Re-View—1918–1958," *Hispanic American Historical Review*, XL (1960), 53–62; G. Connell-Smith, "English Merchants Trading to the New World in the Early Sixteenth Century," *Bulletin of the Institute of Historical Research*, XXIII (1950), 53–67; A. Domínguez Ortiz, "La concesión de 'naturalezas para comerciar en Indias' durante el siglo XVII," *Revista de Indias*, XIX (1959), 227–239.

goods needed at home and that it should serve as a market for goods exported. The Spanish colonies did serve this role through part of the sixteenth century, when basic provisions were still required, and when quantities of hides, dyes, and precious metals were returned to Spain. But by the end of the century, except for silver and a few other goods, colonial and Spanish productions were duplicating one another. Spanish industries were in decline. The formerly great wool trade, the silk trade, all manufacturing and agriculture were conspicuously suffering by 1550. Textiles, grain, and other staples, originally sent to the colonies from Seville, came to be produced by the colonies themselves in quantities sufficient to interfere seriously with the mercantilist relationship.

The colonies and the colonial trade could still of course be taxed, and the imperial government undertook to make up in taxes for what it lost, spent, or squandered in other ways. Royal revenues were collected wherever concentrations of goods or funds permitted a practicable impost. The customs duty (*almojarifazgo*) was levied upon goods exported from Spain and again upon the same goods as they were imported into the American colonies. *Almojarifazgo* history is a record of complex adjustments in collection procedure, all designed to increase royal income. Evaluations were based upon American market conditions, where prices were higher. Percentages were increased and bulk payments were required in efforts to reduce the costs of collection. In the seventeenth century the monarchy shifted irresolutely among a variety of customs procedures, including collection by volume, collection by weight, and collection by number of articles, and equivalent changes were made in the location of customs offices and in the inspection methods.[20]

The sales tax (*alcabala*) underwent similar modifications. Computed originally as a levy of 2 per cent upon goods sold in the colonies, it was subsequently increased and subjected to a variety of new conditions. Most goods (there were some particular exceptions) were liable to *alcabala* at each change in ownership, and the tasks of inspection and regulation became formidable. Merchants, ranchers, and other large-scale buyers and sellers were expected to render

[20] Clarence H. Haring, *The Spanish Empire in America* (New York, 1947), pp. 279 ff.

periodic accounts to the *alcabala* collectors, who were often members of the colonial *consulado* or other contractual agents to whom the collection privilege had been farmed out for a price. Intricate devices involving composite payments by towns or *consulados* were allowed for.⏋

To offset financial drains and to provide needed funds, the monarchy continually sought new ways of raising revenue, the result being a progressive complication of the tax structure. An increasing number of royal offices were sold, eventually including the all-important treasury offices themselves.[21] It was not unusual for officials to embezzle or extort or otherwise acquire treasury funds in order to pay for the offices that allowed them to do so. Other sources of royal income included the Indian tribute; the royal monopolies over quicksilver, gunpowder, salt, playing cards, and stamped paper; the *arrería*, a tax on imports and exports to pay the cost of the *flotas;* the *mesada* and *media anata*, exactions from salaries of royal officers; the ecclesiastical tithe, one-ninth of which was officially designated for the royal treasury; and the *cruzada*, or sale of indulgences. But no single item in this intricate repertory yielded more than a small fraction of what was needed, and the total never sufficed to render the colonies a financially profitable undertaking.[22]

Venality, graft, peculation, and personal use of public funds attended the operation of government at all levels. Tax funds were regularly dipped into by the individuals authorized to make collections. The distinction between fees and bribes became blurred, and financial charges accompanied the performance of all official services. In America officeholders used their positions opportunistically, allowing themselves greater freedom in contraband, speculation, cornering of markets, and covert embezzlement. The funds that

[21] John H. Parry, *The Sale of Public Office in the Spanish Indies under the Hapsburgs* (Berkeley, 1953).

[22] A basic article in English is Clarence H. Haring, "The Early Spanish Colonial Exchequer," *American Historical Review*, XXIII (1917–18), 779–796. C. B. Kroeber, "The Mobilization of Philip II's Revenue in Peru, 1590–1596," *Economic History Review*, X (1958), 439–449, is a documented case study of a critical period. For late colonial times and a general survey of royal income, see Francisco Gallardo y Fernández, *Origen, progresos y estado de las rentas de la corona de España, su gobierno y administración* (8 vols., Madrid, 1805–8).

reached the monarchy were always residual funds, or what remained after a series of governmental officials had taken what they dared. The crown's extravagant use of public money was imitated at all subordinate levels of the hierarchy. It was for these reasons that the monarchy took pains to inspect and regulate the flow of goods at key points, as in the computation and handling of the *quinto*. But at no point could such methods successfully eliminate illegalities.

The situation was not one in which a normal and expectable integrity in officeholding was occasionally violated by a dishonest administrator. The situation was rather one of normal and expectable corruption, within which an occasional figure stood out for resisting temptation. Corruption is of course impossible to measure even when full documentary evidence is at hand, for it depends upon a comparison with a condition regarded as healthy or uncorrupt. In the Spanish colonies there is evidence that certain practices gained acceptance through repetition or gradual extension, as from the prerogatives of patronage through taxation of salaries to outright sale of offices. Within the techniques of office sale, then, the process continued to expand, and office sale extended itself over an ever-widening list of posts. Popular acceptance was further induced by royal action, for the crown was as eager to profit as any bureaucrat, and the crown's position of power facilitated royal exploitation of accepted venality. In confronting the widespread colonial office sales, Philip II sought not to abolish them on ethical grounds but rather to monopolize and profit from them. In general, royal or popular sanction resulted in uncritical acceptance of abuse of office.

The highest posts, and thus the foremost opportunities, in imperial government went to peninsular Spaniards of the aristocratic class. The lower offices of the hierarchy tended to be confined to white colonials.[23] Spanish America is a classic case of authoritarian government administered by a distant mother country. Viceroys, captains general, governors, and presidents were Spaniards who came to the colony for short terms in office and then returned. The brief

---

[23] The term creole (*criollo*) in Spanish American colonial history commonly refers to a person of white ancestry born in the colonies. The implication of a halfbreed or other ethnic mixture is absent.

tenures reflect the demands for royal patronage as well as the common assumption that American officeholding provided occasions for rapid self-enrichment. ⌉

The tradition of rule by peninsulars was justified, from the Spanish point of view, by the argument that peninsulars were better administrators than were colonials. ⌈Colonial government appeared as an extension of Spanish government, and in the absence of any civil service the officeholding class of Spain was regarded as the proper class from which to draw its personnel. Spanish officials were known and trusted; their services to the monarchy deserved reward; colonial positions provided additional opportunities for bestowing such rewards. The monarchy preserved a system of patronage in office assignment. A noteworthy feature of the native American's hostility to peninsulars is that so little attention was paid to it in Spain, where the justice, propriety, and efficacy of peninsular officeholding were everywhere assumed. Only very rarely did responsible Spaniards advance the argument that high colonial positions should be opened to colonials. ⌉

Between the individual and the law in Spanish America there was always a certain irrelevance. Imperial law was issued as a continuous flow of enactments by king and Council and their American subordinates. Occasionally, as in the New Laws, efforts were made to present an innovating legal corpus dealing systematically with a given subject. But most laws appeared as isolated statements only casually related to their context. In its attention to minute detail Spanish imperial law was the direct heir of medieval and fifteenth-century law. Enactments were often lengthy and of much superficial orderliness, but their content might be a series of petty restrictions irrationally arranged. The heterogeneity of law and the extremely detailed, or trifling, quality of individual enactments are especially celebrated in the period of Philip II. But they characterize the whole of Spanish American legislation, and they are clearly manifest in the most successful and comprehensive of the efforts at codification, the four-volume *Recopilación de leyes de las Indias* of 1681.[24]

---

[24] *Recopilación de leyes de los reynos de las Indias* (4 vols., Madrid, 1681); Juan Manzano Manzano, *Historia de las Recopilaciones de Indias* (2 vols., Madrid, 1950–56), of which the first volume deals with preliminary sixteenth-

An interesting feature of Spanish imperial law is that it was so often disobeyed. In a political and economic imperialism so conceived, a natural tendency of both colonists and administrative officials was to escape the controls and to engage in freer forms of action through illegal means. The violations resulted not in the enforcement of existing rules but in the enactment of new ones, and the new ones were in their turn disobeyed. Reiterated prohibitions of the same offense are commonly to be taken as direct evidence of disobedience, and this disobedience is often explicitly commented upon in the laws themselves. One of the more intriguing paradoxes of Spanish American history involves the straight-faced repetition of legal rules in conjunction with the persistent, and expected, violation of them.[25] Quite apart from disobedience, reiteration came to be wholly characteristic of imperial legislation, which found security in legal custom already established and evinced a powerful reluctance to introduce change. Legal repetition was most pronounced between the late sixteenth century and the middle eighteenth century, a long period characterized by proliferation of paper and paralysis of action. Lawmakers were uniformly conservative in this period, and the entire mood of Spanish imperialism was one of caution.

Bureaucracy bred law, and law bred bureaucracy. In Spain and Spanish America the lawyer class was a formidable one in size and

---

century efforts to achieve a compilation, and the second with the seventeenth century. The *Recopilación* edition of 1791 has been reprinted in a modern facsimile (Madrid, 1943).

[25] See the perceptive comments of John Phelan, "Authority and Flexibility in the Spanish Imperial Bureaucracy," *Administrative Science Quarterly*, V (1960), 63–64: "Historians have assumed that the Spanish bureaucracy like other bureaucratic organizations had only one goal or a set of commensurate goals and that standards of conduct for members were not mutually conflicting. If this assumption is cast aside in favor of goal ambiguity and conflicting standards, new light is thrown on the chasm between the law and its observance in the Spanish empire. The wide gap between the two was not a flaw, as has been traditionally assumed. On the contrary, the distance between observance and nonobservance was a necessary component of the system. Given the ambiguity of the goals and the conflict among the standards, all the laws could not be enforced simultaneously. The very conflict among the standards, which prevented a subordinate from meeting all the standards at once, gave subordinates a voice in decision making without jeopardizing the control of their superiors over the whole system."

power. The huge General Archive of the Indies in Seville and the great colonial archives of Spanish America bear witness to the immense quantity of legal documentation that was produced. The student soon discovers that page after page of the documentation is sheer legality, and he learns to recognize the formalities and quickly to pass to what is essential in each legal case. But the formalities are revealing too, for they reflect a living world of legalism every word of which had to be written by hand and copied and recopied for the series of authorities to whom the papers were directed. The very quality of paper and ink is significant in these *legajos,* for the paper is often still a pristine white after three or four centuries, and the ink black and clear. In general colonial papers are better preserved and colonial inks less faded than those of the nineteenth and early twentieth centuries. It was a time when paper and ink were important. All legal forms were taken seriously by this society, and they were recorded in a medium designed to endure.[26]

[26] On lawyers see Javier Malagón-Barceló, "The Role of the *Letrado* in the Colonization of America," *The Americas,* XVIII (1961–62), 1–17.

CHAPTER 6

The Established Colony

SPAIN did not settle the whole of America, or even the whole of Spanish America. Beginning about 1520, Spaniards chose to move much more rapidly than before, and they abandoned or by-passed the locations of lesser interest. Later some of these locations were occupied by other nations, and though Spain retained a theoretical claim she now lacked the resources to make the claim effective. Moreover, Spaniards continued to regard a large part of the claimed area as not worth settling. Few attempts were made to occupy North America beyond the real, as opposed to the claimed, limits of New Spain. In South America, Spanish colonists allowed the Portuguese to triple their original territory at Spanish expense. Spaniards concentrated on the areas where a dense Indian population could do the work, and if the Indian population no longer sufficed, they brought Negroes from Africa to do it. Thus the characteristic Spanish colony was one in which Spaniards dominated Indians or Negroes.

Caucasoids, Mongoloids, and Negroids, the three basic ethnic types, had their first historical confrontation and intermingling in Spanish America. For uncounted millennia the three races had lived in isolation. Their mixture in the sixteenth century occurred in a region that was not "native" to any, but to which the three were drawn, or driven, by circumstances of quite divergent character. The point of significance is not really that Spanish America was the first, for other parts of America soon followed, and the priority

was merely chronological. What is of interest is the special socio-
ethnic accommodation that took place in the Spanish-American environment.

The whites of Spanish America were something less than a full
cross section of the population of the parent country. Members of
the higher Spanish nobility, whose commitment and success at home
tended to inhibit any desire to take up new lives elsewhere, came, if
they came at all, mainly for short terms and to fill administrative
positions, and their experience rather solidified their attachment to
Spain than reconciled them to colonial ways. But second, third, and
fourth sons of the Spanish nobility had only limited opportunity at
home, and to this group America offered a variety of attractions.
Merchants, farmers, and craftsmen who could not claim nobility high
or low occupied a superior position in colonial society, an improvement in status that they obviously found attractive.[1] More whites
came as servants than one might expect, and fewer came as soldiers.
Nothing in Spanish society induced the migration of groups bound
together by special ideological or national loyalties, such as occurred
with the Puritans of Massachusetts Bay or the Germans ("Dutch")
of Pennsylvania. Non-Spaniards and non-Catholics, formally excluded, were frequently able to evade the exclusion, but they migrated as individuals and prudently passed themselves as Spaniards
and Catholics. An extraordinary instance of non-Spanish immigrant
success was Ambrosio O'Higgins, the father of the revolutionary
hero, who was born in County Sligo in northwest Ireland about
1720, and whose career was climaxed by his appointment as viceroy
of Peru in 1796. Finally, for Spaniards the selective processes of
migration operated with impressive consistency in favor of males
over females. Probably 90 per cent of the migrants were men.[2]

[1] See the quotations gathered by Richard Konetzke to the effect that the
poorest and most humble whites regarded themselves as of the colonial nobility.
Richard Konetzke, "La formación de la nobleza en Indias," *Estudios americanos*, III (1951), 356. José Durand, *La transformación social del conquistador*
(2 vols., Mexico, 1953), enlarges upon this subject, pointing out, on the other
hand, the tendency of American *"hidalgos"* to engage in commerce and to
enter into practical economic undertakings.

[2] Rubio y Moreno has published a large number of *informaciones* of emigrants from Spain to America, with some unsystematic data on birthplace,
status, family, and other matters. Luis Rubio y Moreno (ed.), *Pasajeros a*

The Indians of the colony, from a strictly ethnological point of view, were an extremely heterogeneous people, but the differences among them meant little to Spaniards or to the over-all Spanish policy of imperialism. In marginal areas Indians were able to resist Spaniards for long periods. But within the colony native peoples were uniformly subject to Spanish controls. After the fragmentation of the original native empires, local communities continued to hold the Indians' loyalty, and it was with these communities that Spaniards dealt in encomienda and in the other Spanish-Indian institutions to be described in a subsequent chapter. In reaction to the Black Legend there has appeared a tendency to take too literally the humanitarian laws governing Spanish-Indian relations, few of which were observed in practice. Among Spaniards, Indians had a reputation for sullenness, laziness, and meekness, qualities that Spaniards did not admire. With very rare exceptions white society looked down on Indian society. Indian subordination was represented legally in tribute (*tributo*), the American equivalent of the *pecho* paid by white commoners in Spain. Significantly, whites in Spanish America were not *pecheros*.

Negroes were introduced into Spanish America as slaves. In Spanish peninsular society, Negro enslavement developed especially in the fifteenth century as an outgrowth of Spanish-African connections, and it was assumed and unquestioned when carried to the New World in the sixteenth.[3] Slave trading by Spaniards or by others for Spaniards continued through the colonial period. It was encouraged by royal law, which sought to substitute

---

Indias. Catálogo metodológico de las informaciones y licencias de los que allí pasaron, existentes en el Archivo general de Indias. Siglo primero de la colonización de América. 1492–1592 (2 vols., Madrid, 1930). The document provides one of our few sources on the types of Spaniard who migrated. V. Aubrey Neasham, "Spain's Emigrants to the New World, 1492–1592," *Hispanic American Historical Review,* XIX (1939), 147–160, discusses the locations of origin within Spain, concluding, partly on the basis of the *Pasajeros a Indias,* that about half came from the south. The conclusion is qualified on pp. 154–160.

[3] Domínguez Ortiz shows how slavery received a new impetus, in Spain and elsewhere in Europe in the fifteenth century, as a consequence of emergent capitalism, labor need, and African exploitation. Antonio Domínguez Ortiz, "La esclavitud en Castilla durante la edad moderna," in Carmelo Viñas y Mey (ed.), *Estudios de historia social de España* (2 vols., Madrid, 1949–52), II, 369 ff.

Negro slavery for exploited Indian labor in particular industries. Negro slavery was consistent with the royal policy of humanitarianism toward Indians, and it reflected as well a royal financial interest, for the holders of slave-trade permits (*asientos*) returned a share of their incomes to the crown.[4] The conditions of enslavement, transport, sale, and distribution were such as to induce a process of "deculturation" among Negroes. On a characteristic plantation many types and mutually unintelligible African languages might be represented. Because slaves lived in isolated domestic or economic units, the circumstances of their lives depended largely upon their individual owners. In some cases close familiar relations were established between master and slave, and Negroes adopted many traits of white society. At the other extreme a Negro's only awareness of an external society might be the armed overseer who compelled him to work. Under some conditions, though, Negroes might escape from slavery through illegal desertion or through legal purchase of complete or partial freedom. Slave rebellions also occasionally broke the peace of Spanish colonial life. Between masters and slaves the modern literature on Spanish America often postulates a uniform and legalized leniency, but this depends on traditional assumptions in Hispanic law and remains to be tested in the real conditions of the colony. In the complex interrelationships among peoples, it sometimes happened that Indians became owners of Negro slaves.[5]

Combinations of the three original races began to appear in the

[4] It remains somewhat unclear why the crown expressed more humanitarianism toward Indians than toward Negroes. Part of the answer doubtless lies in the earlier Spanish tradition of Negro enslavement, which had become customary. Then too Indians appeared to Spaniards suddenly as a new form of being, a new social entity, and a new ethical problem, whereas Negroes occurred as individuals or in small groups, uprooted from their original environment and distributed in a new. Charles Verlinden, *L'esclavage dans l'Europe médiévale*, Vol. I, *Péninsule Ibérique-France* (Brugge, 1955).

[5] The classic work is José Antonio Saco, *Historia de la esclavitud de la raza africana en el nuevo mundo y en especial en los países Américo-hispanos* (2 vols., Barcelona and Havana, 1879–83). For a brief account and general statistical study in English, see Wilbur Zelinsky, "The Historical Geography of the Negro Population of Latin America," *Journal of Negro History*, XXXIV (1939), 153–221. On Indian slaveholding, see Emilio Harth-Terré, *Informe sobre el descubrimiento de documentos que revelan la trata y comercio de esclavos negros por los indios del común durante el gobierno virreinal en el Perú* (Lima, 1961).

first colonial generation, mixed peoples being known by such names as mestizo, *mulato,* and *casta.* Mestizo referred to a combination of white or part-white with Indian and by extension to any person of mixed ancestry. *Mulato* (mulatto) was most often used for a combination of Negro and white. *Casta* signified an individual of low estate, particularly if he were nonwhite. Other names, including *zambo* and *coyote,* were given to mixtures of Indian and Negro. Attributes or supposed attributes of the hybrid classes are suggested by additional connotations of these terms: bastard, social inferior, slum dweller, member of an indolent and shiftless group. In a nominally monogamous society, with wide liberties countenanced for males and with few white women, a large but undetermined number of mestizos were in fact of illegitimate birth. (In lesser degree the same could be said for other classes.)[6] With respect to the mixed peoples as a whole, modern interpreters tend to postulate a sociopsychic role of some complexity, partly because ethnic mixture is identified with progress and nationalistic values in modern Spanish America, partly because the "discovery" of the mestizo has occurred only in post-Freudian times. Hybridization may be understood as a resolution of ethnic differences, resolution begun but not completed in the colonial period. From this point of view the colonial mestizo appears as an outcast, errant, without real roots in either culture. As a pragmatic opportunist who gained strength and numbers through time, the mestizo offers a richer opportunity for psychological interpretation than the phlegmatic, subordinated Indian.[7]

In terms of population numbers, the various elements of Spanish colonial society were in constant process of change. The Indian

[6] Konetzke has assembled examples of administrative efforts to control the illegitimate birth of mestizos. Richard Konetzke, "Sobre el problema racial en la América española," *Revista de estudios políticos,* Nos. 113–114 (1960), pp. 180 ff.

[7] "It has been reported to me," Philip II announced in a law of 1568, "that there are already large numbers of mestizos and mulattoes in those provinces, and that they increase every day and are inclined to evil . . . and because they are the sons of Indian women, as soon as they commit a crime they dress up as Indians and hide out with their mothers' relatives, and they can't be found." Richard Konetzke (ed.), *Colección de documentos para la historia de la formación social de Hispanoamérica, 1493–1810* (3 vols., Madrid, 1953–62), I, 436–437.

population, which at the beginning stood at perhaps 50 million, fell to about 4 million in the seventeenth century, rising again to about 7.5 million by the end of the colonial period.[8] Whites, who numbered only about 100,000 in the middle sixteenth century, increased to over 3 million by late colonial times.[9] These gross figures on Indians and whites are in themselves telling explanations for what happened to encomienda and the missionary program. Figures on Negroes, mulattoes, and mestizos are notoriously unreliable, both because there were no accurate censuses and because the categories themselves were vague. But there is no doubt that all increased. It is possible that the late colonial gain in "Indian" population represented instead a mestizo increase and infiltration. Between the terms Negro and mulatto, colonial usage was imprecise, and the miscellaneous *casta* category, while undoubtedly appropriate and useful in the colonial context, is not informative for a precise ethnic analysis. Even the term Indian was often used in a cultural rather than a biological sense, as indeed it still is.

Population figures are probably most reliable for the late period, when census procedures, if not more advanced, were more broadly applied. Spanish America as a whole had some 17 million people at the end of the colonial period. Of these about 7.5 million were Indian and about 3.2 million white. Negroes, whose numbers and role in the society have frequently been exaggerated, amounted to perhaps .75 million. And the remaining 5.5 million were mixtures in various degrees. The 17-million figure for the late colonial years compares with about 25 million for France, 11 million for Spain, 8

[8] In recent years our estimate for the aboriginal population of central Mexico prior to white contact has risen from a magnitude between 4 and 7 million to between 19 and 28 million. Sherburne F. Cook and Lesley Byrd Simpson, *The Population of Central Mexico in the Sixteenth Century* (Berkeley and Los Angeles, 1948); Woodrow Borah and Sherburne F. Cook, *The Aboriginal Population of Central Mexico on the Eve of the Spanish Conquest* (Berkeley and Los Angeles, 1963). Angel Rosenblat, *La población indígena de América, desde 1492 hasta la actualidad* (Buenos Aires, 1945), supposes about 13 million for America as a whole at the time of the discovery. But if the increased values arrived at by Cook, Borah, and Simpson for Mexico apply proportionately to America as a whole, the aboriginal population at the time of the discovery may have been four or more times that. It is a measure of the flexible state of American studies that so crucial an item as the aboriginal population of 1492 can be subject to so radical a degree of revision.

[9] Rosenblat, *Población indígena*, p. 36.

million for England, 4 or 5 million for Ireland, 3 million for Brazil, and 2 million for Portugal.[10]]

Mexico, the most populous single territory, had some 7 million people at the end of the colonial period, including, rather surprisingly, nearly half the Indian population and over one-third of the whites of all Spanish America. New Granada, La Plata, Central America with the islands, and the Peruvian-Chilean area each had on the order of 2 to 2.5 million. Mixed classes occupied an intermediate numerical position between whites and Indians in most major mainland regions, the exception being New Granada, where the mixed classes came close to equaling whites and Indians combined. Negroes comprised half or more of the population of the islands and about 2.5 per cent of the mainland population. No Indians and half the Negroes were to be found in Cuba and Puerto Rico.[11]

In the great expanses of rural Spanish America the three races achieved some standardized relationships, always with the white minority in control. Throughout the highland interior, the classic institution was the hacienda, or landed estate, which developed from the late sixteenth century as encomienda declined.[12] Here a primary distinction should be made between the kinds of operation that were essentially agricultural and those that depended on grazing. The agricultural hacienda, appropriate to regions where a sufficient laboring population could support it, was commonly to be found in areas of dense Indian settlement. The hacienda centered upon the "great house" of its white *hacendado* and its lands were

[10] For the Spanish American totals I have relied especially on Alexander de Humboldt and Aimé Bonpland, *Personal Narrative of Travels to the Equinoctial Regions of the New Continent, during the Years 1799–1804*, Helen Maria Williams, trans. (7 vols. in 8, London, 1814–29), VI, Part 2, 835–836. Rosenblat accepts Humboldt's figures in general and modifies them somewhat in particular; see *Población indígena*, pp. 35 ff.

[11] These general remarks also are made on the basis of the figures of Humboldt and Bonpland. Cf. Rosenblat, *Población indígena*, p. 36.

[12] Historians once took the position that hacienda developed directly from the declining encomienda. The two histories are now regarded as distinct. For encomienda see Silvio Zavala, *La encomienda indiana* (Madrid, 1935), and *De encomiendas y propiedad territorial en algunas regiones de la América española* (Mexico, 1940). For hacienda see François Chevalier, *La Formation des grands domaines au Mexique: Terre et société aux XVIᵉ–XVIIᵉ siècles* (Paris, 1952).

characteristically former Indian lands that had been usurped. It abutted, or even enclosed, the native towns that provided its working force. Its crops were the traditional grains of Europe, and it is worth noting that though Indians rarely adopted these for their own use, they continued to furnish the labor that enabled Spaniards to use them. Spanish colonists in turn rarely introduced maize into their own diet. But in particular zones the production of maize by hacienda methods came to be a major operation. So great was the Indian consumers' market for maize in Mexico City in the seventeenth and eighteenth centuries, for example, that hundreds of Spanish-owned haciendas of the vicinity were required to supply it.

With respect to grazing, it will be remembered that the raising of livestock was a prestigious industry in Spain, where it had its own privileged guild (called *mesta*) and where flocks and herds were regarded as property of an especially dignified type.[13] In the colony, cattle production was encouraged by the opportunities for the export of cowhides, used in Iberian and other European leather manufacture, and meat and tallow for local markets were subsidiary products. But cattle were often slaughtered in America for their hides alone, the carcasses being abandoned as of insufficient value for sale. The traditional, often romanticized, independence of *gauchos, llaneros, vaqueros,* and other regional cowboy types quickly became a part of colonial folk culture. Cattle raising was appropriate to extensive grassland or range country of sparse Indian population, for it required only a modest supply of labor in comparison with agriculture. It is especially interesting to observe in sixteenth- and seventeenth-century New Spain how the cattle ranches gradually found their proper environment, as the principal grazing region moved from the populous Indian south and center to the drier and more sparsely settled north.[14]

The West Indies of course illustrate, more than any other part of Spanish America, the disappearance of the original native popula-

---

[13] Charles Julian Bishko, "The Peninsular Background of Latin American Cattle Ranching," *Hispanic American Historical Review,* XXXII (1952), 491–515.

[14] Chevalier, *Formation des grands domaines,* pp. 195 ff.; William H. Dusenberry, *The Mexican Mesta: The Administration of Ranching in Colonial Mexico* (Urbana, Ill., 1963), pp. 24 ff.

tion, the importation of Negro slaves, and the emergence of a plantation culture. Negroes were used as laborers at first for mines and subsequently for sugar plantations. Sugar was a new colonial product, previously unknown in America. Spaniards brought it from the Canary Islands, and its early success was due in part to the utilization of Canary Islanders as planters and processors.[15] Unlike wheat and other crops with which Spaniards were more familiar, sugar could not be produced in the leisurely rhythms of conventional European agriculture. Milling had to take place within one or two days after cutting, and a substantial investment in land, refining machinery, furnaces, and other equipment was required.[16] The European demand for sugar steadily expanded in the sixteenth and seventeenth centuries, and, given the insufficiency of the Indian population, the inevitable result was plantation agriculture with white ownership and Negro labor. Plantations developed in the West Indies and on the low-lying coasts of the tropical and subtropical mainland, and these were, or became, regions of extremely limited native population.

The mines of Spanish America occupied an intermediate position between rural and urban industries, and from certain points of view, including the monarch's, they appeared as the colony's most important economic enterprises.[17] Desire for wealth brought into being

[15] Francisco Morales Padrón, "Colonos canarios en Indias," *Anuario de estudios americanos,* VIII (1951), 399–441.

[16] This should not be taken to indicate that only those who were originally wealthy could become producers of sugar. The necessary capital could be acquired in the process of a colonial career. Thomas Gage, an Englishman who traveled in Guatemala in the seventeenth century, reported on the following case: "There is a rich *ingenio* or farm of sugar belonging to one Sebastian de Savaletta, a Biscayan born, who came at first very poor into that country, and served one of his countrymen; but with his good industry and pains he began to get a mule or two to traffic with about the country, till at last he increased his stock to a whole requa of mules, and from thence grew so rich that he bought much land about Petapa, which he found to be very fit for sugar, and from thence was encouraged to build a princely house. . . . This man maketh a great deal of sugar for the country, and sends every year much to Spain; he keepeth at least threescore slaves." Thomas Gage, *The English-American: A New Survey of the West Indies, 1648,* A. P. Newton, ed. (London, 1928), p. 217.

[17] Our remarks on this subject depend primarily upon Modesto Bargalló, *La minería y la metalurgia en la América española durante la época colonial; con un apéndice sobre la industria del hierro en México desde la iniciación de la independencia hasta el presente* (Mexico, 1955).

the mixed society characteristic of mining communities wherever precious metal deposits were discovered and could be worked. Though the products of mines were crown property, private individuals, usually whites, were given the privilege of discovering lodes, for which the exploitation rights were then granted by royal concession, sale, or rent. The yields, minus the royal *quinto* and other taxes, went to the mine operators in recognition of the expenses and risks involved. Thus the crown granted liberal terms in order to ensure a rapid and full extraction of metals, and opportunities for personal profit were large. As with all major industries, some individuals became very wealthy while others barely made a profit or failed entirely.

Mining, or the prospect of mining, governed much of the internal migration of white society in the early period. For a time in the sixteenth century the South American coast and interior highland were thought to be rich gold-producing regions, and prospectors were attracted in large numbers. Other areas in varying degrees became focal points for white penetration as a consequence of their real or supposed deposits of minerals. Mining received its chief stimulus in the mid-sixteenth century, with the discovery of the rich silver veins of Potosí in the viceroyalty of Peru and of Zacatecas, Guanajuato, and the other Potosí in Mexico.

The ultimate size and composition of any mining community were functions of accessibility, availability of labor, and the state of technological knowledge. In the early period Spaniards followed an essentially Indian procedure of surface gathering, with no great yields. About the time of the main sixteenth-century discoveries, a mercury amalgamation process for separating silver from ore was introduced, with the result that mercury became nearly as critical a material as silver in the mining areas. Significantly, the crown maintained a monopoly over mercury sales.[18] In the late sixteenth and seventeenth centuries the rapid development of mines at Potosí in Mexico and

[18] Peruvian silver was commonly processed with mercury from the Huancavelica mine in Peru. Mercury for Mexican silver ordinarily came from Almadén in Spain. But Huancavelica mercury was sometimes sent to Mexico also. Arthur P. Whitaker, *The Huancavelica Mercury Mine: A Contribution to the History of the Bourbon Renaissance in the Spanish Empire* (Cambridge, Mass., 1941), p. 5.

Peru depended on the existence of elevated "mountains of silver" accessible through lateral or diagonal tunneling. Mines that required deep approaches from low entrances were subject to flooding and the deposits frequently became unworkable by ordinary colonial methods. Technologically, a full exploitation in modern terms was impossible. Despite some large incomes the mining class as a whole lacked sufficient capital for new equipment and sufficient initiative for experimentation with new methods. It is only in modern times that abandoned colonial mines have been profitably reworked.

Potosí in Mexico could be operated at first by the Indians of its vicinity, assembled under compulsion as a concentrated labor force. Subsequently this local labor proved inadequate, and a supplementary Negro work force, both slave and free, was introduced. A voluntary mixed laboring group also came into existence, through the provision that all metallic increment over a designated quota accrued to the individual laborer. Virtually all excavation work was manual. Even a rudimentary mechanization with carts and lifting devices was exceptional. Workers moved ore up the steep portions of the mine shafts, carrying it in baskets and ascending ladders. At Potosí in Peru, a site that under other circumstances would have been regarded as uninhabitable, these same conditions applied, but workers were forced to congregate from more distant areas, and the entire enterprise functioned on a bigger scale.[19] With increased size came the additional complications of supply, services, and class and personal relations, all within the intense atmosphere of avarice generated by the deposits of silver.[20] The rapidly created mining communities housed a spendthrift, unsettled, or lawless class of colonists, a substantial number of whom were always prepared to move to other, and presumably more rewarding, strikes.

It is in the more stable cities of Spanish America that one may

[19] Lewis Hanke, *The Imperial City of Potosí: An Unwritten Chapter in the History of Spanish America* (The Hague, 1956), pp. 24 ff.

[20] "The site [of Potosí in Peru] is arid, cold, very unpleasant, and quite sterile. It yields no fruit or grain or grass, and is naturally uninhabitable. . . . But the power of the silver, which calls forth other things than greed, has populated that hill with the largest population of all those kingdoms and has produced such quantities of foods and supplies that everything one wants can be found there in abundance." Joseph de Acosta, *Historia natural y moral de las Indias,* Edmundo O'Gorman, ed. (Mexico, 1940), p. 233.

examine most successfully the standard varieties of relationship among social classes. In the cities the three basic ethnic types lived in unusually intimate proximity, and the cities were the main breeding grounds for the hybrid populations. Urban traditions had been highly developed among the more advanced Indian peoples, but Spaniards built further upon Indian foundations, as in Tenochtitlan, or founded new cities, such as Lima. Spaniards were city-minded people. Municipalities were sometimes created as the first political act of conquistadores, the assumption being that colonial life could not begin until formalized through municipal authority.[21]

Coastal cities had a special character, for they were dedicated to oceanic commerce and, increasingly, to military defense. The point is illustrated in the history of Santo Domingo, which appeared at first as one of the most Spanish of Spanish-American communities in design, architecture, population, and mode of life. Later, as connections with the colonial mainland were established, and as the Caribbean became an area of international rivalry and piratical attack, Santo Domingo became a fortified trade station and lost much of its original character. Havana, which superseded Santo Domingo and became the largest trading center of the Caribbean, emerged as one of the most fortified of colonial cities. Its population of Spaniards, Negroes, and mulattoes was commercially oriented, for *flotas* from New Spain and Panama convened there before setting out for Cadiz via the Bahama Channel and the Terceras or Bermuda. Havana's harbor was one of the best in the world. "Ships of no matter what size are practically moored to the houses of the city," a visitor stated in the seventeenth century.[22]

Other coastal cities were St. Augustine in Florida, Veracruz on the east Mexican coast, Portobello in Panama, and Cartagena on

---

[21] Richard M. Morse, "Some Characteristics of Latin American Urban History," *American Historical Review,* LXVII (1961–62), 321–322; Víctor Frankl, "Hernán Cortés y la tradición de las Siete Partidas," *Revista de historia de América,* Nos. 53–54 (1962), pp. 9–74.

[22] Erwin Walter Palm, *Los monumentos arquitectónicos de la Española, con una introducción a América* (2 vols., Ciudad Trujillo, 1955), I, 45 ff.; George Kubler and Martin Soria, *Art and Architecture in Spain and Portugal and Their American Dominions, 1500 to 1800* (Baltimore, 1959), pp. 62 ff.; Antonio Vázquez de Espinosa, *Compendium and Description of the West Indies* (Washington, 1942), p. 103.

the South American coast. Like Havana these were military outposts and concentration points for goods in the seventeenth and
eighteenth centuries. Their dominant external features were outsized
fortifications, soldiers' quarters, supply houses, and commercial
buildings. Ultimately, strategic demands kept them from becoming
centers of Hispanic culture save in the most materialistic sense. St.
Augustine, whose modern residents point proudly to a rich Hispanic
heritage, was a small garrison town of a few hundred military families in the seventeenth century.[23] Coastal cities underwent rapid,
brief metamorphoses in the designated period of trade. Veracruz,
the main import and export site for the mainland of New Spain,
housed only a small number of Spanish families in normal periods,
but the population vastly increased when the fleets arrived and an
influx of transients from the ships and from the Mexican highlands
met to handle the goods. Portobello, protected by two fortresses and
normally smaller than Veracruz, became a huge, sprawling campsite
at the time of its fair.[24] Only Cartagena, of all the coastal cities of
the Caribbean and the Gulf, was regularly of a size to rival Havana.
Its urban zone was completely circumscribed by fortified walls and
protected by bulwarks, towers, trenches, and artillery.[25] All the
coastal cities were exposed to foreign attack, and the history of each
includes one or more major assaults by English, French, or Dutch.

Of rather different character were the inland cities, of which
Tenochtitlan-Mexico was the foremost example. Interior populations were larger, and Indian survivals gave the cities a distinctive

[23] John R. Dunkle, "Population Change as an Element in the Historical
Geography of St. Augustine," *Florida Historical Quarterly,* XXXVII (1958–
59), 4–6.

[24] "He who has seen this place (Portobello) during the tiempo muerto, or
dead time, solitary, poor, and a perpetual silence reigning every where; the
harbour quite empty, and every place wearing a melancholy aspect, must be
filled with astonishment at the sudden change, to see the bustling multitudes,
every house crowded, the square and streets encumbered with bales and chests
of gold and silver of all kinds; the harbour full of ships and vessels; some bringing by way of Rio de Chape the goods of Peru, as cacao, quinquina or jesuits
bark, Vicuna wool, and bezoar stones; others coming from Carthagena, loaded
with provisions: and thus a spot, at all other times detested for its deleterious
qualities, becomes the staple of the riches of the old and new world, and the
scene of one of the most considerable branches of commerce in the whole
earth." Jorge Juan and Antonio de Ulloa, *A Voyage to South America,* John
Adams, trans.; Irving A. Leonard, ed. (New York, 1964), p. 56.

[25] Vázquez de Espinosa, *Compendium,* pp. 108–109, 129, 304, 309.

appearance. Even Puebla, which Spanish colonists founded as a city for white settlers, and which grew to be larger than Havana and Cartagena combined, acquired something of an indigenous character. Spanish and native urbanism converged in Mexico and Peru, and the developing population was mestizo to a greater extent than on the coasts. Of the two foremost colonial cities of the Andean area, Lima became a political and commercial capital, with a large mestizo and Indian population. Its rapid growth was the consequence both of its position as a viceregal capital and of its role as a distributor of *flota* goods, for it had the finest Pacific port of any city and it supplied, partly via the great Inca roads of the pre-Spanish period, *flota* goods to Chile and Ecuador and Argentina and Upper Peru. The second Peruvian city, Potosí, the mining community par excellence, is said (though the evidence is unclear) to have been for a time the largest city of all Spanish America.[26]

In the characteristic Spanish American city a central plaza was surrounded by *cabildo* offices, the residence of the *corregidor* or *alcalde mayor,* the church, and the principal commercial establishment, all dominated by the white aristocracy.[27] Particular streets and subdivisions, as in the cities of Spain, were dedicated to individual trades and served both as the residences and the places of business of designated artisans. Thus a city might have its street of bakers, its street of carpenters, its street of leatherworkers, and so on. In propertyholding, social classes distributed themselves outward from the plaza, the persons of highest standing and greatest wealth occupying positions closest to the center. Hence the largest houses, the "palaces," the cathedral, and the public buildings were clustered in the vicinity of the plaza, whereas buildings at the outskirts were smaller and less impressive. Even in a former Indian metropolis such

[26] A population of 160,000 is indicated in 1650, but this may be an exaggeration. Hanke, *Imperial City of Potosí,* pp. 1, 19. Mexico City was probably larger than this at the time of the conquest, but its population in 1650 was substantially less. See Charles Gibson, *The Aztecs under Spanish Rule: A History of the Indians of the Valley of Mexico, 1519–1810* (Stanford, 1964), pp. 377–380.

[27] Robert Ricard makes some relevant observations on the historic Spanish plaza and on differences between American and peninsular concepts of the plaza. Robert Ricard, "La plaza mayor en España y en América española (Notas para un estudio)," *Estudios geográficos,* XI (1950), 301–327.

as Mexico City or Cuzco, white colonists inhabited a new, Hispanicized nucleus outside which Indian populations were scattered in disorderly native barrios.[28]

Partly because of the ethnic composition of the society, partly because of the new opportunities in urban foundation, Spanish-American cities brought about some reversals of European terms. Medieval European towns were labyrinths of narrow, winding streets compressed within walled enclosures. Only in newly founded sites, such as Santa Fe, the siege city of the attack upon Granada in the late fifteenth century, could peninsular Spaniards attempt systematic town planning. In America cities were newly settled, and Spaniards availed themselves of the opportunity to establish long, broad, straight streets with uniform and rectangular blocks. The protective walls, except in the vulnerable areas of the coast, were done away with. It was paradoxically the peripheral Indian wards that preserved the meandering and unplanned features of European urbanism. The Spanish centers, even in the eighteenth century, were rectilinear and rationally designed.[29]

Beneath the superficial orderliness of its upper class, urban society manifested a typical disorder, a want of sanitation, and a human degradation. Certain commercial and artisan types can be identified as a "middle class" in urban society, but their numbers were never large and the most striking feature of the social and economic organization was the separation of its extremes. The rich, who were inordinately wealthy, cultivated a deliberate indolence and a set of values appropriate to an aristocratic minority. The poor, infinitely more numerous, lived in indigence and squalor. Theft, prostitution, murder, and other crimes were common in the alleys and recesses of the cities' poor areas. Descriptions of the developed Spanish-Ameri-

[28] George Kubler, *Mexican Architecture of the Sixteenth Century* (2 vols., New Haven, 1948), I, 68 ff.

[29] George M. Foster, *Culture and Conquest, America's Spanish Heritage* (Chicago, 1960), pp. 34 ff. Dan Stanislawski, "Early Spanish Town Planning in the New World," *The Geographical Review*, XXXVII (1947), 101 ff., demonstrates in parallel columns the dependence of Philip II, or his advisors, on Vitruvius in the ordinances for town foundation of 1573. Both the rectangular plaza and the grid street plan were seemingly derived from Vitruvius. The ordinances are published in Zelia Nuttall, "Royal Ordinances concerning the Laying Out of New Towns," *Hispanic American Historical Review*, V (1922), 249–254.

can cities yield telling insights into the sordid, filth-ridden, fetid conditions in which the majority of urban residents spent their lives.

Economically the Spanish-American cities, like the haciendas and the plantations, depended on a servile class of nonwhites. Every city and town had a market function. Craft guilds (*gremios*) ensured the quality of upper-class products and the control of manufacture by the white class. Ethnic prejudice is nowhere so clearly expressed as in the regulations for *gremios,* which allowed *castas* to be apprentices and reserved the status of master for pure whites. For some guilds, as for the smiths in Mexico City in the eighteenth century, even apprentices were to be "Spaniards, pure and without stain." "Stain" in this sense had originally been measured in Spanish society in terms of non-Christian, Jewish, or Moslem intermixture. In America these traditional peninsular elements were retained, but to them was added the new colonial "stain" of Indian or Negro blood. In the larger cities all crafts were organized as *gremios.* The shoemakers, furniture makers, glassworkers, leatherworkers, and practitioners of other crafts not only inhabited and set up their shops in designated localities but grouped formally to prevent competition. The *gremios* commonly had municipal, religious, or ceremonial functions also, fitting their activities into colonial urban society at many levels.[30]

Most of the products that were made for local sale to white consumers in the Spanish-American colonial cities were made by guild methods and in accordance with guild rules. The rules specified size, color, quality, character of the raw materials, and technique of manufacture in meticulous detail. The result was a dedication to established and conservative standards of craftsmanship, persisting in some trades through the eighteenth century. In textile manufacture, cigar manufacture, and a few other industries, on the other hand, there appeared a kind of production that escaped the handicraft character of guild regulation and approached a sweatshop industrial form. The textile manufactures were called *obrajes* and their purpose was the mass production of woolens, principally for use as blankets and in clothing. *Obrajes* were characteris-

[30] Manuel Carrera Stampa, *Los gremios mexicanos: La organización gremial en Nueva España, 1521–1861* (Mexico, 1954).

tic of highland cities to which raw wool could be brought from adjacent pasture areas. Even in a society of gross labor abuses they were notorious for their exploitative management and for the oppressive conditions under which Indians, Negroes, mulattoes, and others were compelled to work. Probably the largest unit industrial enterprises of the Spanish-American cities were the tobacco and cigar factories operating under royal monopoly in the late colonial period.[31]

Between countryside and town there were always intricate psychological, social, and economic tensions. Large towns looked down on small towns and, despite the luxury of hacienda life, on the countryside in general. "Outside Mexico City, everything is Cuauhtitlan" ran a popular refrain of the capital of New Spain, in reference to a nearby suburb famous for its low status and its thriving, uncultivated, Indian-mestizo population. Yet it was on just such small centers that the great cities depended, for the lesser communities that were fortunately situated were intermediate concentration points for agricultural goods or cattle or mules to carry the supplies. Living was cheaper, and the small towns often found their livelihood in the price differences between urban and rural markets. The price differences and the vulnerability of essential grains to the conditions of the agricultural year offered vast opportunities to middlemen and speculators, who operated illegally (Spanish law was always distrustful of middlemen) and sometimes cornered markets to win an exorbitant profit. In the case of Potosí in Upper Peru, situated at too high an altitude for effective agriculture, inland Argentine towns were the regular providers of foodstuffs and other supplies, with price differentials of hundreds of per cent. Even in the case of Mexico City necessary produce came from surprising distances: pork from Apam fifty miles away, cattle from the great northern ranges at a distance of several hundred miles. The most striking commodity was cacao, regularly sent in the colonial period from Central America and even from Venezuela for the huge Mexico City market.

White society, which dominated all the relationships between

---

[31] The tobacco factory of Mexico City had some nine thousand workers in 1769. Gibson, *Aztecs under Spanish Rule*, p. 401.

town and country, was peculiarly class conscious and peculiarly aware of its own internal composition. The white family included a wide range of peripheral relatives, some of whom might really be mestizos or mulattoes.[32] The family was a closely knit unit evoking loyalties and obligations of a compelling sort. The great houses of city and countryside were filled with relatives, and the ties of consanguinity played a role in every family enterprise, domestic, commercial, political, or of whatever kind. Family connections determined who one's business partners were, and who one's social enemies. The white classes in each colony were interconnected by blood relationships and marriage ties. This was true of the encomienda class in the early period and of the commercial leaders, political officeholders, and landed property owners at a later time. Every major household was an extended intermeshed structure and hierarchy, with the master, the master's wife, their sons and daughters, peripheral relatives, inlaws, servants (who were themselves sometimes poor relations), and intimates acquired in various ways. These bulging domestic units go far to explain the allegiances and factions, and the delegations of subordinate authority, the favors, dependencies, and personnel of the political life of the colony.[33]

The emphasis on white purity in a society that was increasingly mixed brought with it some peculiar evasions and legal fictions. An inquisitorial investigation into the ancestry of a white family could be a frightening prospect, for few persons were so sure of their genealogical history that all doubt concerning earlier indiscretions was eliminated. Against the inquisitorial examiners there emerged professional genealogists who served the interests of their clients at a price and who were willing to suppress or manufacture evidence as needed. Ultimately the crown itself became a party to such needs, offering dispensations called *gracias a sacar* from mestizo or mulatto status. Upon payment of the proper amount one could obtain a

[32] "Even in the second or third generations, when they acquire the European colour, they are considered as Spaniards." Juan and Ulloa, *Voyage to South America,* p. 136. The comment relates to Quito, and the authors contrast the situation with that at Cartagena, where a longer time was required.

[33] Juan Carlos Rébora, "La familia americana," *II° Congreso internacional de historia de América,* III (Buenos Aires, 1938), 66–80. Much remains to be studied on the history of the Spanish American family.

royal document testifying that what Negro blood one possessed was legally "extinguished."[34]

In the seventeenth and eighteenth centuries everywhere the division between Spaniards born in the parent country and Spaniards born in the colony provided the basis for white society's most important internal competitions. Whites born in the colonies were called _criollos_, or creoles. Through most of Spanish America _criollo_ meant a pure white of American birth and carried no implication of mixture with Indian or Negro.[35] Spaniards were known as peninsulars, or by any of a number of derogatory terms, such as _gachupín_ or _chapetón_. The peninsular regarded himself as naturally superior to the creole, who resented the discriminatory distribution of privilege. Creoles could gain wealth through landholding or commerce, but their self-esteem was stifled by the limitations placed upon their careers in government and church. Thus place of birth assumed an extraordinary significance. In a sense the sharp disputes between peninsular and creole were crystallizations of other disputes, between Pizarrists and Almagrists, Castilians and Andalusians, or Franciscans and Dominicans.[36] It is especially noteworthy that a society articulated along ethnic lines should have identified its most consequential schism within its highest social level. But the fact is indicative of the fundamental, assumed, unchanging character of subordinate classifications. Though creoles were inferior to peninsulars in status, they were always superior in numbers. The peninsulars required replacement each generation. In time the peninsular

[34] For Spain, Sicroff speaks of the "persistent obsession" with purity of blood in the seventeenth century. Albert A. Sicroff, _Les Controverses des statuts de "pureté de sang" en Espagne du XVᵉ au XVIIᵉ siècle_ (Paris, 1960), pp. 221 ff. In the late eighteenth century the crown instituted a system of payments for transfer from colored to white status, with a gradation depending on how the white status would be recognized and how it would be utilized. Interesting details are added by James F. King, "The Case of José Ponciano de Ayarza: A Document on Gracias a Sacar," _Hispanic American Historical Review_, XXXI (1951), 640–647.

[35] In a technical sense, and in local areas, creole was not even confined to whites but might be used in reference to a Negro born in America as opposed to one born in Africa. In the church, creole sometimes meant a cleric ordained in the colonies as opposed to one ordained in Europe.

[36] Salvador de Madariaga, _The Fall of the Spanish American Empire_ (London, 1947), pp. 24 ff.

came to be associated with attitudes of Hispanic arrogance and domination, and creoles were able to identify themselves as "Americans" suffering from "foreign" abuse.

Creoles remained extremely sensitive to peninsular criticism. Though provincial in many ways, they betrayed an anxiety to demonstrate and prove their capacity. Their fashions and mode of life were imitative and self-conscious. In the creole society of Mexico City and Lima, high stiff collars were given up, breeches became wide and pleated, beards yielded to goatees and mustaches, exactly as in the Spanish capital. New styles appeared in America after an interval of time, and they tended to persist after their disappearance in the parent country. The American colonials, for all their awareness of European modes, were regarded by Europeans as deficient and out of date. And as if in compensation they developed habits of dress, adornment, house styles, liveries, and other living appurtenances that seemed exaggerated or ostentatious or excessive to peninsular eyes.[37]

Creole institutions reflected the creoles' psychology. Their academies and schools and universities—about twenty universities eventually came into being in the colonies—were modeled on those of Spain and unoriginal in their attitude toward learning. Educational practice is always a sensitive barometer of culture. In Spanish America the universities' systematized, authoritarian pedagogy made them the custodians of a pre-established knowledge. The parading of knowledge became the scholar's goal. Scholarship depended upon intellectual intensification and memorization and verbal manipulation rather than investigation or innovation of any kind. "Unusual

---

[37] This exaggerated creole formalism pervaded many institutions of the society, and it emerges as one key to an understanding of the creole mentality. With respect to funerals, Juan and Ulloa in the eighteenth century first described the elaborate creole practices in Cartagena and then moved to Ecuador, concerning which they reported: "The sumptuous manner of performing the last offices to the dead, mentioned in the description of Carthagena, is frugal and simple, if compared to that used at Quito and all its jurisdiction. Their ostentation is so enormous in this particular, that many families of credit are ruined by a preposterous emulation of excelling others. The inhabitants may therefore be properly said to toil, scheme, and endure the greatest labour and fatigue, merely to enable their successors to bury them in a pompous manner." Juan and Ulloa, *Voyage to South America,* pp. 145–146.

intellects in subtlety and facility . . ." was the judgment, not without respect, of a seventeenth-century visitor to the University of Lima.[38]

Subtlety and facility were qualities highly prized in the creole writing of the seventeenth century. This had not always been the case. American writing of the first century following the discovery had tended toward the simple and the expository, toward practical affairs and deeds accomplished. From the letter of Columbus (1493) through the Royal Commentaries of Garcilaso de la Vega (1609), the distinctive literature had dealt with Spanish American events themselves. The societies of the New World had been described with thoroughness, curiosity, and skill. American flora and fauna had been compared with their equivalents in Europe. Historians chronicled the explorations and the conquests. Friars described, and of course praised, the conversion labors of their orders. Drama was didactic, dedicated to missionary instruction. Even the poetry of the early period, for all its elegiac tone, had a practical message. The first important poem of Spanish America, the *Araucana* of Alonso de Ercilla, was an epic in verse, a historical chronicle of Valdivia's conquest of Chile.

In the seventeenth century this simplicity disappeared, and literary values assumed quite a different character. By 1600 the novelty of America had worn off, and unique New World subjects no longer sufficed to sustain a colonial literature. Poets and dramatists and chroniclers and historians still dealt with American themes, but they did so less in immediate appreciation of new material than in a spirit of self-conscious exoticism or as background scenery for other ends. Writing became complex, stylized, lavish, and involuted. Ambiguity and elaborate metaphor were preferred to simple clarity. Aristocratic cleverness became fashionable, and ordinary language was despised as too literal, too practical, too common. One is tempted to say of seventeenth-century Spanish-American literature that it was preoccupied with cryptic ways of disguising the fact that it had nothing to say. Such a judgment could be connected with the ambivalence of the cultivated creole's attitude toward peninsular

---

[38] Vázquez de Espinosa, *Compendium,* p. 445.

values, an attitude in which respect, fear, envy, and distrust mingled with intense dislike of the patronizing peninsulars.⟩

A few outstanding writers deserve special mention. In the mocking phrases of the Lima poet Juan del Valle y Caviedes, the modern reader—perhaps especially the modern reader—becomes aware of a negation of formalism and a bitter, caustic disillusion with seventeenth-century society. In the works of Pedro Peralta y Barnuevo and Carlos de Sigüenza y Góngora there occur occasional forthright expressions of rationalism. For sheer brilliance and power all other writers of the period fade into insignificance beside the extraordinary Jeronymite poetess Sor Juana Inés de la Cruz. But these were exceptional minds, responding in unusual ways to an environment in which all of them felt ill at ease.[39]

⌊In the second century of colonial life, insignificant matters assumed significance. In religion, the vestments, the details of ritual, the degree of obeisance to an archbishop, the route to be followed by a procession became more important than the basic tenets of religion.[40] In the state, protocol, hierarchy, rank, and its symbols became more important than government. In drama and poetry, the intricacies of a contrived syntax prevailed over and obliterated meaning. In architecture, external decoration was prized above plan and structure.[41] In an excess of categorization, late colonial analysts identified ethnic types that had no real meaning in the society, as between a white person whose great-grandfather had been a Negro and one whose great-great-grandfather had been a Negro.[42] Triviali-

[39] Mariano Picón-Salas, *A Cultural History of Spanish America, From Conquest to Independence*, Irving A. Leonard, trans. (Berkeley and Los Angeles, 1963) ; Irving A. Leonard, *Baroque Times in Old Mexico: Seventeenth-Century Persons, Places, and Practices* (Ann Arbor, 1959).

[40] The statement may appear extreme, and it surely would have been denied by responsible colonial ecclesiastics. But a large number of recorded incidents of the later colonial period suggests that it is indeed true. An example is the *vida común* controversy of the 1770's, summarized in Bernard E. Bobb, *The Viceregency of Antonio María Bucareli in New Spain, 1771–1779* (Austin, Tex., 1962), pp. 63–84. Bobb concludes: "If such a minor change involving so few persons could cause so much excitement and occupy the time of so many officials and clerks, the dangers of a major-reform effort may be more clearly understood."

[41] Pál Kelemen, *Baroque and Rococo in Latin America* (New York, 1951), pp. 15 ff., 23.

[42] Juan and Ulloa, *Voyage to South America*, pp. 27–28.

ties were exalted. Everywhere prominent issues were petty ones. Personal relations were governed by etiquette and intrigue. Formalities were the subject of endless discussion and controversy. The viceregal office seemed to exist in order to announce seating arrangements. One of the striking features of the developed colonial society is the extension of baroque attitudes, originally derived from Spain but given more ample opportunity in the creole atmosphere of Spanish America, through all creative activities and all public manifestations of the society.[43]

The term "baroque" implies a proliferation or refinement or intensification of what is already present, and this is what occurred in Spanish America in the seventeenth century. The "liberal" tendencies of European thought and action either were unknown or affected Spanish Americans only superficially. Royal power was unquestioned. It is as if the conservative tendencies of Spaniards in Europe were accentuated in the distant, protected environment of Spanish America, where a subject people helped to perpetuate a feudal structure. The rigidity of social class was unbroken. Protestantism and other deviations from religious orthodoxy were excluded or suppressed.[44] In each colonial city baroque society was a tiny minority of whites, thrown in upon one another, and suspicious of any change. Students who have sought manifestations of "enlightened" thought in Spanish America prior to the middle eighteenth century have succeeded in detailing only a limited inventory of superficial and disconnected instances. "Avoid innovation" was the expressed or tacit message of innumerable Spanish and Spanish-American laws through the seventeenth century to the eve of independence.

A special interest attaches to the processes through which Spanish habits of attitude and conduct were adapted to creole and other American needs. In the fresh early environment of the colony, a selection or simplification took place. The early American forms were not absolute replicas of the Spanish prototypes but rather standardized versions of them or particular choices taken from a variety of available possibilities. Large portions of the original Spanish culture were not carried overseas. The lowly plow provides

---

[43] Leonard, *Baroque Times in Old Mexico,* pp. 215–228.
[44] Or, in the case of the syncretic Indian religions, ignored.

an intriguing example of colonial selectivity. Of the many Spanish plow designs only one, the *arado dental*, survived in Spanish America. Spanish culture, so rich and various in its totality, may have been excessive for a colony which, though larger in size, was composed of interspersed migrants from every part of Spain. In the redistributions of peoples, local Spanish traditions were given up, and what emerged was a preferred type or a standardized common denominator. In the chronology of cultural selection of this kind, the first colonial decades appear to have been critical, with the last two and a half centuries introducing far fewer changes than would have been the case in an even or equitable distribution through time. The historians' general impression, that the middle period of colonial history was a period of very slow change, is undoubtedly accurate. Much more research is required on topics of regional distribution of traits and the chronology of change. But it appears now that in countless popular ways of life—and in contrast to the creoles' deliberate and superficial imitation of upper-class peninsular modes—the tendency of Spanish-American culture was to crystallize early.[45]

---

[45] Foster, *Culture and Conquest*, pp. 16, 52, 227 ff.

CHAPTER 7

Spaniards and Indians

MOST interpretations of Spanish-Indian relations have been influenced by the Black Legend, the tradition that points an accusing finger at Spain and finds Spaniards guilty of misconduct. The Black Legend has thrived wherever anti-Hispanism has filled a need, as in the English-speaking nations and in modern Spanish America. The opposite tradition—the White Legend—is to be found where the reverse is true, as in Spain itself. The Black Legend states that Spaniards slaughtered thousands of Indians and subjected the remainder to exploitative forced labor. The White Legend states that Spaniards brought Christianity to the Indians, eliminated human sacrifice and cannibalism from their society, and offered them draft animals, plows, and other material benefits. Thus both legends are accurate. But neither gives the whole truth. The content of each is selective. In declaring for one and against the other, much depends upon what one chooses to emphasize and what one chooses to ignore.

Specifically, with regard to the Black Legend, the most common counterargument is that it isolates Spain, concentrating its attention upon Spanish cruelty and disregarding the cruelty of other peoples. This also is true, and it means that the Legend is narrowly conceived as well as peculiarly unfair to Spain. In the counterargument the Indian, far from being an innocent victim, is himself cruel—as well as lewd, superstitious, and dirty. A peculiar feature is that for all its vehemence the Black Legend by no means exhausts the history of Spanish cruelty. For the most part its advocates have not been students of history. They have tended to rely for their material on Las Casas, overlooking subjects that Las Casas did not treat. Both the Black Legend and the White Legend concentrate on the early period of Spanish-Indian relations. Without further analysis of the Legends, it is the purpose of this chapter to discuss relations between Spaniards and Indians in the period after 1550.

In the intellectual realm, the century following 1550 was for a select number of Spaniards a period of appreciation and of research into the character of Indian civilizations. Each of the three major American peoples received its classic study at this time: the Aztec by Bernardino de Sahagún, the Maya by Diego de Landa, and the Inca by Bernabé Cobo. Sahagún, born in 1499, arrived in New Spain in 1529, and devoted himself for the next sixty years to missionary labors in the Franciscan province of central Mexico. He became one of the most proficient of the friars in speaking Nahuatl, and in Tlatelolco he developed his plan for an encyclopedic work on the civilization of the Aztecs to be written in their own language. The result was the *Historia general,* a massive exposition of Aztec religion, society, customs, and language, assembled from Indian responses to systematic, ethnographic questionnaires. Landa, also a Franciscan, arrived in Yucatan in 1549 and became Bishop of Mérida in 1572. His *Relación de las cosas de Yucatán,* composed in the 1560's, is a less detailed and less original work than Sahagún's, but it is an extraordinary achievement none the less and the most distinguished ethnological study of Maya civilization made in colonial times. Cobo, born in Spain, arrived in Lima in 1599 at the age of seventeen, received his education in Jesuit schools, joined the Jesuit society, traveled widely in the Andean area and elsewhere, and compiled his *Historia del Nuevo Mundo* between 1612 and 1653. Though he wrote at a later date than the others (a standard time lag between Mexico and Peru is exemplified here), his work stands as the foremost colonial treatment of Inca society. Like Sahagún and Landa, Cobo knew Indians who remembered the precolonial period, and his *Historia* is a full treatise on the geography, natural history, and aboriginal inhabitants of Peru.[1]

[1] Bernardino de Sahagún, *General History of the Things of New Spain:*

A number of other writings attest to this special Spanish interest in native peoples in the late sixteenth and early seventeenth centuries. The bibliography includes great dictionaries,[2] grammars of Indian languages, and additional histories of preconquest civilizations recorded from Indian informants. The pagan religions, calendars, governments, and social compositions received close study. Educated Indians and mestizos, such as Diego Muñoz Camargo and Fernando de Alva Ixtlilxochitl in Mexico, and Garcilaso de la Vega in Peru, contributed to the writing.[3] The appearance of an indigenous literature in the second generation of the Spanish colony was the natural consequence of the processes of settlement and mestization, for in no area could the first generation have afforded the luxury of such scholarship, and a sizable population of mestizos could not have come into being immediately. The century following 1550 was also a time of Indian population loss, to which this writing was in part a direct response. The fear that native peoples might be eradicated or that their civilizations might be so transformed as to become unrecognizable surely stimulated efforts to recapture and record their original form.

The Spanish state of the period after 1550 likewise made efforts to expand its knowledge of Indian civilizations, partly in a spirit of administrative curiosity, and partly to convince itself that imperialism had benefited the native peoples. In the late 1570's and again in the seventeenth century, the monarchy sent out questionnaires to be answered by the local authorities of every colonial town. The

---

Florentine Codex, Arthur J. O. Anderson and Charles E. Dibble, trans. and eds. (Santa Fe, 1950 *et seq.*); Diego de Landa, *Landa's Relación de las cosas de Yucatán: A Translation,* Alfred M. Tozzer, trans. and ed. (Cambridge, Mass., 1941); Bernabé Cobo, *Historia del nuevo mundo* (4 vols., Seville, 1890–93). Biographies and bibliographies of Sahagún and Landa will appear in the forthcoming ethnohistorical volumes of the *Handbook of Middle American Indians.* For Cobo, see M. González de la Rosa, "Biografía del padre Bernabé Cobo," in *Monografías históricas sobre la ciudad de Lima* (2 vols., Lima, 1935), I, v–xxii.

[2] Important examples of dictionaries are Molina's Spanish-Nahuatl dictionary published originally in 1571 and republished in facsimile in 1944 as Alonso de Molina, *Vocabulario en lengua castellana y mexicana* (Madrid, 1944), and the Motul I and Vienna dictionaries of Maya and Spanish.

[3] Diego Muñoz Camargo, *Historia de Tlaxcala* (Mexico, 1947); Fernando de Alva Ixtlilxochitl, *Obras históricas,* Alfredo Chavero, ed. (2 vols., Mexico, 1891–92); Garcilaso de la Vega, *Obras completas,* Carmelo Saénz de Santa María, ed. (4 vols., Madrid, 1960).

questions related to climate, topography, population, distance from other towns, customs, churches, local government, and a number of other topics.[4] One query elicited from Indian informants a series of comments assessing the comparative values of preconquest and postconquest life, with observations on differences in food, drink, hygiene, dress, burial practices, and other matters. The answers, known as *Relaciones geográficas,* tended only partially to justify Spanish belief in the superiority of colonial institutions. But the questionnaires demonstrate the concern of the administrations of Philip II and his successors with local colonial detail, and the responses constitute now one of the best sources of knowledge for Indian life and history.

In Peru during the administration of Viceroy Francisco de Toledo (1569–81), a body of historical data emerged under viceregal sponsorship, similarly documented from Indian informants. The Toledan investigators sought to show not only that Atahualpa had been a usurper and illegitimate ruler but that all members of the ruling Inca class had been usurpers and illegitimate rulers. The Inca ruling class had accordingly been properly attacked by Pizarro, and the descendants of that class (then preserving the separatist Inca state in an Andean retreat) ought similarly to be attacked by the colonial government of the 1570's. Toledo did in fact destroy this separatist state, executing the surviving Inca, Tupac Amaru I, in 1572. But the Toledan researches proceeded a step farther, concluding that local leaders had been the natural and legitimate rulers (*señores naturales*) in ancient Peru.[5] The king of Spain, himself *señor natural,* had thus displaced the illicit government of the Inca class in order to substitute legal and civilized government. A natural compatibility connected the monarchy with the spokesmen of local affairs. The Peruvian society of the future would be freed from

---

[4] *Relaciones geográficas de Indias: Perú,* Marcos Jiménez de la Espada, ed. (4 vols., Madrid, 1881–97). Howard F. Cline, "The *Relaciones Geográficas* of the Spanish Indies, 1577–1586," *Hispanic American Historical Review,* XLIV (1964), 341–374, is a full discussion of the bibliography, scope, and significance of this corpus.

[5] Robert S. Chamberlain, "The Concept of the *Señor Natural* as Revealed by Castilian Law and Administrative Documents," *Hispanic American Historical Review,* XIX (1939), 130–137.

illegitimate usurpation and would appear as a harmonious blend of Indian ways with Spanish ways and of Indians with Spaniards.[6]

Other Spanish writings emphasized the lengthening colonial period itself less in a spirit of rationalization than in the historical-philosophical context of Spanish decline. By the late sixteenth century the early imperial self-confidence had passed. Sahagún spoke of the excessive and deceptive optimism that had prevailed in the early period of conversion. In the writings of the Franciscan friar Gerónimo de Mendieta (1525–1604), the first century of American colonial history assumed an eschatological meaning whereby Indian history recapitulated and paralleled the history of the world. The pre-Spanish period for Mendieta was the Indians' bondage in Egypt. Cortés was the Moses who had led them to the Promised Land of Christianity. The forty years from 1524 (when the first twelve "apostolic" Franciscans arrived in Mexico) to 1564 (when the pro-Franciscan rule of Luis de Velasco, the second Mexican viceroy, came to an end) comprised the Golden Age of Indian-Spanish relations. But the period following 1564 was a time of troubles or Babylonian Captivity, and by the late sixteenth century the end of the world, the day of doom, was at hand.[7] This sense of pessimism is related to the decay of the early mission endeavor, to the reduced authority of the regular orders, to the progressive economic and other crises that were contributing to the loss of Spanish prestige

[6] Philip Ainsworth Means, "Biblioteca andina, Part One, The Chroniclers, or, the Writers of the Sixteenth and Seventeenth Centuries who Treated of the Pre-Hispanic History and Culture of the Andean Countries," *Transactions of the Connecticut Academy of Arts and Sciences*, XXIX (1928), 271–525; Roberto Levillier, *Don Francisco de Toledo, supremo organizador del Perú: Su vida, su obra (1515–1582)* (2 vols., Buenos Aires, 1935–40), I, 301 ff.; II, 3 ff.; Roberto Levillier (ed.), *Ordenanzas de don Francisco de Toledo, virey del Perú, 1569–1581* (Madrid, 1929), pp. 36 ff., 304 ff. The question of legitimacy is linked with the problem of chronology, in the assumption, common in the colonial period, that legality can be established through evidence over a long period. The Inca dynasty's claim to legitimacy was questionable if its history was short. Interestingly, the foremost defender of Incaic values, Garcilaso de la Vega, argued for a long Incaic history. In general a short history aroused suspicions of unlawful usurpation. Most historians now accept the short, non-Garcilasan history proposed by John Rowe, "Absolute Chronology in the Andean Area," *American Antiquity*, X (1945), 265–284.

[7] John Leddy Phelan, *The Millennial Kingdom of the Franciscans in the New World: A Study of the Writings of Gerónimo de Mendieta (1525–1604)* (Berkeley and Los Angeles, 1956).

and power, and to the continuing epidemics and population decline which were, for the Indian civilizations of America, the most striking feature of the hundred years from 1550 to 1650.

In Mexico and Peru the practical Spanish response to Indian epidemic included the establishment of occasional hospitals, provision for sanitary burial, charitable campaigns principally under ecclesiastical auspices, and rudimentary medical remedies, notably large-scale bloodletting. Yet the whole history of epidemic and mass death received limited attention in Spanish commentary. In comparison with the amount of documentation on viceregal receptions or the ceremonial obsequies for the Spanish kings or the question of perpetuity in encomienda, the record is a meager one. The fact surely reflects the white colonist's normal sense of superiority and his feeling that obligations to Indians were satisfactorily fulfilled through a routine Christianization. Many Spaniards, living separate lives and concentrating their attention elsewhere, were genuinely unaware of the afflictions of Indian peoples. Moreover, in the sixteenth and seventeenth centuries epidemic was not the startling and unfamiliar thing that it would be in our own antibiotic age. In the modern world disease has been brought under control and we are attuned to scientific causes and statistical measurements of the results. In an earlier period epidemic was accepted as a condition of life, and population losses had to be immense before they were recognized as extraordinary. White colonists did not regard the Indian losses as a problem worthy of concentrated attention until the process was far advanced. The deficiencies of the Spanish record mean that students have emphasized the deaths caused by conquest or Spanish cruelty. The tremendous extent and impact of Indian depopulation have in reality come to be recognized only in our own time, when scholars have compared statistical tribute records through the first hundred years of colonial history.

We do have some documentation on Indian reactions to epidemic. Native drawings show the victims and their symptoms, among which skin eruptions, nosebleed, and death receive most frequent comment. Suicide and infanticide and refusal to bear children occurred. Covert hostility to whites surely increased. Indians made efforts to extend the epidemics to Spanish society by secretly kneading infected blood into bread dough or placing the dead bodies of victims in the Spaniards' wells. As the mass deaths left orphaned children, Indians adopted the Spanish institution of *compadrazgo,* by which a godmother and godfather became as important to an individual as his real parents.[8]

⌐ In the main population centers Indian society continued to function in reduced and modified form. Living conditions changed depending on the extent of population loss, distance from Spanish influence, and local types of Spanish exploitation. Indian dress became partly Hispanized. On the other hand, house construction, diet, and most features of domestic life remained traditional and conservative. Native agriculture was little affected by European techniques or crop innovations. Spanish efforts to induce Indians to cultivate wheat and other European grains were unsuccessful, save under specific laboring conditions for white employers. Indian agriculture continued to depend on maize, which, in a variety of forms, was the principal ingredient of Indian diet. Only under compulsion or tutelage, or for the payment of enforced tributes in kind, did Indians admit European plants, and this was normally as an adjunct economy without regard for private Indian needs. Indians preferred to raise pigs and chickens rather than cattle or other animals not easily incorporated into domestic agricultural life. Instances of Indian sheep- and goatherding on a fairly large scale are known, but such undertakings involved a greater initial expenditure and a more radical departure from traditional customs than most Indians were willing to assume. ⌐

On the colonial peripheries, on the plains north of New Spain and on the Argentine pampas, the effect of white colonization was sometimes to influence the habits of Indians who had no firsthand contact with white settlers. Migrant tribes took to hunting on horseback; some agricultural peoples abandoned sedentary life and became mounted hunters and warriors. In other regions European tools and weapons were received as trade objects long before knowl-

---

[8] Agustín Dávila Padilla, *Historia de la fundación y discurso de la provincia, de Santiago de México, de la orden de Predicadores, por las vidas de sus varones insignes y casos notables de Nueva España* (Brussels, 1625), pp. 516–518; George M. Foster, "Cofradía and compadrazgo in Spain and South America," *Southwestern Journal of Anthropology,* IX (1953), 1–28.

edge of Europeans themselves was gained. The new economic possibilities allowed for larger tribal units, and tended to intensify strife among neighboring tribes.

In the regions settled by Spaniards the value of the mass Indian population lay in its capacity for work, and after 1550 the main institution of labor was the corvée or *repartimiento*. The term *repartimiento* means distribution or allotment, and in the present sense it indicated the formal or official allotment of Indian workers to Spanish employers. In its first manifestation in the West Indies, *repartimiento* had been a loosely controlled, exploitative institution, so closely associated with encomienda that the two words were employed interchangeably.[9] So long as encomienda remained an instrument of legal Indian labor, *repartimiento* in the strict sense was that aspect of it that concerned the distribution of Indians among Spaniards, without reference to the element of trust or "commendation." But when the Spanish colonial *encomenderos* were forbidden to exact labor from their Indians, encomienda and *repartimiento* became legally distinct. The distinction, of course, was not everywhere observed in practice. Moreover the term *repartimiento* was still sometimes used in reference to encomienda, since encomienda still involved the distribution of Indians.[10] Labor *repartimiento* occurred also under a number of local names (*coatequitl* in New Spain; *mita* in Peru) and with some alterations from place to place, but its essential principles—coercive apportionment of laborers among jobs and employers—did not vary.

In labor *repartimiento*, a Spanish ranch owner, agriculturist, miner, or other colonist in need of workers first made application to local political authorities—to the *corregidor* or *alcalde mayor*, the *audiencia*, the viceroy, or sometimes a special *juez repartidor*. Hav-

---

[9] Ursula Lamb, *Frey Nicolás de Ovando, gobernador de las Indias (1501–1509)* (Madrid, 1956), pp. 147 ff., 166 ff., *et seq.;* F. A. Kirkpatrick, "Repartimiento-Encomienda," *Hispanic American Historical Review,* XIX (1939), 372–379.

[10] The various distinctions were of importance to colonial legal thinkers and to those concerned with justifying the form of the Spanish colonial state. See the interesting series of observations by Solórzano y Pereyra: "The mita is permissible in the public interest. . . . The republic is a mystical body. . . . No one can be excused. . . . It is one thing to serve, another to be a servant," etc. Juan de Solórzano y Pereyra, *Política indiana* (5 vols., Madrid and Buenos Aires, 1930), I, 169 ff.

ing been granted authorization, he was then entitled to receive a stated number of Indian workers for a designated period and for particular tasks. Indians were allotted to him and to other successful applicants from a labor pool consisting of a percentage of the able-bodied males of each community. The workers were liable to the labor draft in rotation, the frequency of their service depending upon local supply and demand. The employer was obligated to provide humane treatment and to pay the wage prescribed in his permit. Since agricultural and many other labor tasks were seasonal, there was no great regularity in the allotted quotas. *Repartimiento* labor was employed for ranches, haciendas, and mines, and even sometimes for domestic service, although the principle of public benefit might be evoked to disallow the request of any colonist.[11]

Repartimiento functioned most successfully near the viceregal capitals, where Indian populations were most dense, and where appropriate facilities for enforcement were at hand. In more remote areas, after the manner of encomienda, it was subject to abuse. The Spanish crown, aware of abuses and opposed on humanitarian grounds to enforced Indian labor, regarded *repartimiento* as a provisional institution, ultimately to be abolished. In a series of regulations beginning in the late sixteenth century the crown undertook to implement its policies by placing restrictions on *repartimiento* and by encouraging free Indian labor and Negro slavery. Thus in textile factories and sugar mills, where exploitation was likely to take extreme forms, Indian labor was prohibited and *repartimiento* privileges were denied. But as with all such regulations, obedience was irregular and enforcement impossible. Local and traditional prac-

[11] Again Solórzano provides the theoretical, justificatory, apologetic commentary in a very interesting way: "Whether it is proper to require Indians to work at cattle raising . . . what relates to agriculture and what relates to cattle raising . . . Adam was a farmer, Abel a shepherd. . . . Aristotle teaches that raising and grazing animals is truly agriculture," etc. *Ibid.,* pp. 221 ff. Discussions of *repartimiento* may be found in Lesley Byrd Simpson, *Studies in the Administration of the Indians in New Spain,* III, *The Repartimiento System of Native Labor in New Spain and Guatemala* (Berkeley, 1938); Jorge Basadre, "El régimen de la mita," *Letras,* III (1937), 325–364; Donald L. Wiedner, "Forced Labor in Colonial Peru," *The Americas,* XVI (1959–60), 357–383; Silvio Zavala and María Castelo (eds.), *Fuentes para la historia del trabajo en Nueva España* (8 vols., Mexico, 1939–46). The last is a publication of primary documents, beginning in 1575, and the *repartimiento* operation in New Spain is set forth in detail.

tices could not be transformed by royal decree or humanitarian intent. Because the colonists' need for labor exceeded the Indians' willingness to provide it, the system of compulsory native labor continued wherever Indian society remained and wherever work was to be done.

Spanish procedures of labor conscription were complicated by Indian class and status systems, which in some instances persisted for long periods. In the Aztec world a semislave class, generally called *mayeque,* continued to be held in subordination and isolation by the Indian upper class, so that it was only near the end of the sixteenth century that the survivors of this portion of the native population were brought within the labor *repartimiento.* In Peru members of a native Indian class called *yanaconas* were attached to particular properties and remained in this serflike condition to the eighteenth century despite many royal orders declaring their freedom. Here "free" Indians made efforts to become classified as *yanaconas* in order to escape the *repartimiento* of the mines.[12] In the urban areas, where Indians rapidly learned Spanish crafts and trades, a skilled worker could earn an income several times that of the *repartimiento* wage, and elaborate procedures were devised for exemption and the hiring of substitutes. Indian shoemakers, saddlers, and cabinetmakers competed directly with Spanish craftsmen (for a time in Mexico City, Indian saddlemakers successfully passed their products as imports from Spain) and devised ingenious methods for evading the *repartimiento.*

In certain ways the employment of Indian workers became more severe as the seventeenth century advanced. Fewer Indians were available, and the growth of the white population increased the demand for them. Hence competition among employers became more intense, and the employers as well as the Indian craftsmen found ways to overcome the limitations of *repartimiento.*[13] Employers sought private and dependable labor supplies not subject to the

[12] Levillier (ed.), *Ordenanzas,* pp. 241 ff.; John Lynch, *Spanish Colonial Administration, 1782–1810: The Intendant System in the Viceroyalty of the Río de la Plata* (London, 1958), p. 179; Charles Gibson, *The Aztecs under Spanish Rule: A History of the Indians of the Valley of Mexico, 1519–1810* (Stanford, 1964), pp. 220–256.

[13] Woodrow Borah, *New Spain's Century of Depression* (Berkeley and Los Angeles, 1951), pp. 30–44.

political control or the periodic fluctuations of *repartimiento*. In part
this objective was achieved through bribery of *repartimiento*
officials; in part it was accomplished through "free contract labor"
and new private labor systems that developed in the seventeenth
century.⌋

Free contract labor had the apparent advantage that it was con-
scientiously approved by the monarch and hence subject to less restrictive administrative controls than was *repartimiento*. To a
Spanish government concerned with the Hispanization of the
Indian, free wage labor seemed to imply an Indian working class
capable of exercising volition and operating to the material benefit
of the Spanish colony. ⌈From the point of view of the employer, free
contract labor had the real merit that the term of labor (normally
a year or several years) was expressed in a written agreement
drafted according to the employer's specifications and legally agreed
to by the Indian. Once committed, the Indian worker had little
recourse, in spite of official regulations respecting wages and labor
terms. Freedom was further limited by the circumstances that
Indians, illiterate and readily duped, commonly lacked knowledge
of the meaning of the contract.⌋

Free contract labor failed because employers abused their privileges and because Indian laborers were unable sufficiently to influence the labor market. In areas where the monarchy sought to
effect the full change to free labor, the attempt was unsuccessful and
the principle of freedom became farcical. Coercion attended all
efforts to substitute alternative labor forms. *Repartimiento* itself was
persistently evaded. Employers sequestered workers and induced
them to work outside the designated periods. *Repartimiento* officials
connived with the employers, accepted bribes, and entered into
many kinds of irregularity. The crown meanwhile forbade *repartimiento* in additional types of labor and looked forward to its
eventual elimination in all. In 1632 the viceroy of New Spain ruled
the abolition of *repartimiento* labor for all industries except mining.[14]

The termination of so many aspects of *repartimiento* brought

[14] Zavala and Castelo (eds.), *Fuentes*, VI, xxi–xxii, xxx–xxxi, xlii, xliv, 394–
397, 616 ff.

about no such hostile reaction as had the attempted termination of encomienda in the previous century. At the time of the New Laws, the disaffected colonists depended on encomienda and resisted accordingly. The difference is that by 1630 no influential colonial class still based its operation on compulsory rotational labor. The employers of the colony had passed beyond a labor system involving state rationing of workers and had developed the successor institution, peonage or debt labor.

Instances of peonage are known from the sixteenth century, but it was in the seventeenth and eighteenth centuries that peonage spread broadly throughout the colonies and affected all appropriate forms of employment. In peonage, a condition of indebtedness gave an employer a legal (or semilegal) opportunity to compel a laborer to work. Spaniards began by loaning small sums to impoverished Indians, with the understanding that the loan represented an advance on wages. Repayment could be made only through work. But work was what the employer desired, and he saw to it that his position as creditor remained secure. Additional loans were made before the original debt could be discharged, and through recurrent transactions the Indian was held to a lifetime of labor. Indebtedness still outstanding at the time of the worker's death might be inherited by his children, and entire families might thus be held in bondage generation after generation.

Peonage affords another example of the insufficiency of Spanish law. The king and Council tried in many ways to control it. Debts were to be confined to the equivalent of a stated period of labor, were not to exceed a fixed amount, and could be repaid only in labor. An Indian worker was free to work wherever he chose regardless of the debt. Debts for labor were forbidden altogether.[15] But the real history of peonage meanwhile continued unaffected by the legislation. It was to be the most durable of all colonial labor forms.

In these ways native labor, one of the two principal components of the original encomienda, passed from private control to royal control and back to private control. No such full circle was achieved

---

[15] For the debtor in Spain, see Luis Redonet y López, "Condición histórico-social del deudor," in *Estudios de historia social de España,* Carmelo Viñas y Mey, ed. (2 vols., Madrid, 1949–52), II, 479–532.

in the history of the second of the original impositions of encomienda, namely, the tribute that was exacted from each Indian
family head. As individual encomiendas reverted to the crown, their
Indian tributes were taken from the control of *encomenderos* and
directed to the royal treasury without opposition. In the seventeenth century financial income was far more important to the
crown than was the disposition of American labor, and the monarchy
made sure that native tribute was retained as royal revenue. To the
end of the colonial period this tribute continued to comprise an important part of the crown's income. In the history of tribute, no
second or intermediate colonial class, comparable to the class of
white employers, intervened between the Indian population and the
crown.

Indian tribute was collected through the imperial political hierarchy, at the lowest levels of which *corregidores* were appointed as
overseers of the Indian communities. Thus a *corregidor* might be an
individual exercising royal *justicia* in a city or town of Spanish
colonists in the manner previously described, or one exercising a
comparable authority over an area inhabited by Indians. The *corregidores* of the latter type, governing rural or semirural regions
called *corregimientos,* were the main Spanish authorities in the exaction of tribute from native tributaries.[16]

The process involved a considerable Hispanization at local levels.
All the large Indian communities of the seventeenth century came
to be reorganized in accordance with peninsular Hispanic forms,
and their municipal governments were direct imitations of those of
whites. *Cabildos* with Indian *alcaldes* and *regidores* came into being
in the native towns of New Spain and Peru. Meetings were held,
ordinances issued, and minutes kept after the model of Spanish
community governments.[17] The *alcaldes* exercised judicial functions
for minor crimes and civil suits. The *regidores* were councilors legis-
lating rules for local affairs. The actual collectors of tribute were
the *alcaldes* and *regidores* themselves, or particular Indian tax col-

---

[16] José Miranda, *El tributo indígena en la Nueva España durante el siglo
XVI* (Mexico, 1952), pp. 225 ff., 346.

[17] Constantino Bayle, "Cabildos de indios en la América española," *Missionalia hispánica,* VIII (1951), 5–35; Adolfo Lamas, "Las cajas de comunidades
indígenas," *El trimestre económico,* XXIV (1957), 298–337.

lectors designated by them. Tributaries gave a specified amount in money or kind at fixed intervals. The receipts were delivered to the *corregidor,* who was responsible for the full amount and for its delivery to higher Spanish authority.

Two significant features may be noted with respect to these processes of labor and tribute exaction. One is that Indian officeholders were utilized at the subordinate levels of the hierarchy for the enforcement of Spanish rules. Thus the destruction of native government that attended the conquests of Mexico and Peru was in an important degree selective. In both empires it was designedly the large imperial features that were eliminated, while local and lower-class traditions were allowed to persist. The point is further demonstrated by the survival of the community unit called *ayllu* in Peru, and by the survival of the Indian town (*altepetl*) and its component subdivision called *calpulli* in Mexico.

The second is that the Spanish state exercised a controlling influence over the individual lives of a mass population. One might say that Spain responded to the challenge posed by the size and distance of America not simply by expanding its political organization but by intensifying it as well. The task was much facilitated by the local Indian organization. Where possible or expedient, or where they could be closely regulated, native political and social practices were incorporated and retained, and this was uniformly at the functioning levels of original payment of tribute and service. The power and prestige of the pre-Spanish states, and their continuing traditions of popular subservience, made it possible for Spaniards to exact labor and tribute with little opposition. In Mexico and Peru especially, Spaniards took charge of an established society, substituting themselves for the rulers they had deposed or killed. The result was that *repartimiento* and tribute in America demonstrated a degree of organization and control over lower classes unmatched by any nation in Europe.

In the process local native rulers served as intermediaries between the dominant Spanish society and the subordinate Indian society. Spaniards identified such local rulers as "caciques," a West Indian term meaning chieftain and one that Spaniards eventually carried everywhere and applied to all Indian societies in the colonies.

Caciques were granted special privileges, partly as a consequence of the Spanish respect for status, partly to induce them to function as cooperative puppet bosses in their communities. Because legitimate caciques were regarded as *señores naturales,* they were held to be rightfully entitled to authority and high position. Cortés and Pizarro had used caciques to collect treasure and to enlist military allies. *Encomenderos* wielded their power through the caciques of their encomiendas. The ease with which the first Spaniards manipulated huge numbers of native peoples, even the ease with which the first missionaries induced huge numbers of conversions, depended upon the intermediate position of caciques. And the alacrity with which Spaniards overthrew the caciques who displeased them and substituted others indicates the tenuous, theoretical, and expedient character of all such status.

Some of the most striking individual adaptations to Spanish civilization took place at the cacique level. Caciques were in the vanguard in the adoption of Spanish dress, foods, language, and styles of house construction. They were excused from tribute and labor exactions and given special privileges, such as permission to ride horses and carry arms. Caciques' estates, called *cacicazgos,* became subject to mixed Indian and Spanish law and in some instances were inherited generation after generation in accordance with the rules of entail and primogeniture. By the eighteenth century there had emerged a small group of extremely wealthy and aristocratic caciques who were owners of slaves, cattle, and large propertied estates and who made a transition to Hispanic life at an affluent social rank.[18] At the lower end of the scale, in the eighteenth century there existed caciques who were undistinguishable from other Indians save in a meaningless hereditary prestige. But by this time the deliberate Spanish utilization of the cacique class was largely a thing of the past, and individual caciques succeeded or failed to the extent that they could use their positions to facilitate careers in commerce, ranching, financial speculation, or the gentle-

---

[18] Guillermo S. Fernández de Recas, *Cacicazgos y nobilario indígena de la Nueva España* (Mexico, 1961); Carlos A. Vivanco, "Anotaciones para la historia de los cacicazgos ecuatorianos," *Boletín de la Academia nacional de historia* (Quito), XXII (1942), 119–152.

manly management of their properties.

Indian caciques and Spanish *corregidores* joined forces to extract from the mass Indian population whatever wealth it possessed over and above the subsistence level of its economy. In the seventeenth and eighteenth centuries a favorite and universal form of exploitation was the forced-sale *repartimiento,* according to which the principle of allotment was applied to surplus commodities in the Spanish economy while the common Indian became the recipient, at a price, of goods he did not want and could not use. Like the Requirement, but in a much more materialistic way, the forced-sale *repartimiento* assumed a degree of Indian Hispanization in excess of the reality. Caciques and *corregidores*—and frequently ecclesiastics and others who were able to assume positions of local power—earned a regular income through the forced-sale *repartimiento.* They contracted with ranchers and *hacendados* and merchants and other entrepreneurs to dispose of whatever could not be sold through ordinary forms of marketing. Markups of several hundred per cent were common. Indians were compelled to buy farm animals and manufactured goods and luxury items such as shoes and silk stockings (most Indians went barefoot) and were punished if they resisted. History affords many examples of controlled economies, but rarely in history, outside of Spanish America, has such institutionalized provision been made for liquidating surplus stocks at the expense of a lower-class "consumer."[19]

One other Indian possession was exploited by Spaniards, namely land. Spanish usurpation of Indian property holdings took place as a gradual process extending over the entire colonial period. It was also an accelerating process, developing from limited beginnings. The earliest Spanish colonists did not take land, save in small quantities. When Spaniards first arrived, little attention was given to land possession as an individual objective, and the private colonial

---

[19] A manuscript in the New York Public Library entitled "Yndize comprehensibo de todos los goviernos, corregimientos, y alcaldías mayores que contiene la gobernación del virreynato de México," is an eighteenth-century political handbook for local political officials, notifying them of what they may expect by way of forced-sale profit in each jurisdiction. For an account of the forced-sale *repartimiento* in Peru see John Howland Rowe, "The Incas under Spanish Colonial Institutions," *Hispanic American Historical Review,* XXXVII (1957), 164 ff.

estate did not appear as an immediate consequence of conquest, for the wealth of America was seen in other terms. The most conspicuous American resources at first were the elaborate Indian civilizations and subsequently the mines. Indians occupied the lands and Indian agriculture supported the first Spanish colonists. Labor could be organized and white society maintained through control over Indians rather than through control over land, and encomienda was appropriate and sufficient for these purposes in the immediate post-conquest period. Thus Indian landholding was respected in early colonial law, and a Spanish colonist had no need to displace Indian occupants. Indeed, much of the land was so thickly occupied that displacement would have been physically impossible. Forced removal from these regions to the more sparsely settled frontiers would have been self-defeating, for it would have implied a wholesale disavowal of the all-important labor force.

The sequence of events was in reality just the reverse of this. Only as lands became unoccupied through depopulation did Spaniards become interested in acquiring them. As encomienda failed to provide capital in sufficient amounts, a larger and more complex Spanish society required a more varied economy. For a time in the sixteenth century highland Indian land was abandoned more rapidly than Spaniards could assimilate it, and there appeared the open sheep ranges and what were called *tierras baldías,* or empty, unused lands. Sheep multiply more rapidly than people, and sheep filled the vacuum that neither Spaniards nor Indians could fill. One result, on the slopes of the intermontane basins, was trampling and close cropping, and hence erosion in the torrential wet-season rains. The denuded landscape of much of modern Spanish America is thus related to Indian abandonment of land and the replacement of a human population with grazing animals.[20]

For Spaniards land became the symbol of wealth that encomienda had formerly been, and by and large this meant a new colonial aristocracy not related to the earlier conquistadores and *encomenderos.* By the seventeenth century the Spanish demand for land had

[20] Lesley Byrd Simpson, *Exploitation of Land in Central Mexico in the Sixteenth Century* (Berkeley and Los Angeles, 1952); Sherburne F. Cook, *Soil Erosion and Population in Central Mexico* (Berkeley and Los Angeles, 1949), and *The Historical Demography and Ecology of the Teotlalpan* (Berkeley and Los Angeles, 1949).

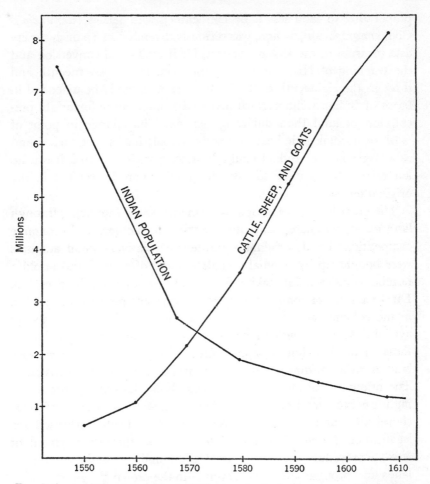

Population and livestock in central Mexico. As the Indian population declined, the numbers of livestock rose. After Simpson, *Exploitation of Land in Central Mexico in the Sixteenth Century*, adjusted in accordance with Borah and Cook, *The Population of Central Mexico in 1548*.

caught up with depopulation, and Spaniards made efforts to free lands from their remaining native occupants, both in legal and in illegal ways. The principal illegal method was forced usurpation. The legal methods included forced concentration (*congregación*) of Indians in new communities[21] and requirements that Indians show

[21] Howard F. Cline, "Civil Congregations of the Indians in New Spain, 1598–

proper title to land lest it be condemned and seized (*denuncia*).
Civil *congregación*, at first, was seriously defended in Spanish society
as a measure in the Indian interest, for it facilitated conversion and
the teaching of Hispanic ways. *Denuncia*, in the seventeenth and
through the eighteenth centuries, could not so easily be defended in
terms of Indian welfare, for it involved a much more forthright pre-
emption of land than did *congregación*. The change in point of
view, or in apologetic base, is wholly typical; for as time passed and
as a larger part of Indian land fell under Spanish control, it was no
longer so necessary, or so easy, to justify Spanish conduct in the
original terms.

The great haciendas of Spanish America came into being through
land grant, purchase, usurpation, accretion, merger, and economic
competition. Lands originally granted in relatively small amounts
were bought up by colonial speculators and often sold and resold a
number of times before taking final form as segments of huge estates.
Land values, like commodity prices, underwent progressive increase
in the colonial period, and land represented an investment always
available to those with money to spend and always disposable by
those in need of liquid capital. Only rarely did viceroys or other
land-granting authorities issue large tracts in the original instance.
The title deeds of most haciendas were bulky files of records covering numerous small properties. Their legal status was often of great
complexity, and the royal government periodically provided for
legalization (*composición*) of defective titles through payment of
fees—a procedure that encouraged additional usurpation of Indian
lands and brought additional revenue to the crown.[22]

1606," *Hispanic American Historical Review*, XXIX (1949), 349–369; Lesley
Byrd Simpson, *Studies in the Administration of the Indians in New Spain*, II,
The Civil Congregation (Berkeley, 1934). *Congregación* procedures are related
in detail for the sample community of San Pedro Yolox in Howard F. Cline,
"Civil Congregation of the Western Chinantec, New Spain, 1599–1603," *The
Americas*, XII (1955–56), 115–137. All these relate to Mexico, which has been
studied in this respect much more thoroughly than Peru. For a statement on
Indian resettlement in Peru, see Rowe, "Incas under Spanish Colonial Institu-
tions," p. 156.

[22] Fabián de Fonseca and Carlos de Urrutia, *Historia general de real hacienda*
(6 vols., Mexico, 1845–53), IV, 399 ff.; Wistano Luis Orozco, *Legislación y
jurisprudencia sobre terrenos baldíos* (2 vols., Mexico, 1895), I, 46 ff.; Enrique
Torres Saldamando "Reparto y composición de tierras en el Perú," *Revista
peruana*, III (1879), 28–34.

The crown of course never openly advocated Spanish land seizures from Indians. The laws were explicit that haciendas should be located at a distance from Indian communities and that all grants should be "without injury" (*sin perjuicio*) to Indian livelihood.[23] But no such rules could be consistently enforced. Other laws, laws of *congregación,* of *denuncia,* and of *composición,* uniformly militated against them. Colonial lawyers were adept at exploiting legislation in their clients' favor and interest. It became physically impossible to separate haciendas from Indian towns. Haciendas employed the inhabitants of Indian towns as *peones* and controlled all their activities. The wealthiest and most powerful persons in the colony—viceroys, high-ranking officials, prosperous merchants, ecclesiastics—became *hacendados.* The process was irrevocable. Laws of entail assured the perpetuation of properties in Spanish hands. Very little land ever reverted to Indian control.

Haciendas repeatedly incorporated and absorbed native towns, and hacienda society emerged in the familiar form as a stratification of white owners and native laborers. The *peones* formed the proletariat of every hacienda. The *hacendado* was its absolute master, euphemized in the term *patrón.* The *hacendado's* house was a magnificent dwelling, the residence of his large family of relatives and the scene of banquets and elaborate receptions. To the *peones* of the hacienda the *patrón* was an apotheosis of authority, immediate in a way that the viceroy and king never were. His ostentatious possessions—his horses and carriages, his elaborate attire, his silver and finery—were visible symbols of wealth. Disobedience to his will brought severe and exemplary punishment. A prudent servility was essential if the hacienda laborer were to adjust peacefully to his condition, and internal revolution was extremely rare in hacienda society. Thus the hacienda fitted the universal character of Spanish America.[24]

Unlike conquest and encomienda, the hacienda did not, in the

---

[23] Eusebio Bentura Beleña, *Recopilación sumaria de todos los autos acordados de la real audiencia y sala del crimen de esta Nueva España, y providencias de su superior gobierno* (2 vols., Mexico, 1787), I (5th pagination), 207 ff.; Mariano Galván Rivera, *Ordenanzas de tierras y aguas ó sea formulario geométrico-judicial* (Paris, 1868), pp. 192 ff.

[24] Eric Wolf, *Sons of the Shaking Earth* (Chicago, 1959), pp. 204 ff.

colonial period, receive criticism based on humanitarian sympathy for its victims. Spanish self-criticism, and the tradition of the Black Legend outside Spain, concentrated on the earlier institutions even while the hacienda developed and prospered. To Spaniards hacienda was a natural, precedented institution. The political power of land-holding noble families in Castile had been broken by Ferdinand and Isabella, but the great landholdings themselves persisted. It remained for the twentieth century to identify and condemn the social inequalities of hacienda life, the forms of which were more subtle and far less overt than those of conquest and encomienda. The nature of hacienda society was such that its oligarchical features were often compromised or disguised, and it has accordingly been the subject of romantic interpretation, as encomienda never has.

From the point of view of its aristocratic proprietor, one can easily understand how hacienda society might be romanticized. But even from the point of view of the Indian worker, it could be argued that the hacienda brought benefits otherwise unobtainable in colonial society. The worker owed a financial debt to the hacienda, in the system of peonage. But this very indebtedness made him an object of economic importance to the *hacendado* and one that had to be cultivated if the *hacendado* were not to lose him through truancy. Thus haciendas ordinarily provided lands (lands, to be sure, that had been taken from Indians) on which *peones* could live and raise crops. They provided local stores at which essential commodities could be obtained, and chapels for the satisfaction of spiritual needs. The laborers formed a community and were provided with a security that they could not have had outside the hacienda. All such benefits were of course limited, and they appear meliorative only in comparison with the practical alternatives. Exploitative and cruel the hacienda certainly was. But conquest, encomienda, and *repartimiento* were far more so, and no other comparable institution offered Indians so much.[25]

The various devices that held Indians to a servile condition in hacienda and throughout the colony were the outcome of many

[25] "It is . . . entirely conceivable that debt peonage meant an improvement in the life of many of the laborers." Borah, *New Spain's Century of Depression*, p. 42.

causes. Reduction by conquest, Spanish disinclination to work, the sense of white superiority, heavy labor needs in a new colonial environment, and the precedent that Indians had served their own Indian rulers all contributed to this end. But within this general situation of Spanish mastery and native subordination, the sequence and timing require special explanation. A basic fact is that whites increased while Indians decreased in numbers. The succession of institutions may be seen broadly as sequential responses to numerical population change. The first solution, encomienda, has most commonly been studied as a derivative of feudalism, which it was. But in relation to the demographic pattern, encomienda appears most appropriate to the earliest conditions, when whites were few and natives numerous. After the material spoils of conquest the principal resource of the colony was its prodigious man power, and encomienda governed the allocation of this resource to those colonists who were deemed deserving. Through it the essential tasks of the early colony were accomplished and a select class of colonists became wealthy.

Repartimiento, after encomienda, represents a more controlled and meticulous exploitation of the Indian population, and the change may be understood as a response to a declining labor force. When a desired commodity is in short supply, a strong state will ration it, and this is what occurred with colonial labor. The matter is, of course, relative. The Indians of the late sixteenth century can be called a commodity in short supply only in contrast to the much larger numbers of the earlier period. We are obviously not dealing here with a situation of labor austerity comparable to Jamestown or Massachusetts Bay, where the colonists themselves were the workers and where no sedentary native population was available for reduction to a proletariat rank. But *repartimiento* provided a method for utilizing a reduced laboring population more economically, and for distributing it among a larger number of white employers.

With debt labor there developed the third stage and one consistent with a still more depleted native population. The labor force eventually became so small, or so relatively small, that the state could no longer ration it. By the time that *repartimiento* was legally limited in the seventeenth century, peonage was already established.

Peonage, which is generally regarded as the classic Spanish-American labor device, had no early history in the immediate aftermath of the conquests because then, with the abundant labor supply, Spaniards did not need to hold any individuals by debt. But a century later the colony consisted of many more white employers and many fewer laborers, and peonage was an employer's way of holding his workers and ensuring that no other employer could utilize them.

With this the series of institutions ends, for peonage continued to the twentieth century. The slowly expanding labor supply of the late seventeenth and early eighteenth centuries was incorporated within the peonage system. By the late eighteenth century, with progressive increase, there was much less need for peonage, as is indicated by the numbers of unemployed. But peonage was an entrenched technique with a life and strength of its own, and it remained. Labor organizations were far more sensitive to population loss than to population gain, as one would expect in a labor economy so thoroughly dominated by the employers.

An analogous history is found with respect to land. If peonage is the classic employment system of Spanish America, the hacienda is surely the classic land system. Both were relatively late developments, not to be found before the late sixteenth century. As Indian depopulation was reflected in a series of labor controls pointing toward peonage, so was it reflected in the gradual process through which hacienda came into being. Depopulation meant a change in native land occupation. An area of a hundred Indians per square mile became an area of twenty-five or ten or five Indians per square mile. In a free society, or one at liberty to be shaped by its environment, such a change might have meant an abandonment of marginal land and a reconcentration of surviving peoples in the most productive regions. But this occurred only rarely in Spanish America, for the Indian society was not free. It was at the mercy of whites, and the result of depopulation was the Spanish pre-emption of the land, and especially of the most productive land. In view of the chronology, it is quite proper that *congregación* and *denuncia* should have been most common in the seventeenth century, when the population was at its lowest ebb. These were less significant in the eighteenth century, for by then Indian population was again increasing, and the available land had already been taken by Spaniards. The eighteenth and nineteenth centuries were the period par excellence of strife between Spaniards and Indians over property. Spaniards were now accustomed to seizures and determined to hold what they had. But Indians now needed more land, for there were more Indians to occupy it and there was less land for them to occupy. As with labor, the sequence of controls culminated in a fixed form. There was no successor to hacienda until the incipient land reform movements of the twentieth century.

In the colonial period, Indian society was brought to the depressed position it holds today. With few exceptions Indians were held to a subsistence level and denied opportunities for escape. The process in Spanish America involved more intimate kinds of white-Indian contact than did the otherwise similar processes in the colonies of the English, French, and Dutch, and it provides for this reason a more complex example of the destruction of a native society. Because Spaniards were more organized and legalistic than other imperial peoples, the white-Indian relations of Spanish America emerge as the most thoroughly documented of American history. Indeed, Spanish America furnishes to an exceptional degree an example of a lower class that can be studied. The fact that advocates of the Black Legend have continued to rely on Las Casas thus provides further evidence, if further evidence is needed, of the inadequacy of the Black Legend.[26]

[26] The last ten or so paragraphs depend essentially on the researches of Simpson, Cook, and Borah demonstrating the population change and, especially in the case of Borah's *New Spain's Century of Depression,* deriving the socioeconomic consequences and implications. There are as yet no comparable researches for the viceroyalty of Peru.

CHAPTER 8

Imperial Readjustments

THE successive episodes of colonial Spanish-American history are related at all points to processes of "rise" and "decline" in the parent country. Rise began with the monarchical centralization of Ferdinand and Isabella and continued through the voyages of exploration and the establishment of colonies. Decline was chronologically less compact. It first manifested itself conspicuously during the reign of Philip II, and it characterized the reigns of all the later Hapsburgs. If the conventional historical periodizations be accepted, most of Spanish American colonial history must be assigned to this period of "decline."

But it is probable that the economic rhythms of the colony and those of Spain should not be equated precisely. Decline in the colony appeared in particular colonial ways and its consequences were less pronounced than in Spain. Here "cultural lag" operated to the colonial advantage. Then too the colony continued to produce wealth; the white population continued to grow; settlement expanded; and the New World in contrast to the Old was still regarded as a land of superior opportunity. With only a slight extension of these thoughts, one might assert that America was a buoyant and stabilizing factor operating to slow the rate of Spanish decline.[1]

[1] A fundamental study of the economy and economic literature of Spanish decline is Jaime Carrera Pujal, *Historia de la economía española* (5 vols., Barcelona, 1943–47). Earl J. Hamilton, "The Decline of Spain," *Economic History Review*, VIII (1937–38), 168–179, provides a succinct economic interpretation. In more recent expressions of the problem, the complexities of the

Spanish prestige earned by the victory of Lepanto (1571), which broke Turkish naval power in the Mediterranean, was offset by unsuccessful wars in the Low Countries and against England. Crop failures, severe plagues, and other internal disasters marked the last years of the sixteenth century. Under Philip III (1598–1621) and Philip IV (1621–65), Spain continued in a state of national bankruptcy. Despite some military victories the monarchy was unable to profit from the Thirty Years' War. Spanish land armies suffered unprecedented defeat in the battle of Rocroi (1643). Decline that had tended at first to manifest itself in economic weaknesses in Castile spread to other areas. Catalonia was lost for a time. The dynastic connection with Portugal (1580–1640) proved unenforceable. The nadir of Hapsburg rule in Spain was reached under Charles II, called El Hechizado, the Bewitched. So intertwined was the Hapsburg genealogy that all four of his paternal great-grandfathers and three of his four maternal great-grandparents were direct descendants of Juana la Loca. Because he had no natural heir, the question of dynastic succession emerged as the dominant political issue at the end of the seventeenth century. The problem was the more acute, for by this time Spanish unemployment had increased, Spanish agricultural and industrial economies had deteriorated, and Spanish government had become progressively more insolvent.

With respect to the overseas world, one important series of events serves as a measure of imperial change prior to the eighteenth century. This was the progressive failure of the concept of a closed Iberian area. When Spain and Portugal signed the agreement of Tordesillas in 1494, no other European nation had been capable of rendering more than formal protest against it. European nations, not at first daring to interfere in regions where Hispanic peoples were obviously in control, had confined their exploits to the margins of the New World, the Newfoundland fishing banks and the un-

---

various phenomena of "decline" have received emphasis. Thus J. H. Elliott, *Imperial Spain, 1469–1716* (London, 1963), pp. 172 ff., identifies the Castilian economic crises and the chain of reactions to them in the seventeenth century, and Woodrow Borah, *New Spain's Century of Depression* (Berkeley and Los Angeles, 1951), p. 29, connects the depression in Spain with Indian depopulation in America.

protected logging coasts of Brazil. In these areas English and French mariners found exploitable products and trafficked in them from an early date. But very quickly America became the scene of direct anti-Hispanic attacks. Forays were made on both sea and land, against the treasure fleets and against seaports. The apogee of French incursion occurred in the mid-sixteenth century, when French pirates made assaults in the Caribbean and held Havana for ransom, and when French Huguenots sought to establish colonies in the Florida-Carolina region. The French incursions declined after the 1560's, partly because the French suffered defeat in conflict with Spaniards, partly because internal French wars limited further enterprises overseas.

The English, who assumed the dominant role in anti-Spanish activity as the French capacity for it was reduced, undertook at first to exploit the economic weaknesses of Spain's overseas system. Both the national and the international situations favored such a course. The period was one of commercial expansion in England. It was a time when Spanish mercantilist policy sought to maintain monopolistic controls and high prices in Spanish America. Hence Spanish colonists were in need of low-cost goods, unobtainable through legitimate transactions with peninsular merchants. When John Hawkins sailed to Hispaniola in 1562–63 with a cargo of African slaves, local officials authorized their sale and Hawkins was able to return to England with a valuable profit. He obeyed the regulations to which Spanish merchant vessels would have been subject in similar circumstances and conducted his negotiations in peace and order.[2] But English intrusion rapidly passed from this peaceful, commercial (though of course from the Spanish point of view illegal) phase to one of outright hostility.

The English naval commander most feared by Spain and Spanish America in the late sixteenth century was Francis Drake. Schooled under John Hawkins and already celebrated for his exploits in Spanish-American waters, Drake was commissioned as a privateer by Queen Elizabeth in 1570 and spent the next twenty-five years

[2] James A. Williamson, *Sir John Hawkins, the Time and the Man* (Oxford, 1927); Rayner Unwin, *The Defeat of John Hawkins: A Biography of His Third Slaving Voyage* (London, 1960).

leading attacks against Spain and establishing English control of the seas. In his voyage of 1572–73, Drake plundered the Panamanian port of Nombre de Dios and captured Spanish treasure on its way from Peru for embarkation to Spain. Later in the 1570's he moved north along the Pacific coast of South America, attacking Spanish coastal cities, seizing Spanish ships, and inflicting all possible damage before turning west across the Pacific and circumnavigating the globe. Again in the 1580's Drake attacked the American coastal cities of Cartagena, St. Augustine, and Santo Domingo. He was a principal figure in the defeat of the Spanish Armada in 1588, and died, appropriately, on shipboard in Panamanian waters in 1596. His achievement demonstrated the weaknesses of Spanish-American defenses and the ready opportunities for depredation. Honored in England and dreaded in the American coastal cities, Drake epitomized the "Elizabethan Age" in Spanish-English relations.[3] Moreover, his example was followed by a host of imitators.

By the early seventeenth century, a little more than a hundred years after the Treaty of Tordesillas, all of the national rivals of Spain were sending colonists to America for settlement. The Virginia Company of London established the first permanent English colony in America at Jamestown in 1607. Champlain founded Quebec in 1608 for France. Agents of the new Dutch West India Company purchased Manhattan Island from local Algonquian peoples in the 1620's. These colonies were on the northern mainland in regions where Spanish interests no longer lay. But the powers intruded also in South America and the Caribbean islands. In the Caribbean the chief English interest was Barbados, first settled in the 1620's and an important slave center and plantation colony later in the century. No other plantation in America realized so well the prevailing English policies of mercantilism. The colonies of Martinique and Guadeloupe in the Lesser Antilles, and Haiti or Saint Domingue, the western part of Hispaniola, played a similar role for France.[4] French and English together settled the island of St. Christopher (Kitts) and the two nations made additional less

---

[3] Julian S. Corbett, *Drake and the Tudor Navy* (2 vols., London, 1898).
[4] Spain recognized the French possession of Haiti, a former Spanish territory, in the Treaty of Ryswick in 1697.

important settlements on the other West Indian islands. A main function of these French and English colonies was in the provision of tobacco and sugar for European markets. But they served also as anti-Spanish bases, and they appeared as direct intrusions into areas close to the Spanish-American lands.[5]

Dutch activity in the West Indies, in its spirit of trade rivalry and naval warfare, paralleled the Dutch operation against the Portuguese in the Far East. To the Dutch West India Company, organized after the model of the Dutch East India Company for the Orient, should be attributed the Dutch attack on and occupation of northeast Brazil between 1624 and 1654, as well as the most successful anti-Spanish depredations in the Caribbean during the second quarter of the seventeenth century. In a major coup, a company fleet intercepted the entire Veracruz treasure convoy of 1628, forcing it into the Matanzas River in Cuba and capturing its rich cargo. Innumerable raids on shipping and on coastal towns yielded smaller but impressive booties. The Dutch took the island of Curaçao in 1634 and employed it as an economic base and slave center and strategic stronghold.

In South America the seventeenth century witnessed the first major clashes between Spanish and Portuguese. The settlers of Brazil, now no longer confining themselves to the coastal regions, pushed westward in search of wealth and Indian slaves and converts. The leaders of the movement were the frontiersmen of São Paulo, the southern district between Rio de Janeiro to the east and the Treaty of Tordesillas line to the west. These were the Paulistas or *bandeirantes* famous as the pioneers of Brazilian history. During the sixty years of royal union after 1580, the Tordesillas division seemed irrelevant and the Paulistas moved inland westward and southwestward toward Paraguay and the Plata. Commercial relations were established with Buenos Aires and Asunción and Peru, and Spaniards and Portuguese colonists came into conflict. After 1640 the Brazilians did not withdraw.

The later seventeenth century was a period of constant imperial

---

[5] Arthur Percival Newton, *The European Nations in the West Indies, 1493–1688* (London, 1933), pp. 131 ff.; John H. Parry and P. M. Sherlock, *A Short History of the West Indies* (London, 1957), pp. 63–93.

clashes in America. England seized Jamaica from Spain in 1655 in an aggressive Puritan assault. Both France and England made use of the international buccaneers of the West Indies whenever policy and opportunity coincided. The coastal cities were repeatedly sacked, and commercial intrusions were continuous. Jamaica, which for a time was governed by Sir Henry Morgan, the foremost of the seventeenth-century English pirates, became a center of the English contraband trade. Colonial officials of all nations joined in the illegal operations and profited from them.[6]

Thus in all ways at the beginning of the eighteenth century, the imperial tasks facing Spain were of a radically different order from those at the beginning of the sixteenth century. In the administration of the Indies, problems of colonial foundation and Christian conversion had yielded to problems of fiscal weakness, bureaucratic maintenance, and the repair of international positions. The adjustments would necessarily be made in the absence of that vast monarchical self-assurance through which the decisions of the earlier period had been reached. The colonial empire was now a far more cumbersome organism. It could not be manipulated with any ease. The monarchs of the eighteenth century, unlike those of the sixteenth, inherited a labyrinthine imperial system to which individual and group interests were firmly attached, and against which anti-Spanish nations were making threats from many sides.

Spanish economic and political thinkers were well aware of what was taking place and powerless to correct it. They commented at length on a variety of causes: intrusion by foreigners, inadequacy of defenses, concentration on precious metals, neglect of manufacturing, political corruption, primogeniture, monetary disorders, and many other matters. Modern historians can add little to the enumeration of deficiencies that Spaniards themselves suggested, and one reason for this is that the Spanish thinkers were no longer speaking

---

[6] A natural tendency is to suppose that the coastal cities bore the entire burden of piratical siege and that the wealthy Spanish colonists were the ones who suffered. But lower classes and Indian communities likewise felt the assaults, which might be raids penetrating many miles into the interior. See the accounts of the attack on Nicoya in 1687 in León Fernández (ed.), *Colección de documentos para la historia de Costa Rica* (8 vols., San José and Barcelona, 1883–1907), VIII, 468 ff.

in sixteenth-century terms. The change in the intellectual climate of imperial management is fundamental to an understanding of late colonial developments.[7]

Like other peoples of western Europe, Spaniards were attracted by the progressive and "enlightened" values of the eighteenth century, the same values that so affect our own historical interpretations. The principal foreign source of the new Spanish thought was France, and its chief spokesman in Spain was the rationalist Benedictine Benito Jerónimo Feijóo y Montenegro.[8] Enlightened thought brought into being a new sense of efficiency, a scientific attack upon ignorance, and a rational institutional reorganization. Practical applications rather than theoretical justifications characterized the new Spanish objective. A new group of economic and political writers appeared—Jerónimo Uztáriz, José del Campillo y Cosio, and Pedro Rodríguez, Conde de Campomanes—all of whom were critical of traditional imperial regulations and the sluggishness that retarded Spanish administration and economic affairs.[9] In comparison with the sixteenth century, the new mood was distinctly secular. Spain remained a highly religious nation, but in the new international competition the religious sanction was not enough. The eighteenth-century challenge required a systematic resistance to international forces of a type that had hardly existed in the sixteenth century. In rival foreign nations these same new values contributed to capitalism and to a capitalist reshaping of the anti-Spanish Black Legend. To a surprising degree the foremost Spanish thinkers now accepted the new arguments, only accommodating to them a patriotic rather than a propagandist and hostile temper.

In Spanish imperial administration the "Bourbon century" be-

[7] Hamilton, "Decline of Spain"; Robert Jones Shafer, *The Economic Societies in the Spanish World (1763–1821)* (Syracuse, 1958), pp. 5–6. An indispensable treatment of the Spanish Enlightenment is Richard Herr, *The Eighteenth-Century Revolution in Spain* (Princeton, 1958).

[8] Gaspard Delpy, *L'Espagne et l'esprit européen; l'oeuvre de Feijóo (1725–1760)* (Paris, 1936).

[9] Ricardo Krebs Wilckens, *El pensamiento histórico, político y económico del conde de Campomanes* (Santiago de Chile, 1960); José Muñoz Pérez, "La idea de América en Campomanes," *Anuario de estudios americanos,* X (1953), 209–264; Jean Sarrailh, *L'Espagne éclairée de la seconde moitié du XVIII⁰ siècle* (Paris, 1954); Luis Sánchez Agesta, *El pensamiento político del despotismo ilustrado* (Madrid, 1953); Shafer, *Economic Societies,* pp. 8 ff.

ginning in 1700 with the reign of Philip V has been commonly interpreted as a century of reform, and it is quite true that the declining Spanish economy of the seventeenth century was in some ways reversed under the Bourbons in the eighteenth. In a mercantilistic imperialism, where economic relations between the colony and the parent country were accorded a primary position, the changes necessarily affected the circumstances of Spanish America as well. The eighteenth century assumes a distinct character in Spanish-American history. Ultimately it brought administrative readjustment, increased social change, a degree of economic recovery, and the emergence of a colonial culture prepared to take advantage of an opportunity to rebel.

Philip V (1700–46) was delayed in accomplishing his program of reconstruction by the wars that attended his accession to the throne. French intrusions in the Spanish colonial trade were extensive during the War of the Spanish Succession (1701–13), and at the Treaty of Utrecht (1713) Spain was compelled to permit England the *asiento* privileges in slave trade. By the year 1720, Philip had lost Gibraltar, the Low Countries, and the Italian possessions, and had admitted defeat in his claim to the French monarchy. Thus the first two decades of his rule were consumed in costly and bootless warfare. But during these wars Philip and his advisers were able to centralize monarchical control over Aragón, Catalonia, and Valencia, and to reorganize some of the financial and military resources of the nation for the reinforcement of royal authority. The creation of "intendancies" in 1718 meant that for an experimental period district administration in Spain would be modeled upon the centralized French system developed by Richelieu and Colbert.

In colonial administration similar centralizing policies under Philip V and his successor Ferdinand VI (1746–59) resulted in the creation of a Ministry of the Marine and the Indies, which usurped some of the most important functions of the Council of the Indies. The Council after 1717 was to confine its activities mainly to judicial matters. The ministry concept was distinctly Bourbon and French, and it contrasted with the conciliar concept of the Spanish Hapsburgs. The ministry became a royal agency for the issuance of orders relating to finance, commerce, war, and other crucial matters of state. At the same time the Casa de Contratación, transferred to Cadiz in 1717–18, came also to be limited in its functions. A number of the Casa's duties were now placed under the control of a maritime intendant general and other royal officers. In the Indies some new jurisdictional areas were created, especially the viceroyalty of New Granada (1717) in northern South America.[10] In the system of commercial controls, import duties were decreased and at some points eliminated altogether. New monopolistic companies were created: the Caracas, or Guipúzcoa, Company for trade, principally in gold, silver, and cacao, between Guipúzcoa and Caracas; the Havana Company for Spanish-Cuban trade; the Santo Domingo, or Catalonia, Company for the Hispaniola trade; the Honduras Company; and several others.[11] Modifications appeared in the inefficient *flota* system, which was temporarily abandoned in 1740 only to be restored later under the strenuous demands of the Cadiz merchants.

These innovations in national and colonial policy were expanded under Charles III (1759–88), the most energetic of the eighteenth-century Bourbon monarchs of Spain. Charles III and his exceptionally able ministers developed a broadly conceived program of imperial readjustment. The authority of the Council of the Indies was reduced still further. The Ministry of Marine and the Indies was divided between two ministers. A new Junta de Estado was created to coordinate ministerial programs. Territorial jurisdictions in South America were again reconstructed, now by the creation of a fourth viceroyalty, La Plata (1776), including roughly what are now Argentina, Uruguay, Paraguay, and Bolivia (Upper Peru).

The most far-reaching of the readjustments effected under Charles III were those relating to commercial connections between Spain and the colonies. The crown's advisers identified a series of accumulated weaknesses, which it became the task of the new monarchical government to correct: the monopoly of Cadiz, which

---

[10] This was soon abolished, but it was re-established in 1739.
[11] The most thorough monographic study is Roland D. Hussey, *The Caracas Company, 1728–1784: A Study in the History of Spanish Monopolistic Trade* (Cambridge, Mass., 1934).

restricted the trade of other ports; the system of carrying by convoys, which reduced the number of operating vessels and raised costs through delays and excessive freight rates; the *tonelada,* or tonnage duty, an export tax on liquors, which raised the American price of Spanish wine and caused the domestic industry to suffer from American competition; the *palmeo,* a duty by volume, which favored goods of quality and small size; the scarcity of Negro slaves in America, which reduced the supplies of American agricultural and other products for importation into Spain; the illegal production of cloth and liquors in America, which prejudiced Spanish products otherwise exportable to the colonies and slowed the flow of silver to the parent country; the high Spanish import duty on colonial products; and the contraband trade, which was regarded as the consequence of the long restrictive policy as well as of the weakness of the protective safeguards.

It would of course be incorrect to state that Charles III was able to resolve all the colonial economic problems or even to effect improvements in all the critical areas designated. Yet the reforms accomplished during his reign were considerable. The opening of American commerce to Spanish merchants other than those in the Cadiz monopoly was undertaken in 1765, when nine Spanish ports were permitted to trade with the cities of the Caribbean islands. In the 1770's and 1780's other Spanish and colonial ports were added to the list, until in 1789 all American colonies were opened to Spanish trade. Meanwhile ad valorem duties of 6 or 7 per cent were introduced, and the regulations relating to ships were reduced or in some instances abolished. Intercolonial trade no longer suffered so heavily from the former restrictions after the 1770's, when New Spain, Guatemala, New Granada, Peru, and La Plata were permitted to engage in reciprocal commerce. Spanish manufacture was encouraged by duty exemptions on textiles, glassware, and other products for the American market, and a variety of American goods, including sugar, cacao, coffee, and leather, were permitted to enter Spain more cheaply.[12]

---

[12] Additional elements in the disruption of commercial controls are summarized by Sergio Villalobos R., "El comercio extranjero a fines de la dominación española," *Journal of Inter-American Studies,* IV (1962), 517–544.

In the political sphere the principal Bourbon reform was the transfer of the intendancy system to the American colonies. This was designed to centralize the colonial administration still further under the crown, to eliminate abuses of officeholding, and to increase the royal revenue. A few years after its formal introduction in Spain in 1718, the intendancy had been abolished, but it was re-created by Ferdinand VI in 1749 and thoroughly implanted in the 1750's and after. Proposals for American intendants were made as early as the 1740's by Campillo and others.[13] The proposals became urgent with the mounting evidence of corruption in local colonial officeholding. About 1750 Jorge Juan and Antonio de Ulloa had graphically described the misdeeds of *corregidores* and others in the celebrated *Noticias secretas de América*. Similar evidence was provided by José de Gálvez for New Spain in the 1760's. An immediate and persuasive circumstance arose also out of the British capture of Havana during the Seven Years' War. The British regime lasted less than a year (Cuba was restored to Spain in the Peace of Paris of 1763), but the brief interval provided an impressive lesson for Spanish administrators. For Havana the few months of British rule brought a prosperity and a volume of traffic that the city had never before experienced. On the restoration of Spanish control, and with a dispatch and efficiency that were themselves unusual in Spanish imperial administration, the intendancy system was extended to Cuba in 1764. This was the first step in a process that by 1790 resulted in intendancies in practically every part of Spanish America.[14]

The colonial intendant was to be a Spanish-born officer in administrative charge of an area known as an intendancy. The latter was to be a jurisdictional region of some size (La Plata was divided

[13] Miguel Artola, "Campillo y las reformas de Carlos III," *Revista de Indias,* XII (1952), 699–705.

[14] William Whatley Pierson, Jr., "Institutional History of the *Intendencia,*" *The James Sprunt Historical Studies,* XIX, No. 2 (1927), 81 ff.; Alain Vieillard-Baron, "L'intendant américain et l'intendant francais: Essai comparatif," *Revista de Indias,* XI (1951), 237–250. On the origin and gradual implementation of the intendancy system, see John Lynch, *Spanish Colonial Administration, 1782–1810: The Intendancy System in the Viceroyalty of the Río de la Plata* (London, 1958), pp. 46–61. For the intendancy in general, see Lillian Estelle Fisher, *The Intendant System in Spanish America* (Berkeley, 1929), and Luis Navarro García, *Intendencias en Indias* (Seville 1959).

into eight, New Spain into twelve), incorporating older and smaller areas, and subdivided into *partidos* governed by *subdelegados*. Intendants and *subdelegados* were to absorb the functions of the local *gobernadores, corregidores,* and *alcaldes mayores,* officers whose positions were now to be abolished. Administrative and especially fiscal efficiency was to be the intendants' chief objective. Their instructions were emphatic on matters of economic concern: the encouragement of industry and agriculture, the promotion of more prosperous trade, and the collection of royal revenue, over which they were to assume full charge.[15]

Intendants in the late colonial period nominally had control within their jurisdictions over four departments of government: administration, finance, justice, and war. In most ways, like other political officials, they were subordinate to the viceroy and *audiencia* within whose areas their jurisdictions fell. But the complex intendancy ordinances allowed for some evasion of traditional viceregal authority. In financial matters a degree of independence from viceregal control was provided for, and intendants could communicate on important subjects directly with the Ministry of the Indies in Spain. Intendants received salaries of four to six thousand pesos per year, in contrast to the three to five hundred pesos per year that had been received by the average *corregidor*—but in contrast also to the sixty thousand pesos that comprised the annual salary of the viceroy of New Spain.

The real effects of the Bourbon legislative enactments are exceptionally difficult to measure. While on the one hand the Bourbons, and especially Charles III, eliminated many of the restrictions of the Hapsburg centuries and allowed a freer economic play, on the other they introduced some tighter political controls and neglected the Christian-humanitarian ideal of the sixteenth century. Theirs was a compromise legislation, which sought at many points to make the

[15] The intendancy instructions for Havana (1764) stated: "The Intendant shall have original jurisdiction over all funds, fiscal services, and taxes of whatever kind or form that may pertain to my royal treasury, with all that is incident, dependent, and annexed to it, whether it is controlled by government administration, or is leased, or is collected in whatever other way." Pierson, "Institutional History of the *Intendencia,*" p. 113. A translation of the intendancy ordinance for New Spain, and a comparison between this and the ordinance for Buenos Aires, will be found in Fisher, *Intendant System,* pp. 97–344.

best eighteenth-century sense of outmoded colonial situations.[16] They did not, of course, admit freedom of trade in a nonmercantilist way. The incipient prosperity was exploited as well as fostered by the monarchy. The American markets were legally opened to non-Spanish nations only when it was diplomatically or practically impossible to exclude them. Severe taxation, especially in the form of the *alcabala,* continued to restrict purchase and sale. Many minor economic tributes were never eradicated. In numerous other ways innovation implied only the addition of a new institution to the structure of the old, without further adjustment and with continued jurisdictional conflict. Spain was still unable to supply the market needs of her American colonies. And the great inequalities in American (and Spanish) society, wealth, and land possession remained at the end of Charles' reign, untouched by the "reform" legislation.

Expectedly, the influence of the new policies differed from area to area. Buenos Aires had been neglected prior to the eighteenth century, both as a commercial port and as a location of power within the Platine system. Now the creation of the Platine viceroyalty and the liberation of trade established the conditions for the area's first period of prosperity. Population and commerce spurted in the 1780's and 1790's. Significantly, the city's economic mainstay remained cattle. The grasslands that were later to be one of the great wheat-producing areas of the world were still unoccupied. Buenos Aires prospered in the late eighteenth century even while it continued to import wheat.

Other towns found the late colonial period less propitious. In the New Granada–isthmian region, Cartagena, Portobello, and Panama had developed under the traditional mercantilist policies of the earlier period, which favored them above would-be competitors. Cartagena was a terminus for the *flota* shipments, dominating the network of exchange in the Magdalena Valley and its surroundings. The adjacent coastal lowland was a plantation region and all three cities were markets and slave centers for the coastal strip. But in the eighteenth century, *flotas* were no longer so important. The regional trade deteriorated. The exposed coastal area was repeatedly attacked

---

[16] On this point see Herbert Ingram Priestley, *José de Gálvez, Visitor-General of New Spain (1765–1771)* (Berkeley, 1916), pp. 388 ff.

by foreign powers. The Portobello Fair suffered as contraband and "free trade" enriched other cities. Cartagena underwent a new prosperity in the late eighteenth century, partly under the stimulus of its *consulado,* but Portobello and Panama never recovered from the liberalization that removed other cities from dependence on them.

Specifically, with respect to the intendancy, it may be said that though the effects differed from place to place, the jurisdictional change did not result in any conspicuous reformation in the political society of the late colony. The intendancy innovation was most successful where the long traditions of viceregal control were not entrenched, as in Buenos Aires. In central New Spain and other established areas the intendancy had much less scope. Though it was designed to replace the *corregimiento* system, in reality a number of former *corregidores* were appointed as intendants, and many others were appointed as *subdelegados.* It is unlikely that the intendancies introduced any substantial modifications in Indian society, or in the way that Indian society was treated by white society. Thus one of the key objectives of the original Spanish policies in the sixteenth century remained untouched. Charges against the *subdelegados* in the 1780's and 1790's strikingly resemble the earlier accusations against the *corregidores.* Conflicts in jurisdiction between intendants and viceroys were common in late colonial times. In Paraguay, where the intendancy was established in 1783, about fifteen years after the Jesuit expulsion, the innovation resulted in further administrative complication and did nothing to solve the problem of the Guaraní.[17] But against these various defects one could say, as one could say of all the Bourbon reforms, that the allotted time was insufficient to provide a real test. Within a few decades of the establishment of the intendancies the revolutions broke out and independence was declared.

Between the theory and the practice of colonial administration many differences remained. Smuggling was still a principal obstacle to a profitable mercantilist commerce in the eighteenth century, as it had been in the seventeenth. The *asiento* privilege in the supply of slaves, granted to England in 1713, was more and more boldly abused thereafter. One English shipload of general merchandise was

---

[17] Lynch, *Spanish Colonial Administration,* pp. 190–191.

allowed each year at the Portobello Fair, but in the course of time the number of ships multiplied far beyond the single privileged vessel.[18] The Spanish monarchy possessed no adequate means of prevention or retaliation. The British established offices and warehouses at Veracruz, Cartagena, and Portobello ostensibly for the regulation of slave imports, but these also expanded their activities until British merchants were in control of many aspects of Hispanic-American economy. The abolition of the *asiento* failed to halt the intrusions. Smuggling was engaged in by the allies as well as by the enemies of Spain, and French, Dutch, Portuguese, and Anglo-Americans all developed commercial relations in Spanish America. Hundreds of British and French merchants were established in Cadiz and other Spanish centers, where illegal or semilegal trade was conducted on a large scale. Spaniards and Spanish colonists themselves participated in it.[19]

The eighteenth-century intrusion of rival powers was not limited to commercial areas. By this time those earlier military attacks by rival European nations had developed into major controversies. In South America, Portuguese and Spanish settlers disputed over lands claimed by both, and they engaged in sharp hostilities at times when the two nations were at war. Colônia, across the Plata River from Buenos Aires, was a focal point of dispute by Argentines after its foundation by Brazilians in 1680 and served as a center of contraband incursion by Portuguese and British as well. The Portuguese threat was responsible for the Spanish foundation of Montevideo (1726), which became a strategic stronghold for the Uruguay region. Colônia and Uruguay were finally secured for Spain during the warfare of the 1770's. The British made forays on the Pacific coast in the eighteenth century as Francis Drake had done in the sixteenth, and the British were active also in the Caribbean, capturing Portobello in 1739 and laying siege to Cartagena in 1741.

The British emerged everywhere in the late eighteenth century

---

[18] See the account of the overladen ship in Jorge Juan and Antonio de Ulloa, *A Voyage to South America,* John Adams, trans.; Irving A. Leonard, ed. (New York, 1964), p. 57.

[19] Jacques Houdaille, "Les Français et les afrancesados en Amérique centrale, 1700–1810," *Revista de historia de América,* No. 44 (1957), pp. 305–330. Parry and Sherlock, *Short History of the West Indies,* pp. 95 ff.

as the chief enemy and most immediate danger. In 1761, near the end of the Seven Years' War, Charles III declared war on Britain, believing that through victory he might control and terminate the British intrusion. But the result was defeat, not victory, and the British intrusions increased. Particularly with the British, but with other nations as well, commercial and military concerns were clearly related. The British spoke openly of the possibility of seizing the Spanish colonies by force, in the belief that conquest would be justified by the expansion of British trade.[20] Spain in turn placed a new emphasis on protection and defensive fortifications in America. Unquestionably it was the British commercial intrusions into Argentina that reversed Spain's traditional policy of neglect toward Buenos Aires in the eighteenth century and raised the late colonial questions of South Atlantic defense, including the defense of the Falkland Islands.[21]

All the new complexities in the imperial policies of Spain and in international rivalries were balanced by new complexities in internal colonial life. Here the available eighteenth-century figures point unmistakably to growth, in population, in economic production, in volume of trade, and in other ways. But growth was attended also by vital qualitative changes in colonial conditions. In reversing the tendencies of the seventeenth century, the eighteenth-century colonies did not in any sense revert to sixteenth-century types. The essential simplicity of sixteenth-century colonization was irrecoverable. "Growth" meant proliferation and complication. Issues were no longer so clearly seen. Corruption continued everywhere and the royal program for simplification and reform was never completely accomplished.

[20] Sir James Gray, British minister to Spain, was instructed in 1767 to furnish precise information on Spanish-American strengths and weaknesses, vulnerable points, and "the nature and degree of the dependence of those provinces on Old Spain." Allan Christelow, "Great Britain and the Trades from Cadiz and Lisbon to Spanish America and Brazil, 1759–1783," *Hispanic American Historical Review*, XXVII (1947), 2–29. Programs for British seizure of Spanish America were familiar from earlier hostilities of the eighteenth century. See Richard Pares, *War and Trade in the West Indies, 1739–1763* (London, 1963), pp. 65 ff.

[21] Julius Goebel, Jr., *The Struggle for the Falkland Islands: A Study in Legal and Diplomatic History* (New Haven, 1927), pp. 174 ff.

In intellectual life the striking development of the eighteenth century was the colony's response to enlightened European thought, notably in philosophy and science. Historians in the twentieth century have abandoned the idea of an immediate connection between European revolutionary doctrine and the Spanish-American wars for independence in favor of a more subtle Enlightenment influence.[22] Spanish Americans did read Montesquieu and Voltaire and Rousseau, but they also read Descartes and Newton, and their response to the Enlightenment involved a gradual intellectual reorientation rather than a sudden inclination toward subversion and liberty. What developed in the intellectual circles of eighteenth-century Spanish America was a new rationalism and empiricism and a concern for progress that modified, though it never replaced, the traditional authoritarian doctrine. The new philosophy is evident in university teaching, in demands for social and political and especially economic reform, in insistence on efficiency in thought and action, and in a willingness to change. It was not, or not necessarily, hostile to the church or the monarchy or the principle of imperial rule. The church was only slightly affected by it, and in the secular sphere such enlightened reformers as José de Gálvez or Viceroy Revillagigedo in New Spain remained wholly loyal to the Spanish monarchy.[23]

The transmission of enlightened science was not impeded by any parent-country policy. Indeed Spain promoted the scientific awareness of the colony by sending botanical and other expeditions and by encouraging the modernization of technology. Inspiration and opportunity were provided by the Bourbon connection with France. The French expedition of 1735 to measure the extent of the earth's

---

[22] Charles C. Griffin, "The Enlightenment and Latin American Independence," in R. A. Humphreys and John Lynch (eds.), *The Origins of the Latin American Revolutions, 1808–1826* (New York, 1965), pp. 38–51.

[23] Jefferson Rea Spell, *Rousseau in the Spanish World before 1833: A Study in Franco-Spanish Literary Relations* (Austin, Tex., 1938), pp. 217 ff.; Roland D. Hussey, "Traces of French Enlightenment in Colonial Hispanic America," in Arthur P. Whitaker (ed.), *Latin America and the Enlightenment* (New York and London, 1942), pp. 23–51; John Tate Lanning, "The Reception of the Enlightenment in Latin America," *ibid.*, pp. 71–93, and *The Eighteenth-Century Enlightenment in the University of San Carlos de Guatemala* (Ithaca, 1956).

distortion from a true sphere marked the first occasion on which non-Spanish scientists were formally authorized to enter Spanish America. The object was to determine the exact measurement of one degree at the equator and then to compare this with the measurement of one degree in Lapland. The subsequent expeditions of Louis Antoine de Bougainville in the 1760's and of José Celestino Mutis in the 1780's continued and fostered the tradition of scientific interest in America. The eighteenth century's idea of science was considerably colored, of course, by exoticism and by an indiscriminate collector's urge. But science was valued also for its practical utility, in medicine, mining, manufacturing, and the enlargement of practical knowledge. New schools of medicine and mining appeared. Botanical gardens became popular. Cities were reorganized "rationally." Streets were paved and street lighting was installed. Thus in limited but still significant ways real changes made their appearance in Spanish America.[24]

José Antonio Alzate in this sense was one of the most characteristic and one of the most distinguished persons of his age. Born in 1729 in Ozumba, a small town south of Mexico City, Alzate became a cleric, edited several journals, and wrote voluminously on applied science. Determined to bring scientific knowledge to the attention of the reading public, he wrote in plain language, rejecting the authoritarian knowledge of the schools and the elaborate theoretical knowledge of the philosophers. His perceptive and far-ranging eye took in Indian ruins and the chemistry of fire and mineralogy and water analysis and the growth patterns of seeds and a thousand other subjects. Alzate championed empiricism and emphasized accuracy of observation. Though he sometimes made mistakes and though he sometimes wrote in a doctrinaire tone, the spirit that he expressed had never before been expressed in Mexico, and his writings remain today among the most interesting and readable of all eighteenth-century Spanish-American literature.[25]

[24] Mining and botanical expeditions are dealt with respectively in Arthur P. Whitaker, "The Elhuyar Mining Missions and the Enlightenment," *Hispanic American Historical Review*, XXXI (1951), 557–585, and Arthur Robert Steele, *Flowers for the King: The Expedition of Ruiz and Pavón and the Flora of Peru* (Durham, 1964).

[25] José Antonio Alzate, *Gacetas de literatura de México* (4 vols., Puebla,

By many routes in the late eighteenth century—by publication, by travelers, by commercial agents, by formal university training, through Freemasonry, through the enlightened associations called "Economic Societies," through journals of information and ideas— new European influences spread to the Spanish-American colonies. The movement was not a "popular" one. The limited literacy and the autocratic social structure prohibited the spread of enlightened ideas to the populace as a whole. At least with respect to social criticism, the new ideas of the Enlightenment met their chief response among the creoles, who trimmed the sophistication of their analysis with the hostile edge of their antipathy to peninsulars in the colony. The emphasis of creole criticism (unlike the emphasis of modern historians) was less on the reforms accomplished in the eighteenth century than on the multitudinous remaining deficiencies, and in general the creoles overestimated the facility with which a modified Spanish administration could correct these deficiencies. Thus the liberalizing commercial measures of the era of Charles III tended to be overlooked as the remnant practices of monopoly and corruption received a concentrated creole denunciation.[26] Americans repeatedly pointed to the imbalance of mining, agriculture, and manufacturing, and to the inequalities in the distribution of goods. The Spanish overemphasis on mining and the prohibitions against manufacturing received a special creole commentary because they materially affected creole welfare. These were the same observations that Spaniards themselves were making (indeed American creoles obtained large parts of their supporting data from Spanish commentary), but in their American form they acquired all the intensity of personal interest and frustrated ambition.

With respect to the larger society, discontent manifested itself in the eighteenth century in a series of popular uprisings. The uprisings had little if anything to do with enlightened ideology. They were directed to the elimination of immediate governmental abuses or the

---

1831). When criticized for the title he gave to his journal, Alzate argued that literature includes science. He was both a scientist and a publicist for science.

[26] Earl J. Hamilton, "The Role of Monopoly in the Overseas Expansion and Colonial Trade of Europe before 1800," *American Economic Review*, XXXVIII (1948), 42–43.

satisfaction of limited local needs. There had been occasional revolts before—the populace of Mexico City rose up on two occasions in the seventeenth century in periods of economic stress and high prices—but the eighteenth-century rebellions were more frequent and their tendencies were more alarming to government officials. In Paraguay in the 1720's and 1730's a so-called *comunero* movement (the name brought to mind the rebellion of Castilian communes against Charles V) was an attempt by creoles to assume power, to eject the Jesuits, and to take control of the mission Indians. The movement was notable for its defiance of established authority and for the support given it by the municipal cabildo of Asunción. In the 1740's and 1750's hostility against the monopolistic Guipúzcoa Company brought revolution in Caracas. Further rebellions in Quito and Chile and other regions were directed against local tax assessments or administrative policies.

The rebellion of José Gabriel Tupac Amaru in Peru climaxed a series of popular uprisings in that viceroyalty extending from the late seventeenth century. The uprisings were expressions of Indian and mestizo animosity immediately stimulated by particular abuses in the exercise of white authority. From 1779 to 1783 the uprisings erupted in successive areas, never clearly organized in accordance with a single plan. Both La Paz and Cuzco were subjected to Indian siege, but the efforts were uncoordinated and both failed. José Gabriel Tupac Amaru took his name from the Inca ruler deposed and executed by Viceroy Toledo in the late sixteenth century, and he espoused an ideology dependent in part on an indigenous, anti-white prejudice. Following his capture and execution, other native and mestizo leaders appeared whose expressed object was the suppression of Spanish authority and the creation of an independent Indian state. The racist elements of the Peruvian rebellions, however, were not their most significant features. In a heavily Indian area any uprising by oppressed people would have had indigenous overtones, and it would be an error to interpret the Tupac Amaru incidents as expressions of neo-Incaic culture in the manner of Tupac Amaru I. The revolutionists conducted themselves within the framework of eighteenth-century society. Tupac Amaru II proclaimed loyalty to king and church, and declared his purpose to be the correction of local administrative exploitation.[27]

Increases in the tax burden, instituted to help pay for the defense of the coasts against English attack during the American Revolution, account for the "comunero" revolts in New Granada in 1780. An increase in the *alcabala,* a poll tax, and other new exactions were made principally to pay expenses occasioned by Spain's declaration of war against England. The methods of collection revealed again the arrogance and severity of tax officials. The war itself was destined to expose New Granada anew to foreign attack. Popular uprisings broke out in Socorro and spread to Bogotá, where the *audiencia* was compelled to capitulate to demands for tax reforms. Here again complaint was directed not against the imperial system as a whole but against local exploitation of it. The revolutionists were people of all classes—creole, Indian, Negro, and mixed—and their opponents were the powerful and the wealthy, whether peninsular or not. Like the simultaneous Tupac Amaru insurrection, the New Granada *comunero* movement represented the Indian cause. It demanded the abolition of tribute, forced sales, forced labor, ecclesiastical fees, *corregimiento* extortion, and other abuses against Indian society. The rapid success of the movement was the occasion for its failure. With the submission of the *audiencia* the revolutionists dispersed, and with this the royal troops again dominated Bogotá and re-established royal and viceregal control.[28]

The full historical significance of these uprisings is not wholly clear. In one sense they may be understood as demands for the same

---

[27] José Gabriel Tupac Amaru, "Genealogía de Tupac Amaru," *Los pequeños grandes libros de historia americana,* serie 1, tomo X (Lima, 1946), pp. 5–59; Francisco A. Loayza (ed.), *Preliminares del incendio: Documentos del año de 1776 a 1780, en su mayoría inéditos, anteriores y sobre la revolución libertadora que engendró y dió vida José Gabriel Túpak Amaru, en 1780* (Lima, 1947); Boleslao Lewin, *Tupac Amaru el rebelde: Su época, sus luchas y su influencia en el continente* (Buenos Aires, 1943); Daniel Valcárcel, *La rebelión de Túpac Amaru* (Mexico and Buenos Aires, 1947).

[28] Pablo E. Cárdenas Acosta, *El movimiento comunal de 1781 en el Nuevo Reino de Granada* (2 vols., Bogotá, 1960), is a full, documented study of the New Granada *comunero* rebellion. Chapter V contains a precise chronology from 1775 to 1795. For the impact of these Spanish-American revolts on Spain's posture in the peace negotiations ending the American Revolutionary War, see Richard B. Morris, *The Peacemakers* (New York, 1965).

kinds of reform as those legislated under Charles III. In another sense they illustrated a popular discontent comparable to that of the Mexico City revolts of the seventeenth century. Independence, though occasionally mentioned, was not a major item in their list of objectives. But they were troublesome events for Spanish authorities and they served as indications that the restlessness of colonial society was not confined to philosophy or science or upper-class rivalries. Whether or not the conditions they opposed were more oppressive than those of an earlier period is a complex question, and it would be a bold historian who would essay a simple answer.

CHAPTER 9

The Borderlands

THE term "Spanish borderlands" refers to northern Mexico and those areas of the southern United States, from Florida to California, that were once colonized by Spain. In the United States Southwest, the Spanish language is widely spoken, and Hispanic toponyms continue to be current as far as Montana and Oregon. In parts of the United States borderlands, land titles and water rights derive from original Spanish grants and surveys. Remnant mission buildings dot the landscape, and the Spanish heritage is still taken seriously in the twentieth century. The tradition embraces Old St. Augustine, Santa Fe, Capistrano, the Alamo, and other appealing elements of our folklore. It is obvious that borderlands culture has influenced our conception of all Spanish America. But there were important differences between the northern frontier and the more developed parts of the Spanish colony, and it is for this reason, as well as because sections of the United States itself are involved, that we devote our final chapter to this subject.

We do not know who discovered Florida. Juan Ponce de León was the first Spaniard who sought to explore it, in part in response to Indian rumors of the legendary Fountain of Youth (1512–13). Ponce de León coasted Florida on both sides, returned for a second attempt in 1521, lost a number of men on both expeditions, and never established a true colony. Lucas Vásquez de Ayllón and others then explored the Atlantic coast from Florida northward, and in 1528 Pánfilo de Narváez landed on the Gulf coast and continued westward on makeshift rafts. In a famous exploit Núñez Cabeza de Vaca, a survivor of the Narváez expedition, found his way back to central Mexico by water and on foot. Subsequently Hernando de Soto landed in Florida and moved on to discover the Mississippi.[1]

Fifty years after Ponce de León, Florida remained unsettled. Missionary and other expeditions achieved only temporary footholds. Many Spaniards were killed in battles with Indians, and those who survived went westward or retreated southward. The outstanding failures of the midcentury period were those of Tristán de Luna y Orellano, most of whose fleet was destroyed by storms at Pensacola, and Angel de Villafañe, whose efforts to plant a colony on the Carolina coast were abandoned in 1561. Both these attempts were occasioned by fear that the French would occupy positions on the Florida coast from which attacks might be made upon Spanish shipping in the Bahama Channel.

It was an intensification of the French threat that finally brought about permanent Spanish settlement in Florida. In 1562 a Huguenot party under Jean Ribaut landed in the northern part of the peninsula and settled on an island off the coast of what is now South Carolina. Another party of Huguenots under René Laudonnière constructed Fort Caroline at the mouth of the St. Johns. In immediate response, Pedro Menéndez de Avilés established a Spanish colony in St. Augustine Bay and proceeded to wipe out the Fort Caroline settlers as intruders and Lutherans. (Spaniards frequently had trouble in distinguishing one Protestant group from another.) In 1565, Menéndez de Avilés founded St. Augustine, the earliest continuous settlement within the present limits of the United States, and a base from which Spanish missionaries created additional posts in Florida and Georgia. Further expansion northward was ultimately blocked by the English colonies in Virginia and South Carolina, and after the Georgia missions were abandoned the Spanish occupation came to be concentrated at St. Augustine and a few other nearby locations. In the later colonial period Florida was an

---

[1] Leonardo Olschki, "Ponce de León's Fountain of Youth: History of a Geographic Myth," *Hispanic American Historical Review*, XXI (1941), 361–385; Morris Bishop, *The Odyssey of Cabeza de Vaca* (New York, 1933); Edward Gaylord Bourne, *Spain in America, 1450–1580* (New York and London, 1904), pp. 159–168.

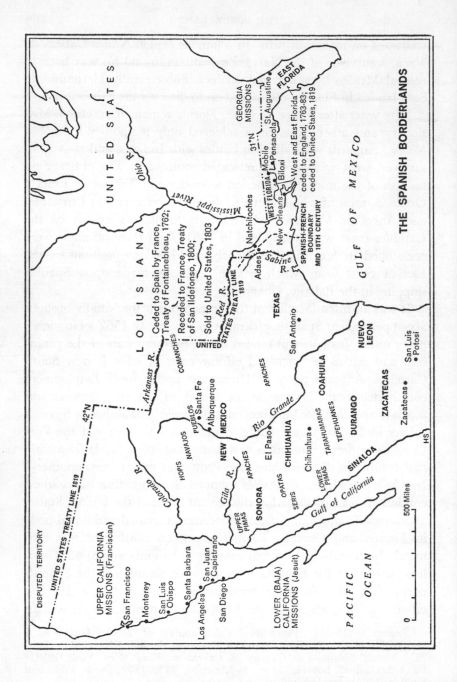

THE SPANISH BORDERLANDS

UNITED STATES

Ohio R.

Mississippi River

LOUISIANA

Ceded to Spain by France,
Treaty of Fontainebleau, 1762;
Receded to France, Treaty
of San Ildefonso, 1800;
Sold to United States, 1803

GEORGIA
MISSIONS

St. Augustine

EAST
FLORIDA

31°N

Pensacola

Mobile

WEST FLORIDA

Biloxi

West and East Florida
ceded to England, 1763-83;
ceded to United States, 1819

New Orleans

Natchitoches

SPANISH-FRENCH
BOUNDARY
MID 18TH CENTURY

GULF OF MEXICO

Red R.

Sabine R.

Adaes

UNITED STATES TREATY LINE 1819

TEXAS

San Antonio

COMANCHES

APACHES

Arkansas R.

42°N

UNITED STATES TREATY LINE 1819

DISPUTED TERRITORY

Colorado R.

PUEBLOS

Santa Fe

Albuquerque

NEW MEXICO

HOPIS

NAVAJOS

Rio Grande

El Paso

APACHES

Gila R.

CHIHUAHUA

Chihuahua

NUEVO
LEON

COAHUILA

San Luis
Potosi

ZACATECAS

Zacatecas

DURANGO

TARAHUMARAS

TEPEHUANES

LOWER
PIMAS

SINALOA

SONORA

OPATAS

SERIS

UPPER
PIMAS

Gulf of California

UPPER CALIFORNIA
MISSIONS (Franciscan)

San Francisco

Monterey

San Luis
Obispo

Santa Barbara

San Juan
Capistrano

Los Angeles

San Diego

LOWER (BAJA)
CALIFORNIA
MISSIONS (Jesuit)

PACIFIC
OCEAN

0   500 Miles

HS

impoverished military outpost, incapable of supporting itself by agriculture or the raising of stock, and dependent upon an annual royal subsidy irregularly paid.[2]

New Mexico, the other northern area occupied by Spain in the sixteenth century, was approached overland from the south. The original attraction was wealth, for Spaniards envisioned native civilizations here as lavish as those of the Aztec and Inca empires. Later the purpose became the propagation of the faith and the creation of a frontier mission society. What prompted the earliest colonists in Mexico to believe that rich cultures lay to the north is a historical mystery still unresolved. The fact in any case provides further demonstration of the impact of European myth upon minds predisposed to understand America in exotic terms. Cabeza de Vaca and several other survivors of the Narváez expedition to Florida, arriving back in Mexico City in 1536, gave currency to rumors that seven cities of great size and luxury were situated in the north. Fray Marcos de Niza, leading a party into or toward the Zuñi territory of western New Mexico in 1539, similarly issued exaggerated reports of what he had seen. Finally Coronado on his expedition of plunder and discovery in 1540–42 brought an end to the fanciful rumors and furnished more accurate and more prosaic descriptions of the peoples of the region.[3]

The missionary phase in New Mexico began in 1581, when the Franciscan friar Agustín Rodríguez set out on a campaign of conversion. This and a supporting party under Antonio de Espejo were preliminary to the major colonization movement of Juan de Oñate, who made the first foundations in 1598. Santa Fe, the capital, was founded about 1610.[4] Additional churches were built and new Spanish settlers entered the region in the seventeenth century. In

---

[2] Woodbury Lowery, *The Spanish Settlements within the Present Limits of the United States: Florida, 1562–1574* (New York and London, 1959); John Jay Te Paske, *The Governorship of Spanish Florida, 1700–1763* (Durham, N.C., 1964).

[3] Bourne, *Spain in America*, pp. 169–174; Herbert Eugene Bolton, *Coronado, Knight of Pueblos and Plains* (New York, 1949).

[4] George P. Hammond and Agapito Rey, *Don Juan de Oñate, Colonizer of New Mexico, 1595–1628* (2 vols., Albuquerque, 1953); Lansing B. Bloom, "When Was Santa Fe Founded?" *New Mexico Historical Review*, IV (1929), 188–194.

1680 the great Pueblo revolt forced the white residents to abandon the New Mexican settlements and to retreat to El Paso—one of the notable instances in colonial history of the reversal of an original conquest. Reoccupation took place after military invasion by Spanish soldiers in the 1690's,[5] and from this time on Spaniards preserved a durable, wary control.

Colonial expansion into Arizona and Baja California was for the most part a missionary movement. Baja California had been coasted as early as the 1530's under the direction of Cortés, but the move was premature from the point of view of permanent occupation, and it was not until the late sixteenth century that Jesuits entered the Sinaloa section of northern Mexico. Here also an element of myth intruded. Ignorance and delusion concerning this part of the coast persisted for a long time. "California is an island and not continental as it is represented to be on the maps," soberly declared Vázquez de Espinosa, one of the most informed colonial writers of the seventeenth century.[6]

The foremost pioneer in Arizona and Baja California was a remarkable Jesuit named Eusebio Francisco Kino. Born of Italian parents about 1644, educated in Austria, and sent as a Jesuit missionary to Mexico, Kino arrived in Pimería Alta in 1687. He founded the mission of Nuestra Señora de los Dolores and from there extended the mission frontier into Arizona to the Gila and Colorado rivers. By 1702 he had explored the Colorado from near Yuma to the Gulf of California. Repeatedly he crisscrossed the country between the Magdalena and the Gila.[7] Kino's reputation illustrates again the persistent regionalism of American history. Famous in Arizona, his name is frequently unrecognized in other parts of the country.

[5] Charles W. Hackett, "The Revolt of the Pueblo Indians of New Mexico in 1680," *The Quarterly of the Texas State Historical Association,* XV (1911–12), 93–147; Charles W. Hackett, "The Retreat of the Spaniards from New Mexico in 1680, and the Beginnings of El Paso," *Southwestern Historical Quarterly,* XVI (1912–13), 137–168, 259–276; Charles W. Hackett and Charmion C. Shelby, *Revolt of the Pueblo Indians of New Mexico and Otermín's Attempted Reconquest, 1680–1682* (2 vols., Albuquerque, 1942).

[6] Antonio Vázquez de Espinosa, *Compendium and Description of the West Indies,* Charles Upson Clark, trans. (Washington, 1942), p. 189.

[7] Herbert Eugene Bolton, *Rim of Christendom: A Biography of Eusebio Francisco Kino, Pacific Coast Pioneer* (New York, 1936).

In the intermediate region between Florida and New Mexico, Spanish occupation took place in the late seventeenth and eighteenth centuries. In response to French and English settlement in the interior of North America, Spaniards moved both westward from Florida and northeastward from Mexico. The French explorers Joliet and Marquette descended the Mississippi to the Arkansas in 1673, and a decade later Robert Cavelier de la Salle planted a French colony at Matagorda Bay on the Texas coast. In the final years of the century, Pierre le Moyne d'Iberville was commissioned to found the colony of Louisiana on the Gulf of Mexico, and the prompt Spanish reaction was an expedition from Veracruz to establish a stronghold on Pensacola Bay. The French countered with a military fort at Biloxi and moved into Mobile Bay.[8] New Orleans was founded in 1718. The French briefly held Pensacola, and from their garrison at Natchitoches in Louisiana they threatened Texas, Coahuila, and New Mexico. The Spanish borderlands were thus cleanly split by the French in the early eighteenth century between an eastern flank in Florida and a western flank south and west of Texas.

The Spanish response to this new French incursion was to send missionaries and soldiers into east Texas. San Antonio and the Alamo mission were founded in 1718, contemporaneously with New Orleans. A Spanish movement from New Mexico extended as far as the North Platte River, in Nebraska or Wyoming, in search of the French enemy. Additional mission and garrison settlements were introduced into Texas, and the capital of the Spanish province of Texas was fixed at Los Adaes (now Robeline, Louisiana), only a few miles from Natchitoches. Toward the mid-eighteenth century Spain and France faced each other across the boundary of the Arroyo Hondo in Louisiana.[9] Though further French penetration westward was limited by Apache and Comanche tribes, occasional French explorers were able to enter New Mexico from the north.

[8] William Edward Dunn, *Spanish and French Rivalry in the Gulf Region of the United States, 1678–1702: The Beginnings of Texas and Pensacola* (Austin, Tex., 1917).

[9] Herbert Eugene Bolton, *Texas in the Middle Eighteenth Century: Studies in Spanish Colonial History and Administration* (Berkeley, 1915). The eastern boundary of Texas became the Sabine in 1819.

French-Spanish confrontation in this interior zone was sharply changed by the Seven Years' War. The city of New Orleans and the huge territory of Louisiana, extending from the Gulf of Mexico indefinitely northward and bounded by the Mississippi on the east, were now formally recognized as Spanish possessions. Some local French resistance in New Orleans still had to be crushed, but the war brought an enormous territorial increment to northern New Spain and an effective elimination of the French frontier.[10] Instead of a divided Spanish colony penetrated by a French wedge on the lower Mississippi, there now emerged a solid Spanish territory to the west and a solid English territory, including Florida, to the east. Though England was to give back Florida in 1783, this new balance of power of the 1760's was to be the decisive one. It was hardly an equal balance. Spain was never able to fulfill the implications of 1763. The interior of North America remained Spanish in name only, and Spain was shortly to return Louisiana provisionally to France and to yield it permanently to the United States. The events of the late eighteenth century thus reveal the practical weakness of Spain's imperial position. A series of complex decisions opened the whole trans-Mississippi west to Spanish occupation, but Spanish physical and human resources were inadequate to the task.

Of all the northern lands available after 1763, only California was settled by Spanish colonists, and here it was not California as we know it but only the coastal strip from San Diego north to San Francisco. This last Spanish move in North America was the result in part of the continuing mission labors organized by Kino and in part of further foreign threats, for Russian traders were moving southward from Bering Strait, and English traders were moving westward from the Great Lakes and the Ohio. These were remote dangers, unlikely in themselves to provoke Spanish counteraction. In the 1760's, however, both the king and his energetic *visitador*, José de Gálvez, who was then conducting a survey and administrative reform in northern Mexico, interpreted the occasion as one

[10] Vicente Rodríguez Casado, *Primeros años de dominación española en la Luisiana* (Madrid, 1942); James Alexander Robertson, *Louisiana under the Rule of Spain, France, and the United States, 1785–1807: Social, Economic, and Political Conditions of the Territory represented in the Louisiana Purchase* (2 vols., Cleveland, 1911).

requiring new colonization. While investigating Baja California, Gálvez formulated plans for joint occupation of Upper California by missionaries and soldiers, with San Diego and Monterey the principal points of occupation. After the Jesuit expulsion the missionary phase of the movement was entrusted to the Franciscan friar Junípero Serra, who set out for San Diego Bay in 1769. The garrison and mission of San Francisco were established in 1776, San José was founded in 1777, Santa Barbara in 1782. Some twenty California communities were founded during the "mission period" from 1769 to 1823.[11]

All borderland areas have been subjected to intense study. Our summary is a mere skimming of the enormous number of facts known about the region, for it is probable that no other part of colonial Spanish America has stimulated so extensive a program of research. That this is the case is due chiefly to the work of Herbert E. Bolton and his students, who have explored the archives with diligence and reconstructed the course of events in detail.[12] Local historical societies in the United States have done much more than their counterparts in Mexico to make information available. Bolton knew that the borderlands were not a typical or even an important part of Spanish America.[13] His interest, like ours, depended heavily on the United States connection. But the differences do tell us some-

[11] Herbert Ingram Priestley, *José de Gálvez, Visitor-General of New Spain (1765–1771)* (Berkeley, 1916), pp. 253–254; Zephyrin Engelhardt, *The Missions and Missionaries of California* (4 vols., San Francisco, 1908–15).

[12] Bolton was the successor of Hubert Howe Bancroft, who published some of the most thorough studies ever made of borderlands areas. But it was Bolton who first used and emphasized the term and who created the school of borderlands study.

[13] "With a vision limited by the Rio Grande, and noting that Spain's outposts within the area now embraced in the United States were slender, and that these fringes eventually fell into the hands of the Anglo-Americans, writers concluded that Spain did not really colonize, and that, after all, she failed. The fallacy came, of course, from mistaking the tail for the dog, and then leaving the dog out of the picture. The real Spanish America, the dog, lay between the Rio Grande and Buenos Aires. The part of the animal lying north of the Rio Grande was only the tail. Let us first glance at the dog." The quotation is from a paper by Bolton in 1929. See John Francis Bannon (ed.), *Bolton and the Spanish Borderlands* (Norman, Okla., 1964), pp. 32–64. The point is further developed in Howard F. Cline, "Imperial Perspectives on the Borderlands," in *Probing the American West, Papers from the Santa Fe Conference* (Santa Fe, 1962), pp. 168–174.

thing of the motives and methods of Spanish expansion elsewhere. At first glance it will seem strange that Spaniards found Florida so difficult to settle and that they took so long to move from central Mexico to California. Florida especially would seem an easy environment for European occupation. Its native inhabitants were sparsely settled, its climate was balmy, and it was far more accessible than the capitals of the Aztec and Inca empires. The apparent advantages, however, implied some of the most practical obstacles. Unlike central Mexico and central Peru, Florida and the other northern regions offered no great incentive. Spaniards needed people to dominate. The borderlands, with few exceptions, lacked wealth and organized civilizations. Their native societies were too loosely structured for Spain to incorporate readily into a functioning colonial organization.[14] Encomienda and *repartimiento,* while they were not entirely absent, never had the importance that they had in the south.[15]

Towns in the north were of smaller size and more distant from one another than the towns of central and southern Mexico. In the Valley of Mexico and its environs, aboriginal peoples were members of pre-existing communities, and they could be utilized in community form for Spanish purposes. In the north, Spaniards found settlements of this kind only in a few places, chiefly among the Pueblos of the Rio Grande and Colorado River region. In Sonora and Georgia and California and elsewhere, original Indian settlements were either far less compact and developed or totally nonexistent, and the Spaniards' task was one of creating settlements in the *reducción,* or mission, form. Tepehuanes and Tarahumaras and most other peoples of northern Mexico lived a half-sedentary, half-nomadic existence. Whether under religious or civil authority, a dominant effort of Spaniards in the north was to establish towns, and the success of Spanish relations with natives could be measured to a considerable degree in terms of town foundation. Spanish fail-

[14] Charles W. Arnade, "The Failure of Spanish Florida," *The Americas,* XVI (1959–60), 271–281.

[15] Encomiendas in the borderlands developed chiefly in the Rio Grande valley. For a summary, see Lansing B. Bloom, "The Vargas Encomienda," *New Mexico Historical Review,* XIV (1939), 366–417.

ures in controlling native peoples were most pronounced where Indians refused to submit to community life.

The most important towns from the ordinary secular Spanish viewpoint were the mining towns, particularly those in the central corridor north from Zacatecas. Here the dates of foundation reflect the steady movement northward: Zacatecas and Durango in the sixteenth century, Parral in the seventeenth century, Chihuahua in the early eighteenth century. The principal mining towns were also administrative and social centers, as well as markets and depots for supplies other than silver. Their layouts were in the familiar Spanish pattern, with plazas, official buildings, churches, and residential houses clustered around the central plaza. Their Indian inhabitants were laborers or servants in the homes of their Spanish masters. Indian or mestizo mine workers also occupied entire barrios, to which they were attracted by the prospect of wages, for a considerable part of the labor force was "free." A few of the upper Rio Grande towns—El Paso, Albuquerque, Santa Fe—were smaller versions of the towns of northern Mexico.[16] But the chief economic motive for all northern expansion—mining—was conspicuously lacking in the areas that form part of the United States, and the momentum of town foundation accordingly slowed and eventually ceased altogether.

A distinctive type of Spanish frontier community, on the other hand, was the presidio, or garrison. The line of protective northern fortifications eventually extended across the entire continent from Florida to California. St. Augustine had the largest and most important fortification and the one with the longest tradition, but this came to an end in 1763 with the English occupation, and St. Augustine never regained its former importance for Spain. The Louisiana garrisons of the eighteenth century had the special function of protecting Spanish territory against the French. The characteristic presidios of the inland borderlands were those designed as

[16] France V. Scholes, "Civil Government and Society in New Mexico in the Seventeenth Century," *New Mexico Historical Review*, X (1935), 71–111; Edward H. Spicer, *Cycles of Conquest: The Impact of Spain, Mexico, and the United States on the Indians of the Southwest, 1533–1960* (Tucson, 1962), pp. 298–303.

outposts on the moving frontier for protection against the attacks of marauding Indians. The type first appeared in the sixteenth century, as a safeguard on the roads from Mexico City to Querétaro, Guanajuato, and Zacatecas. In the Chichimeca area of the central plateau, almost all presidios of the sixteenth century were still located south of the northernmost points of Spanish occupation. The chain of forts at this time ran in a northwesterly direction, and a main function of the soldiers was to escort travelers and silver trains from station to station.[17] But with the end of the Chichimeca War and with the more deliberate expansions of the seventeenth and eighteenth centuries, the presidio became a genuine frontier fortress. Presidios of northern Mexico and the United States borderlands were staffed by up to about sixty Spanish soldiers, living in or near small mud fortifications, and surrounded by their families, Indian servants, and a miscellany of hangers-on. The soldiers were equipped with horses and firearms, with which they went out on punitive expeditions against unpacified Indian peoples. Indian soldiers frequently accompanied the Spaniards in forays against other Indians. In addition to their primary defense function, the soldiers were used as mail carriers, military escorts, police, and guards. Supplying the unproductive presidios was one of the principal administrative problems of the frontier.[18]

In the history of ranches and haciendas as in the history of towns and presidios, an essential pattern was that of expansion northward from southern and central Mexico. Settlement of the Chichimeca area allowed for an extension of cattle raising on a large scale. Fortunes made in mining were invested in land and animals, and the virgin land supported great herds. Single ranchers in some cases

[17] When they were added, new presidios were commonly introduced into the south rather than the far north. In the 1570's the new presidios were constructed on the roads to Panuco and Guadalajara, hundreds of miles south of Zacatecas, and the Chichimeca raiders were attacking farther to the south than ever before. Philip Wayne Powell, *Soldiers, Indians, and Silver: The Northward Advance of New Spain, 1550–1600* (Berkeley and Los Angeles, 1952).

[18] Oakah L. Jones, Jr., "Pueblo Indian Auxiliaries in New Mexico, 1763–1821," *New Mexico Historical Review*, XXXVII (1962), 81–109; Max L. Moorhead, "The Presidio Supply Problem of New Mexico in the Eighteenth Century," *New Mexico Historical Review*, XXXVI (1961), 210–229; Te Paske, *Governorship of Spanish Florida.*

had a hundred thousand cows by the late sixteenth century. The immense grasslands of Zacatecas, Durango, and Nueva Vizcaya attracted not only ranchers but herds of wild cattle and horses, which increased so rapidly that they soon outdistanced humans. Herds roamed at will in the unfenced unsettled areas, occasionally invading frontier settlements as wild bands. Herding, horsemanship, the open ranges, the rodeo, the accouterments of silver, the "Charro" psychology, became permanent features of the area.[19]

The rodeo was a Mexican solution to the problem of unconfined animals. The Mexican rodeo has analogies in other parts of the world, but it probably developed independently and in any case it acquired special traits. The original rodeo, not at all the public display of skill in roping and riding that we now know, was literally a roundup, with mounted cowboys arranged in a circle large enough to surround the animals and to enclose them in a progressively smaller area. In the center, different brands were identified and allocations of unbranded animals were made among the owners. The rodeo left a permanent Spanish legacy in the cattle areas of the United States. Some of our most familiar terms—bronco (wild), lassoo (Sp. *lazo*), rodeo itself—are loan words. Others have been modified but can be readily traced to Spanish originals: chaps are *chaparejos,* protective leggings to guard against the chaparral scrub; lariat is *la reata,* the rope; buckaroo is the Anglo-American version of Spanish *vaquero,* or cowboy.

Indians also became raisers of cattle and horses. In the south in the sixteenth century Indians had taken to small-scale sheep farms, but few raised horses or cattle. In the north the Yaquis and Tarahumaras and Pueblos and some other peoples adopted both sheep and cattle. They did so partly under missionary auspices, but partly

---

[19] Donald D. Brand, "The Early History of the Range Cattle Industry in Northern Mexico," *Agricultural History,* XXXV (1961), 132–139, identifies the periods of cattle expansion and furnishes a map of the expanding cattle frontier. See also Richard J. Morrisey, "The Northward Expansion of Cattle Ranching in New Spain, 1550–1600," *Agricultural History,* XXV (1951), 115–121. There were some cattle ranches in Florida in the period from about 1655 to about 1702. They appear to have been permanently destroyed by English raids in the War of the Spanish Succession. See Charles W. Arnade, "Cattle Raising in Spanish Florida, 1513–1763," *Agricultural History,* XXXV (1961), 116–124.

also because the opportunities were greater, the herding areas larger, and the danger of damage to agriculture by feeding and trampling less. Among the Navajos and Apaches, remote from direct Spanish influence, these animals had far-reaching consequences. Navajo and Apache raiders attacked Spanish and other Indian settlements, taking sheep, cattle, and horses. Some Navajos in the eighteenth century became efficient sheepmen, raising their own herds and developing the techniques for making woolen blankets for which they are celebrated today.[20] The Apaches continued to be nomadic raiders, using their horses for quick attacks and getaways, and generally rejecting the kind of adaptation effected by the Navajo shepherds. On the other hand, the great difference in current reputation between the predatory, merciless Apaches and the gentle, blanket-weaving Navajos is largely a result of later adjustments and selective modern identification. These differences were much less pronounced in the eighteenth century, when both peoples lived by raiding. One of the ironies of borderlands history is that the Apaches were not originally a belligerent or aggressive people. Their raids were the outcome of colonial pressures and opportunities. They became aggressive after Spaniards introduced horses that they could ride and after Spaniards established communities, including Indian communities, that they could attack.[21]

The climactic institution of the borderlands, as everyone knows, was the religious mission. Differing from the establishments of central and southern Mexico, the mission was appropriate to the frontier region, where, as Bolton observed, Indians "were hostile, had few crops, were unused to labor, had no fixed villages, would not stand still to be exploited, and were hardly worth the candle."[22] Accordingly, in addition to its religious function, the mission served secondarily some of the same objectives as the civilian town and the presidio. Justifications for new mission foundation were expressed in terms both of religious need and of strategic imperial expansion,

---

[20] This became an industry catering to a tourist market in the late nineteenth century. At about the same time the Navajos began to use imported, machine-made blankets in their own domestic life.

[21] Spicer, *Cycles of Conquest,* pp. 210–261; Jack D. Forbes, *Apache, Navaho, and Spaniard* (Norman, Okla., 1960).

[22] Bannon (ed.), *Bolton and the Spanish Borderlands,* p. 191.

and missionaries themselves argued the one purpose as well as the other. Both Texas and California had been looked to as mission fields long before the occupations of the eighteenth century, the ultimate timing, however, depending on an assessment of new imperial requirements.[23]

Ecclesiastical labor in the missions fell to Franciscans and Jesuits. Franciscans were the principal Spanish missionaries in Florida and Georgia, and they were present at the discovery of the Zacatecas lodes in 1546. Later they carried their labors into other regions of northern and northeastern Mexico—Coahuila, Nuevo León, Nuevo Santander, and the Concho region of Chihuahua—as well as into Texas. Franciscans accompanied the Oñate expedition of 1598 and maintained the New Mexico field continuously after this except for the period of rebellion in the late seventeenth century.[24] Franciscans also were the missionaries among the Pimas, in California, and in other places after the expulsion of the Jesuits.

The Jesuits received a favorable viceregal attention at a crucial time in the late sixteenth century, when the original Chichimeca hostilities were at an end and when the official policies of "pacification" were shifting from a military to a missionary emphasis. Jesuits came to central Mexico first in 1572, rapidly establishing their position and reputation as the most vigorous and disciplined of the missionary bodies. They were in Guanajuato by 1582 and in the San Luis Potosí area in 1592. Though they failed in Florida, they were preferred over the Franciscans by Viceroy Velasco and others on the northern frontier, and from the conclusion of the Chichimeca War until 1767 they dominated the labors in the north central plateau and in the Sinaloa area to the west. Conversion work among

---

[23] "It is seen every day that in missions where there are no soldiers there is no success, for the Indians, being children of fear, are more strongly appealed to by the glistening of the sword than by the voice of five missionaries." This is a missionary's statement of 1772, quoted in Bannon (ed.), *Bolton and the Spanish Borderlands*, p. 202. The combined religious-imperialist character of the mission is developed in Bolton's famous article, "The Mission as a Frontier Institution in the Spanish American Colonies," reprinted *ibid.*, pp. 187–211.

[24] Maynard Geiger, *The Franciscan Conquest of Florida (1573–1618)* (Washington, 1937); John Tate Lanning, *The Spanish Missions of Georgia* (Chapel Hill, N.C., 1935); Powell, *Soldiers, Indians, and Silver*, p. 10; Spicer, *Cycles of Conquest*, pp. 157 ff.

the Tepehuan, Tarahumara, Yaqui, Mayo, Pima, Opata, and Seri Indians of the northwest Mexican coast was exclusively a Jesuit undertaking, and it is probable that Jesuits rather than Franciscans would have been the missionaries of California but for the general Jesuit expulsion.[25] Thus although the Jesuits were the principal missionaries of the moving frontier in northern Mexico, a coincidence of causes assigned most of the borderlands of the present United States to the Franciscans.

Of the other two leading missionary bodies in south-central Mexico—Dominicans and Augustinians—neither was a major force in the Chichimeca country or the borderlands. Augustinians were in the Pame region east of Guanajuato and San Luis Potosí, but they did not move northward with the expanding frontier as Franciscans and Jesuits did. The Dominicans were critical of the Chichimeca War from the start, regarding it as the consequence of unwarranted Spanish aggression, and they played practically no role in the frontier movements until the late eighteenth century, when they were selected to substitute for the ejected Jesuits in Baja California.

Spaniards had always conceived of religious conversion in America as a broadly civilizing process, and on the northern frontier as elsewhere they aimed at a full social and cultural reorientation of native life. The difference was that on the frontiers Indians had much more to learn. Jesuits and Franciscans were active promoters of the *congregación*, in the belief, undoubtedly accurate, that without it religious conversion would have been impractical or impossible. Community life implied a reorganizing of the economy, and Indians accordingly were taught agriculture and stock raising and a variety of crafts. In some areas, as among the Pimas under Kino's direction, the mission cattle ranches advanced more rapidly than the missions themselves.[26] Franciscans in California developed elaborate

[25] Powell, *Soldiers, Indians, and Silver,* pp. 192, 197, 209; Gerard Decorme, *La obra de los jesuítas mexicanos durante la época colonial, 1572–1767* (2 vols., Mexico, 1941); Peter M. Dunne, *Pioneer Black Robes on the West Coast* (Berkeley and Los Angeles, 1940); Peter M. Dunne, *Pioneer Jesuits in Northern Mexico* (Berkeley and Los Angeles, 1944), and *Early Jesuit Missions in Tarahumara* (Berkeley, 1948).

[26] Spicer, *Cycles of Conquest,* pp. 126, 131.

economic complexes, the native inhabitants of which built aqueducts, dams, and reservoirs and cultivated gardens, grain fields, orchards, and vineyards. Indians constructed buildings, learned carpentry and masonry, operated gristmills, raised cattle and sheep, tanned hides, wove textiles, and made wine, shoes, soap, and candles, all under Franciscan supervision. Cattle raising was the foremost industry, and hides and tallow the principal sources of income. Not all the missions of the borderlands were so thoroughly involved in economic activities as were those in California. But labor, agriculture, construction, crafts, granaries, cattle, and orchards were features of the Franciscan foundations in Texas[27] and elsewhere, and it was chiefly in New Mexico that the ecclesiastics lacked official control over Indian economic life. Even in New Mexico, however, the friars taught stock raising and crafts, and everywhere in the borderlands they introduced plows, European plants and seeds, and new agricultural techniques in addition to Christianity.

Characteristically the congregated Indian houses were laid out in an orderly pattern within the mission confines. Surrounding the central quadrangle were the smith's shop, workshop, granary, tannery, and stables. The church was the largest building, dominating all others. This standard physical form was developed by Jesuits for northern Mexico and it achieved its culmination in the Franciscan establishments of California. In New Mexico, on the other hand, the tendency was to retain existing Indian communities intact, to build the churches on the edge of the settlements, and to divide Indian life between a town-oriented secular aspect and a church-oriented religious aspect.[28] These differences were less the result of differing preconceptions and philosophies among the religious bodies than of the nature of Indian societies. In New Mexico the Franciscans adapted their methods to sedentary Indian peoples. In California they dealt with natives who had no permanent communities,

---

[27] Billie Persons, "Secular Life in the San Antonio Missions," *Southwestern Historical Quarterly*, LXII (1958–59), 45–62.

[28] It is perhaps relevant to observe that Pueblo society survived relatively intact to the twentieth century, whereas California Indian society disintegrated in the nineteenth century. There were of course other reasons for this in addition to the differences in mission form.

who knew neither agriculture nor pottery making, and who lived on acorns and whatever else they could gather.

Indians from the south were introduced on the frontiers as aides in these processes of civilization. They came as colonists, teachers, and models, the purpose being to instruct by example in orderly social living, agriculture, and political officeholding. Tlaxcalans were used in this way at various locations in northern Mexico and Texas. Tarascans were moved north to Sonora, and Opatas from Sonora were moved to Arizona. Politically the mission communities came to be organized, as were Indian towns to the south, with offices of *gobernador, alcalde, regidor,* and *alguacil.* Indian officers were appointed by the missionaries or elected by the community. The full native community had judges and police, a *cabildo,* a jail, and other institutions for the maintenance of internal order, all under the supervision of Spaniards. But it should be added that these programs often lapsed, most missionaries had little understanding of the social organization of the peoples among whom they worked, and appointments to native office were sometimes made arbitrarily and thoughtlessly.[29]

In the north, more than in the center and south, the teaching of the Spanish language became an important part of the religious program. The particular problem was that many languages were spoken by a relatively small number of people. In the Valley of Mexico and its surrounding area, only a few languages were spoken, and a friar who learned one or two of these could communicate with thousands of converts. In the north, peoples only a few miles apart might speak mutually unintelligible languages. It was uneconomical, indeed it was impossible, for missionaries to learn all the languages and dialects of the borderlands. Jesuits were more successful in learning languages than were Franciscans and they took the obligation more seriously. But the common effort even among Jesuits was to teach Spanish to Indians. The result for a variety of reasons was only partially successful. The observation of a

[29] "Usually such appointments were made on the most meager knowledge of the groups. Indians who presented themselves as friendly and helpful to the Spaniards were given the appointments, often immediately with a cane as badge of office, and without any inquiry into the status of the individual in his group." Spicer, *Cycles of Conquest,* p. 390.

Franciscan friar in California suggests some of the limitations and frustrations: "They find it difficult to learn to speak Spanish at this Mission, since each year pagans arrive to become Christians and the greater number of these are old people. A suitable method to get them to talk Spanish is the one we follow, namely, we exhort and threaten them with punishment, and in the case of the young, we punish them from time to time. We do not know what reasons keep them from using Spanish."[30]

It is obvious that the religious and civil society of the borderlands contained many potentialities for strife. Conflicts between ecclesiastics and political authorities were common from the beginning. Civil governors sought to take Indians as laborers, to exact extralegal tribute from them, and to profit from them in other ways. Private *hacendados* and ranchers were always alert to the possibilities of sequestering Indians from the religious communities. Conflict with the garrison soldiers was also frequent. Royal administrators and civilian colonists repeatedly criticized the clergy for their severity with Indians, for their exploitation of native labor, and for their laxity in moral behavior, and missionaries in their turn criticized civilians and administrators with these same accusations.[31]

Disputes with outsiders were paralleled by internal tensions within the communities. No matter how benevolent and Christian, conversion was a program designed to impose European standards upon non-European peoples. The common attitude of the clergy was one of authoritarian paternalism, and in various degrees the regime that they imposed was maintained by force, with whipping posts, stocks, and prison cells. Missionaries disagreed among themselves concerning the degree of conformity required, and concerning the degree of compulsion necessary to achieve it. Sudden and arbitrary campaigns against residual pagan practices alternated with periods of toleration and leniency. One of the great strengths of Kino and one of the major reasons for his success was his tolerance

---

[30] Maynard Geiger (ed.), "Questionnaire of the Spanish Government in 1812 concerning the Native Culture of the California Mission Indians," *The Americas*, V (1948–49), 487. For a full summary of the mission language program and its effects in northern Mexico and the United States Southwest, see Spicer, *Cycles of Conquest*, pp. 422–430.

[31] Spicer, *Cycles of Conquest*, pp. 288–308.

of existing Indian practices. But it is obvious that no program could be too tolerant, for this would defeat the purpose and weaken the effort to substitute Christianity for paganism.

Indians responded to Christian life in complex ways. The writings of Franciscans and Jesuits refer repeatedly to the problems raised when Indians accepted some Spanish conditions but not all. The Christian program for individual conversion conflicted with Indian kinship organizations. The Christian concept of sin conflicted with Indian fertility concepts. These and many other differences tended to be understood by the clergy in European terms. Indians were "sly and crafty . . . hypocrites." They had "no diligence, or stability . . . nor capacity to understand the Christian mysteries." Particularly disturbing were the acts of withdrawal, when Christianized or apparently Christianized Indians without warning escaped the mission confines and fled back to their original society.[32]

At other times outright rebellion broke out. The Tepehuanes, the Tarahumaras, the Pueblos, and others rose in serious insurrections, looting and killing, blaspheming holy objects, and maintaining their resistance for long periods. Over a thousand Spaniards were killed in a Yaqui uprising of 1740. The Hopis, Christianized in the seventeenth century, became the most successful of the rebellious peoples, holding out against Spanish counterattack from the time of the New Mexico revolt in 1680 to the end of the colonial period. In California, with the Mexican secularization of 1833, the mission Indians defied the friars, slaughtered thousands of cattle, and fled.[33]

The outstanding differences between borderlands society and the society of central Mexico and Peru were differences of degree and emphasis, and they depended more on Indian society than on Spanish. The fact suggests how sensitively Spaniards responded everywhere in America to the circumstances of native life. Where Indians could be a lower class, Spaniards immediately became an aristocratic class, capable of developing the elaborate urban cultures of Mexico City and Lima. In northern Mexico, native peoples were less well equipped to perform this supporting role, and in so far as

[32] Ibid., pp. 311, 313.
[33] Ray Allen Billington, The Far Western Frontier, 1830–1860 (New York, 1956), pp. 7–8.

they could perform it the tendency of Spaniards was to concentrate Indian services in primary economic tasks, especially in the mining of silver. Undoubtedly if rich mines had been discovered in Texas or California, Spaniards would have been stimulated to far greater exertions in their manipulations of native peoples. Without this motive secondary objectives came into play: Christianization and civilization of Indians, resistance to imperial threats by foreign nations, and economic activities involving lesser commodities such as cattle. It should not be forgotten that the borderland was a frontier. What made it a frontier was precisely the reduced intensity of Spanish concern with it, and in this sense it paralleled other frontiers, such as southern Chile and southern Argentina, where Indians were sparse and hostile, and where Spaniards found no mines to work. Borderlands society was naturally selective and diluted in comparison with the central capital society, and all Spanish life in the north was appropriately provincial.

The Christian effort of the borderlands reminds us again that Christianity, though of less interest to many individuals, was an important element in Spanish imperialism. For particular missionary personalities the frontier was a challenge, the more so *because* its Indians were primitive or hostile. Neither the religious nor any other impulse was sufficient to promote expansion farther north, and this means that the Christian effort, like the secular, was defined and limited at fixed points. But the religious drive was strong in northwest Mexico and California, where missionaries were impelled to create wholly new societies, with adjunct economic and political and social institutions. The peculiar features of the frontier called forth and intensified this part of the Spanish purpose, which in the seventeenth and eighteenth centuries was one of self-sacrifice and spiritual values in excess of those of the south.

Other aspects of the borderlands should not be overlooked. There is the danger of romantic simplification in understanding mission society, and a tendency to exaggerate its peaceful and idyllic qualities. The frontier was an area of strife. The creation of peaceful enclaves provoked aggressions that had not existed before. Christianity and peace and order were preserved by force, and opposing forces repeatedly undermined them.

"Perfect in independence, isolation, and peace" were the words James Steele used in a nostalgic effusion in 1889 to characterize the California missions.[34] One of the interesting features of borderlands history is the process of growing recognition and idealization in the United States during the nineteenth and twentieth centuries, a process that may be understood in part as an aspect of the recognition and idealization of the West as a whole. But it has a distinct Hispanic as well as an Indian cast, and with the addition of Florida it appears as a special phenomenon. The first visitors from the United States to comment on their experiences in the Southwest adopted a very different tone. James Ohio Pattie, the author of a "Personal Narrative" in the 1820's, expressed an unglamorous viewpoint that was to be standard for several generations. Pattie was surprised and disappointed that the people of New Mexico were so different from himself. His deprecatory and critical attitudes were common among the Anglo-American merchants of the period and among the soldiers of the Mexican War in the 1840's. Prior to the Treaty of Guadalupe Hidalgo in 1848, the southwest borderlands were parts of independent Mexico, and Mexico was regarded by the observers from the North as impoverished, bigoted, uncivilized, and degenerate. To the many soldiers and merchants and travelers of the middle nineteenth century, the towns of the Southwest appeared as collections of mud huts, unkempt, unproductive, indolent, backward, and soon to be displaced by a more progressive civilization. "The people lack that neatness and show of wealth, that taste and refinement which we left in 'the States,' " wrote George Gibson, a cultivated Missouri lawyer and editor who served as a soldier in New Mexico.[35]

California was something of an exception, even in the 1840's. In *Two Years Before the Mast* (1841), Richard Henry Dana gave a vivid impression of its Spanish life. Hubert Howe Bancroft, arriving in California in 1852, immediately took its traditions seriously and began the accumulation of materials for his detailed borderlands

[34] Quoted in Edith Buckland Webb, *Indian Life at the Old Missions* (Los Angeles, 1952), p. 2.

[35] Burl Noggle, "Anglo Observers of the Southwest Borderlands, 1825–1890: The Rise of a Concept," *Arizona and the West*, I (1959), 105–131, furnishes material on the individuals mentioned and others of the period.

histories. A significant figure was Bret Harte, whose tales of California society included familiar features of the Hispanic image: missions, mission bells, padres on horseback, proud dons, señoritas, serenades, fandangos, fiestas. Harte's people were literary characters playing expectable roles, but they injected a certain concreteness into the California setting that New Mexico and Texas and Arizona still lacked. It remained only for Helen Hunt Jackson to infuse the Spanish society of California with a sentimental aura. A less accomplished writer than Bret Harte, she expressed in a single popular novel, *Ramona* (1884), a message that her readers could not ignore: United States expansion into California stood in crude and tragic contrast to its genteel Spanish heritage.[36]

In other parts of the Southwest recognition came more slowly, but the essential pattern was the same. In Arizona and New Mexico the commentary became steadily more critical of the United States intruders and more appreciative of local color. John Bourke in the 1870's observed ironically that the streets of Tucson were quite as dirty as the streets of New York. Noble L. Prentis in the 1880's found a symbol of Anglo-American civilization in the empty tin cans scattered throughout New Mexico. Charles F. Lummis, author of *Some Strange Corners of Our Country* (1892) and *The Land of Poco Tiempo* (1893),[37] proved a passionate and faithful devotee of the whole Southwest, including California. From the 1890's to the present the volume of publication has continuously increased, and the Spanish-Indian charm of the Southwest has become familiar to all.

Thus in a period of little more than fifty years the romance of the Spanish world, not at first thought to be applicable to the borderlands, came to be applied to them. What Washington Irving had felt at the Alhambra, others felt at Santa Fe or Capistrano. In prose and poetry the borderlands were Alhambrized. Programs for restoration of neglected missions were developed before the end of

---

[36] United States writers on California in the nineteenth century are discussed in Stanley T. Williams, *The Spanish Background of American Literature* (2 vols., New Haven, 1955), *passim*.

[37] Noggle, "Anglo Observers," pp. 125, 129. In *The Spanish Pioneers* (Chicago, 1893), Lummis was one of the first writers in the United States to combat the Black Legend in Spanish American history.

the nineteenth century. Spanish styles in furniture and architecture became fashionable and popular. The Southwest experienced its cultural renaissance. Florida gave attention to the Spanish past, and in Georgia the remains of nineteenth-century sugar mills were publicized as mission ruins, an unfortunate error to which some serious students of history lent their support.[38] As everyone knows, this awakened interest has not entirely escaped commercialism or vulgarity or romantic distortion. But it should be said also that particular communities—Santa Barbara and Santa Fe may be cited as examples—have been exceptionally successful in translating their Spanish traditions into meaningful twentieth-century compatibility with the very different civilization of the United States.

[38] E. Merton Coulter, *Georgia's Disputed Ruins* (Chapel Hill, N.C., 1937).

Epilogue

THE movement for Spanish-American independence in the early nineteenth century was disunified, and one properly speaks of its revolutions rather than of a single revolution. Uprisings in different localities remained separate or competed with one another. Simón Bolívar and José de San Martín, the two principal leaders in South America, met only in 1822, and the result of their meeting was personal alienation and further withdrawal on both sides. In Mexico the struggle against Spain developed its own series of leaders and had no contact with South America. The area from Guatemala to Costa Rica remained at peace and ultimately declared itself free from Spain without having to support its decision in battle. The island colonies failed to develop independence movements until much later and remained dependencies of Spain. Thus Spanish America did not declare its independence as a unit. There were a number of declarations, each applying to a limited region, and the first result was not one new nation but seven.

The original objective of the revolutionists was not political independence. Warfare broke out after the army of Napoleon invaded the Iberian peninsula and after Napoleon forced Charles IV and his son Ferdinand VII to renounce the Spanish throne. The first insurrections were protests in support of Ferdinand VII and against Napoleon, and they brought forth more eloquent assertions of loyalty to the crown than had appeared in the previous three centuries of unquestioned colonial rule. Only after the wars were well advanced and after the American patriots had become disillusioned with the monarch and his Spanish supporters did independence become their purpose.

The failure to integrate and the failure to identify independence as an early objective are historical "facts" of the Spanish American revolutionary period. Their implication is that political separation itself was more accidental and less basic than it might otherwise have been. But what this means in its turn is by no means clear. The Anglo-American patriotic armies achieved unity only with difficulty, and the British colonies, long after Lexington and Concord, likewise denied that they were fighting to break a political connection. Historians are agreed that the Napoleonic invasion of Spain was the immediate stimulus for the Spanish-American uprisings. But obviously this single incident cannot serve as a full historical explanation. The less direct or more far-reaching causes are complex, and, as with British America, scholars have failed to reach consensus. After Anglo-American independence was achieved, a similar independence for Spanish America could be, and was, predicted, both in Spain and in foreign countries. Indeed the British minister George Canning stated that in view of the Anglo-American example the disruption of the Spanish empire was inevitable. But again this is quite different from a historical explanation.

A large number of "causes" have been proposed. Among the most frequently mentioned are the ideologies stemming from the European Enlightenment, the hostility of creoles to peninsulars, the gradual development of a unique "American" identity, the authoritarian and corrupt character of the imperial government, and the Bourbon reforms, which fell short of what was needed and served to create a demand for additional change. As might be expected, the historical problem is not one of identifying causes, for these are present in abundance, but rather of evaluating the causes already identified and arriving at an understanding of their interrelationships.[1]

The revolutions were not spontaneous popular uprisings against

---

[1] R. A. Humphreys and John Lynch (eds.), *The Origins of the Latin American Revolutions, 1808–1826* (New York, 1965), is an anthology of writings on this subject.

Spanish oppression. The people—Indians, Negroes, mestizos, mulattoes, and all subordinate classes—fought when they were required to fight by their white leaders, and if their leaders were royalists rather than revolutionists, the same people were soldiers for the king. The absence of a spontaneous popular sentiment is illustrated in the celebrated landing of Francisco de Miranda, one of the precursors of independence, on the Venezuelan shore in 1806. Miranda, a talented career soldier and an agent of romantic international intrigue, expected that he would receive general support in Venezuela. When no such response was forthcoming, Miranda was compelled to withdraw. The ideologies of the revolutions, as well as their active leadership and financial support, were provided by creoles, and creoles were not representatives of the mass society. They were among the least oppressed of all peoples of Spanish America.

These facts are related to the nature of the society of Spanish America in the national period. Neither the revolutions nor anything else subverted the existing social order. Lower classes remained subordinate, and significant change occurred only between creoles and peninsulars at the uppermost level of social rank. The creoles won the revolutions, and the result was the elimination of the peninsulars and the assumption of new powers by the creoles. A case could be made for the proposition that lower classes were more severely oppressed after the revolutions than before, much as creoles sought to out-peninsular the peninsulars in other ways. The various declarations of independence and the new constitutions expressed principles of egalitarianism, but egalitarianism was never achieved and no serious effort was made to practice it. It is true that certain symbols of oppression, such as the Indian tribute and an economically unnecessary Negro slavery, were locally abolished. But where Indian tribute was financially significant and where Negro slavery served a genuine need, these remained. Nowhere did a principle of egalitarianism affect the realities of social or economic life. No middle class appeared. Thus the polarities of the colonial class system and the gulf between rich and poor survived the independence movement. The displacement of peninsular by creole meant only a limited, circumstantial modification in the philosophy of the ruling class.

The history of Spanish America, like the history of Anglo-America, is commonly divided into two periods, colonial and national, the turning point being the achievement of independence. In recent years students have questioned this periodization—on the grounds that political independence is an insufficient criterion on which to base a division.[2] Independence is important from a narrowly political or from a nationalistic point of view. It is less important in the economic and social and cultural emphases that have gained favor in twentieth-century historical thinking. Modern historians, unlike those of two or three generations ago, are not bound by political or military events. Their effort is to find meaningful interpretations through all the categories of historical happening.

Independence did result in a formal fragmentation of Spanish America into the seven nations of the early 1820's. It could be argued that the implications of these transcend a purely political interpretation, for the nations evoked new loyalties, and new patterns of geographical clustering came into being. Through independence an ostensibly unified society became overtly disunified. Persons familiar with Spanish America frequently emphasize this disunity, pointing out that a unitary Spanish America is an illusion and that great social and cultural differences separate the Mexican from the Venezuelan and the Peruvian from the Argentine. But the connection betwteen these differences and the period of independence is also somewhat deceptive. It is as easy to exaggerate the unity of the colonial period as it is to exaggerate the disunity of the national period. There was unquestionably a common colonial allegiance to Spain. But administratively the area was already divided into *audiencias* and other subdivisions, and these served as precedents for the national areas of the nineteenth century. The boundaries of the colonial subdivisions coincided, exactly or approximately, with

---

[2] Some of the foremost students of Latin-American history have now questioned the traditional periodization. See Richard M. Morse, "The Heritage of Latin America," in Louis Hartz (ed.), *The Founding of New Societies* (New York, 1964), p. 165; Woodrow Borah, "Colonial Institutions and Contemporary Latin America: Political and Economic Life," *Hispanic American Historical Review*, XLIII (1963), 372; Howard F. Cline's bibliographical section on Latin America in *The American Historical Association's Guide to Historical Literature* (New York, 1961); and Pierre Chaunu, *L'Amérique et les Amériques* (Paris, 1964).

the boundaries of the independent nations—not in every case, but in a sufficient number of cases to allow one to speak of continuity. An attitude frequently observable in Spanish-American writings of the late colonial period is the loyalty, even patriotism, expressed toward these geographical entities, these protonations. Thus the unity of the colony may appear as a rather superficial thing. It has an external quality, imposed from without. The matter is related to the disparate character of the revolutions for independence. If unity consisted principally in the common attachment to Spain, disunity naturally made its appearance when that attachment was dissolved.

Modern Spanish America is sometimes spoken of as a backward, or euphemistically as an underdeveloped, part of the world. The implication is that in comparison with other areas, whose rates of change are more rapid and whose status is advanced, Spanish America has failed to keep pace. Backwardness per se is, of course, regarded as an undesirable condition. In relation to the colonial past, backwardness means that insufficient change has taken place during the past century and a half, and that Spanish America remains too much the way it was in the colonial period. Hence the failure of the revolutions to introduce a new society or a new culture also carries a meaning for the present.

The argument is perhaps most clearly made with respect to economics, always a prominent subject when backwardness is under discussion. Here the phrase "colonial economy" is regularly used to refer to an export trade of raw materials, with a dependence upon foreign nations for manufactured goods and a high degree of sensitivity to foreign market conditions. Spanish America had such an economy during its colonial centuries, and, with some modifications, it has such an economy still. It is a common conception of United States history that the Revolutionary War brought about political independence and that the War of 1812 was a war for the economic independence that had not been won in the Revolution. In this sense Spanish America had no War of 1812. It continued to be dependent upon foreign purchases of raw materials and upon foreign sales of finished goods. The dependence was not upon Spain, and, as we have observed, it had been only partially upon Spain in the colonial period. Rather Britain and the United States and other nations filled the role that Spain had hoped to fill. But the trade remained "colonial."

With respect to political life, it is obvious that the national period has been a time of turbulence and constant change, in contrast to the political stability of the colonial centuries. The student's immediate impression is of a sequence of political misadventures so grotesque as to constitute a caricature of political life, a comedy of politics that, despite the sober efforts of historians, can hardly be taken seriously. But in many ways the political contrast with the colonial period is a superficial one. Beneath the surface of disorder and recurrent revolution exist important elements of continuity. A connection is expressed in the statement of Bolívar that Spanish Americans were politically unprepared for self-government. They sought to govern themselves in the nineteenth century, but they continued to be unprepared. The matter could be understood not as absolute contrast between colonial and national epochs but as a pre-existing condition becoming manifest, or as a continuous disability at first latent and then exposed. As in the matter of unity and disunity, it is as if the imperial government of Spain functioned as a cover or screen, the removal of which in the revolutions for independence permitted a variety and freedom of political activity previously forbidden.

Lack of political preparedness fitted the creole argument. To creoles it was Spain's fault that they were unprepared, for Spain had denied them the kinds of political experience that would have given them an appropriate education. Unpreparedness is suggested also in the inability to unite the several areas of revolution and in the ease with which wars in support of the monarchy became wars in opposition to the monarchy. There was a sense in which some of the most meaningful features of the independence movement were not natural or native to Spanish America at all but were imported and adapted. An incompatibility between the creoles' real proclivities and such foreign principles as constitutionalism, federalism, and democracy goes far to explain why these principles have not flourished in the Spanish-American environment. The inexperienced new governments of Spanish America lacked discretion and experimented with bizarre forms. Paraguay modeled its new government on ancient Rome, with two consuls and a congress of a thousand delegates.

In the absence of orderly democratic procedures, revolution became a standard Spanish-American device for bringing one political administration to an end and initiating its successor. Insurrection accomplished what the more "developed" nations accomplished by popular election. Only very rarely, as in Mexico after 1910, can one identify a revolution that transcended political bounds and transformed the society. The typical Spanish-American uprising since independence has been a palace or barracks revolt, and the larger society has had nothing to do with it. It is possible to be near the center of a Spanish-American revolution and not know that it is taking place. Spectators have been known to mistake a change in Spanish-American government for a parade.

With respect to dictatorship, which is a second obvious feature of the national governments following independence, we cannot draw so sharp a line between the apparent and the real. We cannot pretend that the dictatorships have not been genuine. Dictators have sometimes governed tiny nations, and their political techniques have sometimes assumed opéra bouffe forms, but there can be no mistaking the fact that they have been dictatorial. There was nothing quite like them in the colonial period. Were they then wholly new in the nineteenth century, or is there something in the colonial period that provides an antecedent condition or in other ways accounts for them?

One need not look far in the colonial period to find expressions of authority, political and of other kinds. The general atmosphere of dictatorship—its preoccupation with personal power and with self-assertion, its neglect of the "rights" of individuals—existed from the beginning. A large subordinate population, exploitable and already exploited, was ready at hand. The creole class craved an unrealized power. In the plantations and haciendas of Spanish America, political states existed in microcosm and their *hacendados* were dictatorial masters. Out of the further competitions of these—caudillo vs. caudillo—in the nineteenth century, national dictators emerged. Here again the Spanish imperial government may be understood as a repressive force or cover, under which the components of dictatorship accumulated. With the removal of the imperial government, dictatorship found a congenial environment in the jurisdictions of the new nations. It received an additional impetus from the militarism of the revolutions, for the first dictators were revolutionary officers, and they were supported in power by their own armies. Those that failed to achieve a national stature became "caudillos" in their own districts, a fact that helps to explain why the original seven nations of independent Spanish America further fragmented into sixteen.

Law has continued to occupy an ambiguous position in the Spanish-American political view of the past hundred and fifty years. On the one hand, law has been accorded great respect. The lawyer is an honored and ubiquitous professional type. Most of the higher degrees granted in Spanish-American universities are legal degrees. Laws are proclaimed with impressive solemnity. Constitutions are honored as fundamental expressions of national policy, and cases are argued on the basis of constitutional law as they were on the basis of the Recopilación in the late colonial period. But the relation between law and actual human behavior is not what it is in the Anglo-American experience. There is a certain impracticality and inflation in the respect paid to constitutions, and a tendency to discard existing documents and start afresh. A Spanish-American nation may issue a series of constitutions within a few years' time, and one is hard put to decide whether this reflects a respect or a disrespect for constitutions. Law leads a life of its own, much as historical scholarship does in the United States. It is an academic subject, separated from reality by the continuing assumption that its significance and application are in doubt. Routine business is conducted around the law, in fees and bribes, in personal loyalties, in official compromises, in codes of honor, in tax evasion, and in embezzlement. Such activities continue to be regarded as natural and expectable, as in the colonial period.[3] The view implies a certain

---

[3] Robert Potash remarks on the similarity between the modern Argentine *blanqueo de capitales* and the colonial *composición:* "Just as Philip II's government, pressed for funds, was willing to update land titles and overlook past irregularities in return for present payments, so the Argentine government in its desperate search for funds whitewashes past tax irregularities and regularizes the status of those who will come in and make payment of current taxes." Robert A.

tolerance of human frailties and is not unrelated to the pride that foreigners frequently attribute to Spanish-American personalities. It offers the sharpest of contrasts with the self-conscious ethic of Puritan New England, which insisted upon direct, personal, and literal obedience of law by individuals acutely aware of their own depravity.

Part of the reason that human law is treated at once so respectfully and so lightly in Spanish America relates to the ancient concept of natural law. It is no accident that the law of nature was introduced into the debates concerning the justice of the Spanish imperial effort or that in modern times Spaniards and Spanish Americans have been outstanding in the fields of international law and abstract legal theory. The law of nature plays a part in all Hispanic legal thinking. A human law merits respect in so far as it constitutes a reflection of natural law. But it is natural also for human conduct to fall short of perfection. Thus one could say that United States observers fail to appreciate the significance of the Spanish-American attitude toward law. The Spanish American's disobedience of law is not lawlessness or irresponsibility in the narrow sense. It is rationalized and justified in terms of obedience to another law, and the Spanish American's understanding of law is both Catholic and catholic. The Protestant convention is to emphasize not the "humanity" of the Spanish-American attitude toward law but rather its antisocial or defiant side. The English loan word desperado means not a person in despair but an outlaw.

Individualism is an element in the psychology of Spanish America, just as it is in the United States. But in the United States it is a political and social and economic concept, whereas in Spanish America individualism is ethical and religious and personal. Individualism dictates not so much an equality of opportunity or obligation in relation to others as a fulfillment of one's own inner integrity, one's *dignidad,* one's honor, one's *alma.* Spanish American individualism is not inconsistent with an established and continuing class system. It has not promoted democracy. It allows the indi-

Potash, "Colonial Institutions and Contemporary Latin America: A Commentary on Two Papers," *Hispanic American Historical Review,* XLIII (1963), 393.

vidual, or a small group of individuals, to take advantage of others and to exploit rather than change the society.[4]

In Spanish America some additional constants in the relation of the individual to the state connect the early colonial period with the present, and much that is liberal in the history of the national period—meaning much that is derived from the eighteenth-century Enlightenment—runs counter to these. The concept of a republic consisting of equal citizens is one. The belief in practical progress is another. A functioning party system with its concomitant of political elections, particularly honest political elections, likewise fits the pattern. Spanish America's authoritarian structure, its popular indifference to civic needs, and its sense of fatalism are legacies that progressive liberals have opposed. "Colonial period" has a more pejorative meaning in Spanish America than in Anglo-America precisely because so large a liberal effort has been devoted to rejecting it and because it has not yet been completely rejected.

Like the liberalism of the Bourbon legislation under Charles III, liberalism in nineteenth-century Spanish America repeatedly found itself in conflict with antiliberal traditions. In a society unprepared for self-government, opportunistic dictators shifted easily between liberalism and conservatism. Change occurred at a slow pace, and the practical meaning of the terms liberal and conservative remained vague. Federalism became a travesty when espoused by a unitary figure like Juan Manuel de Rosas in Argentina. An Indian class of private landholders, legislated into existence under Benito Juárez in Mexico, was denied its legal opportunity in a complete distortion of the legislation's intent. No national government after independence ever evoked the universal loyalty that had been attached to the king of Spain. Significantly, honest elections became the immediate goal of liberalism. José Batlle, who instituted the far-reaching Uruguayan reforms of the early twentieth century, and Francisco Madero, who initiated Mexico's major revolution of 1910, both assigned the most prominent place in their programs to electoral reform.

The first institution on which liberalism was able to focus a clear

---

[4] John Gillin, "Ethos Components in Modern Latin American Culture," *American Anthropologist*, LVII (1955), 488–500.

attention after independence was the church. The church survived the revolutions as it had survived all earlier crises of the colonial period. Ecclesiastics were divided on the question of separation from Spain, but the issue was hardly more disruptive than the many other issues on which ecclesiastics were divided. What was significant for the church was the loss of royal support. Patronato Real came to an end. For the first time since the liberal measures of Charles III in defiance of the Jesuits, ecclesiastical properties and privileges were in danger. The liberal opposition to the Spanish-American church attacked not simply a single ecclesiastical order but the entire ecclesiastical complex. Immediate conflicts between the new states and the church related to tithe collection, special courts, education, charitable funds, cemeteries, and marriage—matters in which the church suffered repeated secular inroads. Occasional conservative regimes restored the ecclesiastical privileges—the prime example is the government of Gabriel García Moreno (1860–75) in Ecuador, under whom the church was in some respects stronger than in the colonial period—only to see them relinquished again under liberal regimes. The conflicts were in part ideological. Extreme liberals went beyond anticlericalism to the position that the church was in all ways an obstacle to progress and that ecclesiastics were enemies of the state. What rendered the church especially vulnerable was its property and wealth, which had been assembled in the colonial period as an inalienable possession, but which could be abruptly sequestered and liquidated by secular governments that were chronically in need of funds.

Within its own terms Spanish America has changed enormously since the colonial period. The change is cumulative and accelerating. As the distance from the colonial past increases, conservatism comes to be devoted to the preservation of more recent positions than the colonial ones, and Spanish Americans are able to view the colonial period more as a fixed historical and less as a polemical contemporary subject. But the process of escape from the colonial past remains much less complete than in the United States, and the difference reinforces the view that Spanish America is underdeveloped.

Underdevelopment itself is a modern concept, historically and philosophically dependent upon the eighteenth-century faith in progress. It reflects an extension of the egalitarian principle from the society of individuals to the society of nations—for the whole purpose of recognizing underdevelopment is to correct it and to raise the underdeveloped nations to the level of the developed nations.[5] It is in part the United States' commitment to progress that makes Spanish America so difficult to understand. So powerful is the United States' concern with progress that we are not content to confine the concept to our own country, but feel the obligation to export it to underdeveloped areas, including Spanish America. What our information media emphasize in the Spanish-American scene is the relation between selected subjects—revolution, industrialization, dictatorship, education—and the presence or absence of progress. What our government proposes as its policy is an "alliance" for progress. But what the colonial and modern history of Spain in America so steadfastly informs us is that Spanish America is less concerned with progress than we are.

[5] Title I of the Charter of Punta del Este (Alliance for Progress) states the initial objective as follows: "To achieve in the participating Latin American countries a substantial and sustained growth of per capita income at a rate designed to attain, at the earliest possible date, levels of income capable of assuring self-sustaining development, and sufficient to make Latin American income levels constantly larger in relation to the levels of the more industrialized nations. In this way the gap between the living standards of Latin America and those of the more developed countries can be narrowed. Similarly, presently existing differences in income levels among the Latin American countries will be reduced by accelerating the development of the relatively less developed countries and granting them maximum priority in the distribution of resources and in international cooperation in general. In evaluating the degree of relative development, account will be taken not only of average levels of real income and gross product per capita, but also of indices of infant mortality, illiteracy, and per capita daily caloric intake." Organization of American States, *Alliance for Progress: Official Documents Emanating from the Special Meeting of the Inter-American Economic and Social Council at the Ministerial Level Held in Punta del Este, Uruguay from August 5 to 17, 1961* (Washington, 1961), p. 10.

Bibliography

Abundant bibliographical resources exist for studies of Spanish-American history. English-speaking students ordinarily turn first to Robin A. Humphreys, *Latin American History, A Guide to the Literature in English* (London, New York, and Toronto, 1958), which lists and comments on the principal writings in all fields of the subject. A basic general bibliography in Spanish is Benito Sánchez Alonso, *Fuentes de la historia española e hispanoamericana* (3 vols., Madrid, 1952). The Hispanic American portion of the *American Historical Association's Guide to Historical Literature* (New York, 1961) is a carefully selected bibliography with commentary by Howard F. Cline and others. For recent and current materials, students depend on the *Handbook of Latin American Studies,* of which twenty-seven volumes have now been published (Cambridge, Mass., and Gainesville, Fla., 1936–65), and which continues to appear at the rate of one volume per year under the editorship of Earl J. Pariseau. The *Handbook* covers archaeology, ethnology, art history, political science, economics, literature, and a number of other fields, and for most purposes it is the most comprehensive and useful guide in existence. A critical and selective bibliography for history, entitled *Latin America, A Guide to Historical Literature,* is now being compiled under the general editorship of Charles C. Griffin.

Bibliographies of special subjects, mainly prepared by scholars in the United States, include Cecil K. Jones, *A Bibliography of Latin American Bibliographies* (Washington, 1942); Raymond L. Grismer, *A New Bibliography of the Literatures of Spain and Spanish America* (7 vols., Minneapolis, St. Louis, and Dubuque, 1941–46); E. G. Cox, *A Reference Guide to the Literature of Travel,* of which the second volume (Seattle, 1938) deals with America; R. C. Smith and Elizabeth Wilder,

Guide to the Art of Latin America (Washington, 1948); Ralph S. Boggs, *Bibliography of Latin American Folklore* (New York, 1940); José Alcina Franch and Josefina Palop Martínez, *América en la época de Carlos V* (Madrid, 1958), a listing of books and articles that have appeared since 1900; and Paul Baginsky, *German Works Relating to America, 1493–1800* (New York, 1942).

Students should be aware of the work of two great Spanish-American bibliographers: Joaquín García Icazbalceta, whose *Bibliografía mexicana del siglo XVI* has been reprinted with additional new materials by Agustín Millares Carlo (Mexico, 1954); and José Toribio Medina, whose publications include *La imprenta en Lima* (4 vols., Santiago de Chile, 1904–7), *La imprenta en Quito* (Santiago de Chile, 1904), and other valuable works of colonial bibliography.

Archival calendars of manuscript sources on Spanish America are available for a large number of depositories. The most convenient guide to all this material is Lino Gómez Canedo, *Los archivos de la historia de América: Período colonial español* (2 vols., Mexico, 1961), which provides descriptive and bibliographical data on archives in Spanish America, Europe, and the United States.

Contemporary colonial maps are assembled in a publication of the Royal Academy of History in Madrid, *Mapas españoles de América, siglos XV–XVII* (Madrid, 1951), with a full analytic commentary. *A Catalogue of Maps of Hispanic America* (4 vols., New York, 1930–33), published by the American Geographical Society, is the most ample reference work on Latin American cartography, listing maps in various collections as well as in scientific books and periodicals. The most widely used map for Latin America is probably the Millionth Map, for which Earl P. Hanson has edited a one-volume guide, *Index to Map of Hispanic America, 1:1,000,000* (Washington, 1945). Mention should also be made of the *Planos de ciudades iberoamericanos y filipinas existentes en el Archivo de Indias* (2 vols., Madrid, 1951), which reproduces town maps and city plans. The second volume contains commentary by Julio González y González.

General works on colonial Spanish-American history have been prepared from a variety of points of view. E. G. Bourne's *Spain in America, 1450–1580* (New York and London, 1904), in the first American Nation Series, has recently been reprinted in an edition by Benjamin Keen (New York, 1962). Bourne emphasized the periods of discovery and exploration and conquest, but he did not neglect later subjects and his interpretation is distinguished by a detachment that was unusual sixty years ago. More recently, the foremost treatments in English are Clarence H. Haring, *The Spanish Empire in America* (New York, 1947), and Bailey W. Diffie, *Latin-American Civilization: Colonial Period* (Harrisburg, 1945). The former is a factual, systematic work useful for reference on any aspect of the subject. The latter is a more personal interpretation keyed to the relation between the historic human society and the geographical environment.

Textbooks covering the whole of Latin-American history to the present include Hubert Herring, *A History of Latin America from the Beginnings to the Present* (New York, 1961); Donald E. Worcester and Wendell G. Schaeffer, *The Growth and Culture of Latin America* (New York, 1956); Mary W. Williams, Ruhl J. Bartlett, and Russell E. Miller, *The People and Politics of Latin America* (Boston, 1955); Alfred B. Thomas, *Latin America, A History* (New York, 1956); and John E. Fagg, *Latin America, A General History* (New York, 1963). All contain useful sections on the Spanish colonial period.

Two works by William L. Schurz, *Latin America, A Descriptive Survey* (New York, 1949), and *This New World, The Civilization of Latin America* (New York, 1954), are well-informed, popular accounts, with keen insights into the character of the history. Two studies by Salvador de Madariaga, *The Rise of the Spanish American Empire* (New York, 1947), and *The Fall of the Spanish American Empire* (New York, 1948), reflect the interpretation of a highly literate and perceptive Spanish historian. General treatments in Spanish are Ricardo Levene, *Historia de América* (14 vols., Buenos Aires, 1940–41); Diego Barros Arana, *Compendio de historia de América* (2 vols., Santiago de Chile, 1865); Francisco Morales Padrón, *Manual de historia universal*, of which the fifth volume, *Historia general de América* (Madrid, 1962), deals with colonial Spanish America; and the multivolume *Historia de América y de los pueblos americanos*, edited by Antonio Ballesteros y Beretta, which began publication in Barcelona in 1936. These large-scale Spanish works, in addition to their other merits, are notable for their maps and illustrations.

Comparisons among the various colonizing nations in America were introduced first in a serious way by Herbert E. Bolton and Thomas M. Marshall in *The Colonization of North America, 1492–1783* (New York, 1920), and in Bolton's presidential address before the American Historical Association in 1932, "The Epic of Greater America," *American Historical Review,* XXXVIII (1932–33), 448–474. The resulting commentary on unity and disunity is collected and edited by Lewis

Hanke in *Do the Americas Have a Common History?* (New York, 1964). The subject has received recent renewed attention under the auspices of the Pan American Institute of Geography and History, the various studies culminating in the work of Silvio Zavala, *Programa de historia de América: Epoca colonial* (2 vols., Mexico, 1961), of which a summary in English has been made by Max Savelle under the title *The Colonial Period in the History of the New World* (Mexico, 1962). In *L'Amérique et les Amériques* (Paris, 1964), Pierre Chaunu has imaginatively interpreted the Spanish colonies in relation to the whole of hemispheric history.

Published primary materials for colonial Spanish-American history occur mainly in collections issued in the original language. The *Colección de documentos inéditos para la historia de España,* Martín Fernández Navarrete *et al.,* eds. (112 vols., Madrid, 1842–95); the *Colección de documentos inéditos relativos al descubrimiento, conquista y organización . . . de Indias* (42 vols., Madrid, 1864–84); and the *Colección de documentos inéditos para la historia de Ibero- (Hispano-) América* (14 vols., Madrid, 1927–32) are three fundamental anthologies of documents. Primary texts on the social history of Spanish America have been edited by Richard Konetzke, *Colección de documentos para la historia de la formación social de Hispanoamérica, 1493–1810* (3 vols., Madrid, 1953–1962). Numerous documentary works exist for particular areas, such as the *Epistolario de Nueva España, 1505–1818,* edited by Francisco del Paso y Troncoso (16 vols., Mexico, 1939–42), and the *Documentos históricos y geográficos relativos a la conquista y colonización rioplatense* (5 vols., Buenos Aires, 1941).

The larger European background of colonization is the subject of a separate volume in the New American Nation Series with its own bibliography. Specifically for Spanish history, the classic older work in English is Roger B. Merriman, *The Rise of the Spanish Empire in the Old World and the New* (4 vols., New York, 1918–34). Of a number of recent studies the most notable are J. H. Elliott, *Imperial Spain, 1469–1716* (London, 1963), and John Lynch, *Spain under the Habsburgs* (New York, 1964). Outstanding works in Spanish include Rafael Altamira, *Historia de España y de la civilización española* (4 vols., Barcelona, 1928–29); Antonio Ballesteros y Beretta, *Historia de España y de su influencia en la historia universal* (11 vols., Barcelona, 1943–56); and Fernando Soldevila Zubiburu, *Historia de España* (8 vols., Barcelona, 1959–64). A brilliant modern study of Spain together with other parts of the Mediterranean world is Fernand Braudel, *La Méditerranée et le monde méditerranéen à l'époque de Philippe II* (Paris, 1949). One of the most influential of recent Spanish historians has been Jaime Vicens Vives, whose *Manual de historia económica de España* (Barcelona, 1959), and *Historia social y económica de España y América* (5 vols., Barcelona, 1957–59) are impressive efforts to modernize the terms and concepts of Spanish history. The latter contains contributions by a number of Vicens Vives' disciples, and it deals with Spanish America as well as with Spain.

Specific Spanish origins of American institutions have been studied by Robert S. Chamberlain in "The *Corregidor* in Castile in the Sixteenth Century and the Residencia as Applied to the *Corregidor*," *Hispanic American Historical Review*, XXIII (1943), 222–257, and in "Castilian Backgrounds of the Repartimiento-Encomienda," *Carnegie Institution of Washington Publication* No. 509 (Washington, 1939), pp. 19–66. Another important article on Spanish antecedents is Charles Julian Bishko, "The Peninsular Background of Latin American Cattle Ranching," *Hispanic American Historical Review*, XXXII (1952), 491–515. With respect to intellectual history, all students should be aware of the authoritative study of Marcel Bataillon, *Erasme et l'Espagne: Recherches sur l'histoire spirituelle du XVIᵉ siècle* (Paris, 1937). The Spanish translation of this by Antonio Alatorre, *Erasmo y España, estudios sobre la historia espiritual del siglo XVI* (Mexico, 1950), contains an additional chapter on Erasmus and the New World. Two substantial studies concerning Spain in the sixteenth century are Ramón Carande Thobar, *Carlos V y sus banqueros* (Madrid, 1943), and José Miranda, *España y Nueva España en la época de Felipe II* (Mexico, 1962). The entire subject of Spanish history in reference to the colony is considered with expert bibliographical control in Charles Julian Bishko's article, "The Iberian Background of Latin American History: Recent Progress and Continuing Problems," *Hispanic American Historical Review*, XXXVI (1956), 50–80.

The other "background," that of the native American Indian societies, constitutes an enormous and complex subject. The nonspecialist, who cannot expect to keep abreast of the rapid archaeological advances, ordinarily contents himself with surveys, which are always more or less out of date. The largest and most comprehensive survey so far is Julian H. Steward (ed.), *Handbook of South American Indians* (7 vols., Washington, 1946–59). A companion series, *Handbook of Middle American Indians*, is now in process of publication under the general editorship of Robert Wauchope. Its first volume, *Natural Environment and Early Cultures* (Austin, Tex., 1964), is edited by Robert C. West. George Vaillant, *Aztecs of Mexico* (New York, 1941), and Sylvanus G. Morley, *The Ancient Maya* (Stanford, 1956), remain standard, though they are outdated, treatments. Walter Krickeberg, *Altmexikanische Kulturen* (Berlin, 1956), is a thorough and critical text of Mexican prehistory. A single-volume survey of the entire subject is Salvador Canals Frau, *Las civilizaciones prehispánicas de América* (Buenos Aires, 1955).

General literature on colonization embraces writings of numerous kinds. Wilbur C. Abbott is one of several who deal in a comprehensive way with *The Expansion of Europe* (New York, 1938). J. N. L. Baker, *A History of Geographical Discovery and Exploration* (London, 1937); A. P. Newton (ed.), *The Great Age of Discovery* (London, 1932); and Boise Penrose, *Travel and Discovery in the Renaissance* (Cambridge, 1955), are pre-eminent among recent writings on the age of discovery. J. H Parry's two works, *Europe and a Wider World, 1415–1715* (London, 1949), and especially *The Age of Reconnaissance* (London, 1963), are lucid accounts that admirably summarize this field, and Adolf Rein, *Die europäische Ausbreitung über die Erde* (Potsdam, 1931), contains many perceptive observations. Antecedents may be studied in C. R. Beazley, *The Dawn of Modern Geography* (3 vols., Oxford, 1897–1906), and G. H. T. Kimble, *Geography in the Middle Ages* (London, 1938). Subsequent voyaging is dealt with by Edward Heawood in *A History of Geographical Discovery in the Seventeenth and Eighteenth Centuries* (Cambridge, Eng., 1912). Primary accounts of most of the major expeditions appear in English in the great series of the Hakluyt Society. Portuguese exploration in Africa and the east are treated in Edgar Prestage, *The Portuguese Pioneers* (London, 1933); J. W. Blake, *European Beginnings in West Africa, 1454–1578* (London, New York, and Toronto, 1937); C. R. Beazley, *Prince Henry the Navigator* (New York, 1895); and K. G. Jayne, *Vasco da Gama and His Successors* (London, 1910). A volume of exceptional interest is A. L. Locke and B. J. Stern (eds.), *When Peoples Meet* (New York, 1942), with articles such as "The Effects of Western Culture upon Primitive Peoples" by Raymond Firth, and "Europeanization and Its Consequences" by George Young.

Columbus may be studied in older works such as Henry Harrisse, *Christoph Colomb* (2 vols., Paris, 1884–85), and John Boyd Thacher, *Christopher Columbus* (3 vols., New York and London, 1903–4), and especially the superb modern biography by Samuel E. Morison, *Admiral of the Ocean Sea* (2 vols., Boston, 1942). The *Journal* of Columbus has been translated by Cecil Jane (New York, 1960), and Ferdinand Columbus' biography of his father, *The Life of the Admiral Christopher Columbus,* has been translated by Benjamin Keen (New Brunswick, 1959). In "The Meaning of 'Discovery' in the Fifteenth and Sixteenth Centuries," *American Historical Review,* LXVIII (1962–63), 1–21, Wilcomb E. Washburn offers some fresh interpretations concerning word meanings of the period. A modern and intriguing account, with interesting views on the "Italian" preconceptions of Columbus with respect to royal monopoly and the question of private enterprise, is Richard Konetzke, *Entdecker und Eroberer Amerikas* (Frankfurt, 1963). Texts relating to post-Columbian voyages are available in Martín Fernández de Navarrete (ed.), *Colección de los viajes y descubrimientos* (5 vols., Buenos Aires, 1945–46), and in the Hakluyt Society publications. The older bibliography on post-Columbian voyages is amply cited by E. G. Bourne in *Spain in America,* and to it we should now add only a few major works such as Roberto Levillier, *América la bien llamada* (2 vols., Buenos Aires, 1948), and Kathleen Romoli, *Balboa of Darién* (Garden City, N.Y., 1953).

Like discovery and exploration, conquest has been among the most popular of all subjects in Spanish-American history. William H. Prescott's classic studies, *History of the Conquest of Mexico* and *History of the Conquest of Peru,* occur in many editions. Prescott's narratives are of epic proportions, and though written over a hundred years ago remain accurate and valuable. A special issue of the *Hispanic American Historical Review,* February, 1959, reviews and evaluates Prescott's writing and provides some additional bibliography. Everyone enjoys reading the firsthand accounts of conquest, such as Cortés' letters and the *Historia verdadera* of Bernal Díaz del Castillo, both of which have been published many times. Philip Ainsworth Means, "Biblioteca andina," in *Transactions of the Connecticut Academy of Arts and Sciences,* XXIX (1928), 271–525, is a bibliography of the sources for pre-Spanish Peru, but it incidentally describes the principal writings on the conquest as well. Raúl Porras Barrenechea, *Los cronistas del Perú* (Lima, 1962), deals with Peruvian sources from the conquest period into the seventeenth century. For other areas special mention may be made of two scholarly works by Robert S. Chamberlain, *The Conquest and Colonization of Yucatan* (Washington, 1948) and *The*

Conquest and Colonization of Honduras (Washington, 1953). The Germans in Venezuela are the subject of Germán Arciniegas, *Germans in the Conquest of America* (New York, 1943), and of Juan Friede, *Los Welser en la conquista de Venezuela* (Caracas, 1961). Both Arciniegas and Friede have also contributed new data on the conquest of New Granada—the former in *The Knight of El Dorado* (New York, 1942), a biography of Gonzalo Jiménez de Quesada, and the latter in *Vida y viajes de Nicolás Federmann* (Bogotá, 1960). In *Los grupos de conquistadores en Tierra firme* (Santiago de Chile, 1962), Mario Góngora examines the social and economic conduct of conquistadores. Finally mention may be made of the interesting study of conquest weapons and militarism, *Las armas de la conquista* (Buenos Aires, 1950), by Alberto Mario Salas. A large number of other writings on the conquests might be cited.

The various issues raised by conquest have occupied the attention of numerous historians in recent years. *The Spanish Struggle for Justice in the Conquest of America* (Philadelphia, 1949) by Lewis Hanke is a fascinating study of Spanish theories of war and colonization and the efforts to implement them in America. Many other works by Hanke, such as *The First Social Experiments in America* (Cambridge, Mass., 1935) and *Aristotle and the American Indians* (London, 1959), as well as numerous shorter articles by the same author, bear on this theme. J. H. Parry, *The Spanish Theory of Empire in the Sixteenth Century* (Cambridge, Eng., 1940), competently summarizes Spanish imperial doctrine. Along the same lines should be mentioned Silvio Zavala, *The Political Philosophy of the Conquest of America* (Mexico, 1953). The theory and reality of the imperial state in its relation to conquest, encomienda, *corregimiento, repartimiento,* and other post-conquest institutions are developed in Mario Góngora, *El estado en el derecho indiana, época de fundación, 1492–1570* (Santiago de Chile, 1951). Theological aspects are treated by Venancio D. Carro in *La teología y los teólogos-juristas españoles ante la conquista de América* (2 vols., Madrid, 1944).

The special subject of Las Casas runs through and through the works just mentioned. The older biography by Sir Arthur Helps, *Life of Las Casas* (London, 1868), is mainly of antiquarian interest now. Students have at their disposal two very different modern biographies in *Bartolomé de Las Casas* by Manuel Giménez Fernández, of which two volumes have been published (Seville, 1953–60), and *El padre Las Casas: Su doble personalidad* (Madrid, 1963) by Ramón Menéndez

Pidal. The latter is an exhaustive condemnation, a large summary of the anti-Las Casas literature of the last 400 years with some new criticism by the author. Las Casas' *Brevíssima relación* has been reprinted many times, principally in the tradition of the Black Legend. Of various editions of Las Casas' *Historia de las Indias*, that of Agustín Millares Carlo and Lewis Hanke (3 vols., Mexico, 1951) is recommended. The same editors have issued Las Casas' *Del único modo de atraer a todos los pueblos a la verdadera religión* (Mexico, 1942). Two special writings on the Vera Paz experiment may be consulted: *Die Verapaz im 16. und 17. Jahrhundert* (Munich, 1936) by Karl Sapper, and "La Vera Paz, roman et histoire," *Bulletin hispanique*, LIII (1951), 235–299, by Marcel Bataillon. Interest in Las Casas and the Black Legend has much increased in recent years, and this is reflected in the large number of monographic and periodical writings.

Fundamental works on encomienda are Leslie Byrd Simpson, *The Encomienda in New Spain* (Berkeley and Los Angeles, 1950), which deals with the origins of encomienda in the West Indies and its development in Mexico, and Silvio Zavala, *La encomienda indiana* (Madrid, 1935), a general treatment emphasizing the early Mexican form. Elman R. Service, "The *Encomienda* in Paraguay," *Hispanic American Historical Review*, XXXI (1951), 230–252, and Eduardo Arcila Farías, *El régimen de la encomienda en Venezuela* (Seville, 1957), give other descriptions. A useful note on terminology is contained in F. A. Kirkpatrick, "Repartimiento-Encomienda," *Hispanic American Historical Review*, XIX (1939), 372–379. Kirkpatrick's article, "The Landless Encomienda," *Hispanic American Historical Review*, XXII (1942), 765–774, points out the distinctions between encomienda privileges and land possession, the subject also of Silvio Zavala's detailed work, *De encomiendas y propiedad territorial en algunas regiones de la América española* (Mexico, 1940). There exists very little on encomienda after the sixteenth century, though a revealing seventeenth-century document has been published by Leslie Byrd Simpson, "A Seventeenth-Century Encomienda: Chimaltenango, Guatemala," *The Americas*, XV (1959), 393–402. Recent encomienda literature has been surveyed in a bibliographical article by Robert S. Chamberlain, "Simpson's The Encomienda in New Spain and Recent Encomienda Studies," *Hispanic American Historical Review*, XXXIV (1954), 238–250.

The basic works in English on church and state are John Lloyd Mecham, *Church and State in Latin America* (Chapel Hill, N.C.,

1934), the first part of which deals with the colonial period, and William E. Shiels, *King and Church: The Rise and Fall of the Patronato Real* (Chicago, 1961). Mariano Cuevas, *Historia de la iglesia en México* (5 vols., Mexico, 1946–47), and Rubén Vargas Ugarte, *Historia de la iglesia en el Perú* (3 vols., Lima, 1953–61), are detailed treatments for those two viceroyalties. Relations between the American church and the papacy are studied by Pedro Leturia in *Relaciones entre la Santa Sede e Hispanoamérica* (3 vols., Caracas, 1959–60). Rafael Gómez Hoyos, *La iglesia de América en las leyes de Indias* (Madrid, 1961), contains information on the church as an institution in Hispanic law.

Outstanding studies of the missionary period are, for Mexico, Robert Ricard, *La "Conquête spirituelle" du Mexique* (Paris, 1933), and, for Peru, Antonine Tibesar, *Franciscan Beginnings in Colonial Peru* (Washington, 1953), and Fernando de Armas Medina, *Cristianización del Perú (1532–1600)* (Seville, 1953). The role of the nonmonastic clergy in missionary work, is examined by Constantino Bayle in *El clero secular y la evangelización de América* (Madrid, 1950). John L. Phelan, *The Millennial Kingdom of the Franciscans in the New World, A Study of the Writings of Gerónimo de Mendieta* (Berkeley and Los Angeles, 1956), affords many insights into the decline of the missionary effort and the tradition of millennial thought relating to the American colonies. Additional aspects of proselytization history are studied by Ursula Lamb in "Religious Conflicts in the Conquest of Mexico," *Journal of the History of Ideas*, XVII (1956), 526–539, and Constantino Bayle, "La comunión entre los indios americanos," *Revista de Indias*, IV (1943), 197–254.

In later ecclesiastical history the literature concentrates on the Inquisition and the Jesuits. Henry C. Lea, *The Inquisition in the Spanish Dependencies* (New York and London, 1908), and José Toribio Medina, *Historia del tribunal del Santo oficio de la inquisición en Lima* (2 vols., Santiago de Chile, 1887), are valuable older works. An extreme view of the Jesuits is voiced by Louis Baudin, *Une Théocratie socialiste: l'état jésuite du Paraguay* (Paris, 1962). Magnus Mörner, *The Political and Economic Activities of the Jesuits in the La Plata Region* (Stockholm, 1953), is the most objective and best scholarly examination of this debated subject.

Colonial political organization is a subject to which some of the most basic researches have been devoted. Clarence H. Haring, *The Spanish Empire in America*, previously noted, is the outstanding treatment in English. Mention may be made again also of Mario Góngora, *El estado en el derecho indiano,* a well-constructed survey of Spanish colonial institutions. The Council of the Indies has been fully examined by Ernesto Schäfer, in *El Consejo real y supremo de las Indias* (2 vols., Seville, 1935–47). Significant researches on specific political offices and institutions include Lillian Estelle Fisher, *Viceregal Administration in the Spanish-American Colonies* (Berkeley, 1926); C. H. Cunningham, *The Audiencia in the Spanish Colonies* (Berkeley, 1919); J. H. Parry, *The Audiencia of New Galicia in the Sixteenth Century* (Cambridge, Eng., 1948); John P. Moore, *The Cabildo in Peru under the Hapsburgs* (Durham, 1954); Constantino Bayle, *Los cabildos seculares en la América española* (Madrid, 1952); Guillermo Lohmann Villena, *El corregidor de indios en el Perú bajo los Austrias* (Madrid, 1957); José María Mariluz Urquijo, *Ensayos sobre los juicios de residencia indianos* (Seville, 1952); and J. H. Parry, *The Sale of Public Office in the Spanish Indies under the Hapsburgs* (Berkeley, 1953). The *relaciones* or *memorias* written by viceroys to their successors have been published in part. See, for Mexico, *Instrucciones que los vireyes de Nueva España dejaron a sus sucesores* (2 vols., Mexico, 1873), and, for Peru, the systematic survey by Guillermo Lohmann Villena, *Las relaciones de los virreyes del Perú* (Seville, 1959).

A few of the political figures of the colony have been studied biographically. Ursula Lamb is the author of an important life of the governor of Hispaniola, *Frey Nicolás de Ovando, gobernador de las Indias, 1501–1509* (Madrid, 1956). There exist several studies of viceroys: Arthur S. Aiton, *Antonio de Mendoza, First Viceroy of New Spain* (Durham, N.C., 1927); Roberto Levillier, *Don Francisco de Toledo, supremo organizador del Perú* (2 vols., Buenos Aires, 1935–40); and Bernard E. Bobb, *The Viceregency of Antonio María Bucareli in New Spain, 1771–1779* (Austin, Tex., 1962).

The principal compilations of colonial law, such as Diego de Encinas, *Cedulario indiano* (4 vols., Mexico, 1596; facsimile edition, Madrid, 1945), and the *Recopilación de leyes de los reynos de las Indias* (4 vols., Madrid, 1681; various later editions), were published in the colonial period itself for the use of lawyers, judges, and political officials. A readily available text of the Laws of Burgos is Rafael Altamira, "El texto de las Leyes de Burgos de 1512," *Revista de historia de América,* No. 4 (1938), 5–79. The New Laws may be examined in several publications, including Francisco Morales Padrón, "Las leyes nuevas de 1542–1543," *Anuario de estudios americanos,* XVI (1959),

561–619. The history of the various efforts to achieve the Recopilación has been traced by Juan Manzano Manzano in *Historia de las recopilaciones de Indias* (2 vols., Madrid, 1950–56).

Clarence H. Haring was the outstanding United States student of the maritime and financial aspects of Spanish imperialism, and these subjects receive full and detailed treatment in his *Spanish Empire in America*. Earlier articles by Haring include "American Gold and Silver Production in the First Half of the Sixteenth Century," *Quarterly Journal of Economics*, XXIX (1915), 433–479; "The Early Spanish Colonial Exchequer," *American Historical Review*, XXII (1917–18), 779–796; and "Ledgers of the Royal Treasurer in Spanish America in the Sixteenth Century," *Hispanic American Historical Review*, II (1919), 173–187. In *Seville et l'Atlantique (1504–1650)* (8 vols., Paris, 1955–59), Huguette and Pierre Chaunu have provided readers with a prodigious mass of data on ships, cargoes, commerce, and the economic role of Seville in Spanish imperialism. *Consulados* are discussed in Robert S. Smith, "The Institution of the Consulado in New Spain," *Hispanic American Historical Review*, XXIV (1944), 61–83, and German O. E. Tjarks, *El consulado de Buenos Aires, y sus proyecciones en la historia del Río de la Plata* (2 vols., Buenos Aires, 1962). The works of Earl J. Hamilton on prices and American silver are classics of meticulous scholarship; see especially his *American Treasure and the Price Revolution in Spain, 1501–1650* (Cambridge, Mass., 1934). Finally it should be noted that forty years of scholarship on these subjects were reviewed by C. H. Haring in "Trade and Navigation between Spain and the Indies: A Re-View—1918–1958," *Hispanic American Historical Review*, XL (1960), 53–62.

François Chevalier, *La Formation des grands domaines au Mexique* (Paris, 1952), is a rich and suggestive history of the formation of *latifundia*. General land policies are dealt with by José M. Ots Capdequí in *El régimen de la tierra en la América española durante el período colonial* (Ciudad Trujillo, 1946). For mining, Robert C. West, *The Mining Community in Northern New Spain* (Berkeley and Los Angeles, 1949), and Walter Howe, *The Mining Guild of New Spain and Its Tribunal General* (Cambridge, Mass., 1949), are excellent. Modesto Bargalló, *La minería y la metalurgia en la América española durante la época colonial* (Mexico, 1955), is a technical history with a good bibliography of the subject. Emilio Romero, *Historia económica del Perú* (Buenos Aires, 1949), is one of the few regional economic histories.

The term ethnohistory has now come into common use with reference to precolonial, colonial, and postcolonial history involving Indians, and in the early period it is distinguished from archaeology by its dependence upon written sources. During the last few years H. B. Nicholson has been contributing a special section to the *Handbook of Latin American Studies* on ethnohistory. For the colonial period there is no comprehensive survey of the subject, though the themes have been blocked out by Pedro Armillas in *Program of the History of American Indians* (2 vols., Washington, 1958–60). The Indian history of Mexico is the subject of *Sons of the Shaking Earth* (Chicago, 1959) by Eric Wolf. For Peru the outstanding contribution is "The Quechua in the Colonial World" by George Kubler, in the second volume (pp. 331–410) of the *Handbook of South American Indians*. The forthcoming *Handbook of Middle American Indians* is to have several volumes on ethnohistory.

The most comprehensive work on Indian demography is Angel Rosenblat, *La población indígena y el mestizaje en América* (2 vols., Buenos Aires, 1954). For central Mexico, Lesley Byrd Simpson, Woodrow Borah, and Sherburne F. Cook have been producing some of the most original and imaginative scholarship in the entire field of Latin-American studies. These include *The Population of Central Mexico in the Sixteenth Century* (Berkeley and Los Angeles, 1948) by Cook and Simpson; *The Population of Central Mexico in 1548: An Analysis of the Suma de visitas de pueblos* (Berkeley and Los Angeles, 1960) by Borah and Cook; *The Indian Population of Central Mexico, 1531–1610* (Berkeley and Los Angeles, 1960) by Cook and Borah; and *The Aboriginal Population of Central Mexico on the Eve of the Spanish Conquest* (Berkeley and Los Angeles, 1963) by Borah and Cook. Mexican population studies have been carried into the seventeenth century by José Miranda, "La población indígena de México en el siglo XVII," *Historia mexicana,* XII (1962–63), 182–189. Comparable studies have not yet been made for Peru, but suggestive materials are presented by Henry F. Dobyns in "An Outline of Andean Epidemic History to 1720," *Bulletin of the History of Medicine,* XXXVII (1963), 493–515.

For social history and questions of class and race in colonial Spanish America, a valuable survey is the work of Vicens Vives noted above. Sergio Bagú, *Estructura social de la colonia* (Buenos Aires, 1952), is a comprehensive analysis of social and economic classes. Of numerous articles on these subjects the student should be aware of Richard

Konetzke, "La formación de la nobleza en Indias," *Estudios americanos,* III (1951), 329–357, for the historical stages involved in the transplanting of a "nobility," and "Sobre el problema racial en la América española," *Revista de estudios políticos,* Nos. 113–114 (1960), 179–215, on the legal position of mestizos; Elman R. Service, "Indian-European Relations in Colonial Latin America," *American Anthropologist,* LVII, Part I (1955), 411–425, which identifies the determinant role of the Indian societies for colonial history; and Lyle N. McAlister, "Social Structure and Social Change in New Spain," *Hispanic American Historical Review,* XLIII (1963), 349–370, an exceptionally perceptive study identifying classes from various points of view. The origins of white society in Spain may be examined in Luis Rubio y Moreno (ed.), *Pasajeros a Indias* (2 vols., Madrid, 1930), and in V. Aubrey Neasham, "Spain's Emigrants to the New World, 1492–1592," *Hispanic American Historical Review,* XIX (1939), 147–160.

Special mention should be made of the works of John Tate Lanning on colonial universities: *Academic Culture in the Spanish Colonies* (London and New York, 1940); *The University in the Kingdom of Guatemala* (Ithaca, 1955); and *The Eighteenth-Century Enlightenment in the University of San Carlos de Guatemala* (Ithaca, 1956).

Bernard Moses, *Spanish Colonial Literature in South America* (New York, 1922), is still useful for literary history. Two works of Irving Leonard, *Books of the Brave* (Cambridge, Mass., 1949) and *Baroque Times in Old Mexico* (Ann Arbor, 1959), combine literary and historical themes. José J. Arrom, *El teatro de Hispanoamérica en la época colonial* (Havana, 1956), is a basic survey. For the history of art there are some exceptionally fine studies: George Kubler, *Mexican Architecture of the Sixteenth Century* (2 vols., New Haven, 1952); George Kubler and Martin Soria, *Art and Architecture in Spain and Portugal and Their American Dominions, 1500 to 1800* (Baltimore, 1959); Harold E. Wethey, *Colonial Architecture and Sculpture in Peru* (Cambridge, Mass., 1949); and Pál Kelemen, *Baroque and Rococo in Latin America* (New York, 1951). Diego Angulo Iñiguez, *Historia del arte hispanoamericano* is a multivolume history published in Barcelona since 1945.

Luis Sánchez Agesta, *El pensamiento político del despotismo ilustrado* (Madrid, 1953); Jean Sarrailh, *L'Europe éclairée de la seconde moitié du XVIIIᵉ siècle* (Paris, 1954); and Richard Herr, *The Eighteenth-Century Revolution in Spain* (Princeton, 1958), are basic studies for Spain itself in the eighteenth century. Various essays on the effects of the Enlightenment have been edited by Arthur P. Whitaker in *Latin America and the Enlightenment* (Ithaca, 1961). Lillian E. Fisher, *The Intendant System in Spanish America* (Berkeley, 1929), and Herbert I. Priestley, *José de Gálvez, Visitor-General of New Spain* (Berkeley, 1916), are standard monographs in English. John Lynch, *Spanish Colonial Administration, 1782–1810* (London, 1958), investigates the intendancy in the Platine region. Roland D. Hussey, *The Caracas Company* (Cambridge, Mass., 1934), is one of the few detailed examinations of the eighteenth-century corporations.

Few persons have created and defined a historical field so successfully as Herbert E. Bolton. Bolton's own writings continue to occupy a prominent place in the literature of the borderlands, and his volume in the Chronicles of America series, *The Spanish Borderlands* (New Haven, 1921), is still the only general summary. Like other writings of Bolton, and like many other writings on the borderlands, it is strongest in the areas of exploration, settlement, and international implications, and weakest in economic and social history. Selections from Bolton's writings, including some previously unpublished sections, have been edited by John Bannon in *Bolton and the Spanish Borderlands* (Norman, Okla., 1964), and this is a convenient work to consult for Bolton's famous articles on "The Mission as a Frontier Institution" and on "The Epic of Greater America," both originally published in the *American Historical Review*.

Works on the northern expansion of New Spain include John Lloyd Mecham, *Francisco de Ibarra and Nueva Vizcaya* (Durham, N.C., 1927); Philip W. Powell, *Soldiers, Indians, and Silver* (Berkeley and Los Angeles, 1952); Alfred B. Thomas, *Teodoro de Croix and the Northern Frontier of New Spain, 1776–1783* (Norman, Okla., 1941); Vito Alessio Robles, *Coahuila y Texas en la época colonial* (Mexico, 1938); and a number of works on the northern Jesuits by Peter Masten Dunne. Biographies of the major missionary figures—*Rim of Christendom: A Biography of Eusebio Francisco Kino* (New York, 1936) by Bolton, and *The Life and Times of Fray Junípero Serra* (Washington, 1959) by Maynard J. Geiger—are distinguished contributions to borderlands studies. Spanish Florida is the subject of Verne E. Chatelain, *The Defences of Spanish Florida, 1565 to 1763* (Washington, 1941); Maynard J. Geiger, *The Franciscan Conquest of Florida (1573–1618)* (Washington, 1937); Helen H. Tanner, *Zéspedes in East Florida, 1784–1790* (Coral Gables, Fla., 1963); John Jay Te Paske, *The Governorship of Spanish Florida, 1700–1763* (Durham, N.C.,

1964); and a number of articles and monographs by Charles W. Arnade, including *Florida on Trial, 1593–1602* (Coral Gables, Fla., 1959), and *The Siege of St. Augustine in 1702* (Gainesville, Fla., 1959). For Texas, Bolton's *Texas in the Middle Eighteenth Century* (Berkeley, 1915) remains a very substantial work of scholarship. The ethnohistory of the borderlands is the subject of two important recent works: *Apache, Navaho, and Spaniard* (Norman, Okla., 1960) by Jack D. Forbes, and *Cycles of Conquest* (Tucson, 1962) by Edward H. Spicer. The items mentioned are only a small fraction of the total number of studies of the borderlands.

Index

HARPER 🔥 TORCHBOOKS

HUMANITIES AND SOCIAL SCIENCES

American Studies: General

American Studies: Colonial

American Studies: From the Revolution to 1860

CLEMENT EATON: The Freedom-of-Thought Struggle in the Old South. *Revised and Enlarged. Illus.* TB/1150

CLEMENT EATON: The Growth of Southern Civilization: 1790-1860. † *Illus.* TB/3040

LOUIS FILLER: The Crusade Against Slavery: 1830-1860. † *Illus.* TB/3029

DIXON RYAN FOX: The Decline of Aristocracy in the Politics of New York: 1801-1840. ‡ *Edited by Robert V. Remini* TB/3064

WILLIAM W. FREEHLING, Ed.: The Nullification Era: *A Documentary Record* ‡ TB/3079

FELIX GILBERT: The Beginnings of American Foreign Policy: *To the Farewell Address* TB/1200

FRANCIS GRIERSON: The Valley of Shadows: *The Coming of the Civil War in Lincoln's Midwest: A Contemporary Account* TB/1246

FRANCIS J. GRUND: Aristocracy in America: *Social Class in the Formative Years of the New Nation* TB/1001

ALEXANDER HAMILTON: The Reports of Alexander Hamilton. ‡ *Edited by Jacob E. Cooke* TB/3060

THOMAS JEFFERSON: Notes on the State of Virginia. ‡ *Edited by Thomas P. Abernethy* TB/3052

JAMES MADISON: The Forging of American Federalism: *Selected Writings of James Madison. Edited by Saul K. Padover* TB/1226

BERNARD MAYO: Myths and Men: *Patrick Henry, George Washington, Thomas Jefferson* TB/1108

JOHN C. MILLER: Alexander Hamilton and the Growth of the New Nation TB/3057

RICHARD B. MORRIS, Ed.: The Era of the American Revolution TB/1180

R. B. NYE: The Cultural Life of the New Nation: 1776-1801. † *Illus.* TB/3026

JAMES PARTON: The Presidency of Andrew Jackson. *From Vol. III of the Life of Andrew Jackson. ‡ Ed. with an Intro. by Robert V. Remini* TB/3080

FRANCIS S. PHILBRICK: The Rise of the West, 1754-1830. † *Illus.* TB/3067

TIMOTHY L. SMITH: Revivalism and Social Reform: *American Protestantism on the Eve of the Civil War* TB/1229

ALBION W. TOURGÉE: A Fool's Errand. ‡ *Ed. by George Fredrickson* TB/3074

A. F. TYLER: Freedom's Ferment: *Phases of American Social History from the Revolution to the Outbreak of the Civil War. 31 illus.* TB/1074

GLYNDON G. VAN DEUSEN: The Jacksonian Era: 1828-1848. † *Illus.* TB/3028

LOUIS B. WRIGHT: Culture on the Moving Frontier TB/1053

American Studies: The Civil War to 1900

W. R. BROCK: An American Crisis: Congress and Reconstruction, 1865-67 ° △ TB/1283

THOMAS C. COCHRAN & WILLIAM MILLER: The Age of Enterprise: *A Social History of Industrial America* TB/1054

W. A. DUNNING: Essays on the Civil War and Reconstruction. *Introduction by David Donald* TB/1181

W. A. DUNNING: Reconstruction, Political and Economic: 1865-1877 TB/1073

HAROLD U. FAULKNER: Politics, Reform and Expansion: 1890-1900. † *Illus.* TB/3020

HELEN HUNT JACKSON: A Century of Dishonor: *The Early Crusade for Indian Reform. ‡ Edited by Andrew F. Rolle* TB/3063

ALBERT D. KIRWAN: Revolt of the Rednecks: *Mississippi Politics, 1876-1925* TB/1199

ROBERT GREEN MC CLOSKEY: American Conservatism in the Age of Enterprise: 1865-1910 TB/1137

ARTHUR MANN: Yankee Reformers in the Urban Age: *Social Reform in Boston, 1880-1900* TB/1247

WHITELAW REID: After the War: *A Tour of the Southern States, 1865-1866. ‡ Edited by C. Vann Woodward* TB/3066

CHARLES H. SHINN: Mining Camps: *A Study in American Frontier Government.* ‡ *Edited by Rodman W. Paul* TB/3062

VERNON LANE WHARTON: The Negro in Mississippi: 1865-1890 TB/1178

American Studies: 1900 to the Present

RAY STANNARD BAKER: Following the Color Line: *American Negro Citizenship in Progressive Era. ‡ Illus. Edited by Dewey W. Grantham, Jr.* TB/3053

RANDOLPH S. BOURNE: War and the Intellectuals: *Collected Essays, 1915-1919. ‡ Edited by Carl Resek* TB/3043

A. RUSSELL BUCHANAN: The United States and World War II. † *Illus.* Vol. I TB/3044; Vol. II TB/3045

ABRAHAM CAHAN: The Rise of David Levinsky: *a documentary novel of social mobility in early twentieth century America. Intro. by John Higham* TB/1028

THOMAS C. COCHRAN: The American Business System: *A Historical Perspective, 1900-1955* TB/1080

FOSTER RHEA DULLES: America's Rise to World Power: 1898-1954. † *Illus.* TB/3021

JOHN D. HICKS: Republican Ascendancy: 1921-1933. † *Illus.* TB/3041

SIDNEY HOOK: Reason, Social Myths, and Democracy TB/1237

ROBERT HUNTER: Poverty: *Social Conscience in the Progressive Era. ‡ Edited by Peter d'A. Jones* TB/3065

WILLIAM L. LANGER & S. EVERETT GLEASON: The Challenge to Isolation: *The World Crisis of 1937-1940 and American Foreign Policy* Vol. I TB/3054; Vol. II TB/3055

WILLIAM E. LEUCHTENBURG: Franklin D. Roosevelt and the New Deal: 1932-1940. † *Illus.* TB/3025

ARTHUR S. LINK: Woodrow Wilson and the Progressive Era: 1910-1917. † *Illus.* TB/3023

GEORGE E. MOWRY: The Era of Theodore Roosevelt and the Birth of Modern America: 1900-1912. † *Illus.* TB/3022

RUSSEL B. NYE: Midwestern Progressive Politics: *A Historical Study of Its Origins and Development, 1870-1958* TB/1202

WILLIAM PRESTON, JR.: Aliens and Dissenters: *Federal Suppression of Radicals, 1903-1933* TB/1287

WALTER RAUSCHENBUSCH: Christianity and the Social Crisis. ‡ *Edited by Robert D. Cross* TB/3059

JACOB RIIS: The Making of an American. ‡ *Edited by Roy Lubove* TB/3070

PHILIP SELZNICK: TVA and the Grass Roots: *A Study in the Sociology of Formal Organization* TB/1230

IDA M. TARBELL: The History of the Standard Oil Company: *Briefer Version. ‡ Edited by David M. Chalmers* TB/3071

GEORGE B. TINDALL, Ed.: A Populist Reader ‡ TB/3069

TWELVE SOUTHERNERS: I'll Take My Stand: *The South and the Agrarian Tradition. Intro. by Louis D. Rubin, Jr., Biographical Essays by Virginia Rock* TB/1072

Anthropology

JACQUES BARZUN: Race: *A Study in Superstition. Revised Edition* TB/1172

JOSEPH B. CASAGRANDE, Ed.: In the Company of Man: *Twenty Portraits of Anthropological Informants. Illus.* TB/3047

W. E. LE GROS CLARK: The Antecedents of Man: *Intro. to Evolution of the Primates.* ° △ *Illus.* TB/559

CORA DU BOIS: The People of Alor. *New Preface by the author. Illus.* Vol. I TB/1042; Vol. II TB/1043

RAYMOND FIRTH, Ed.: Man and Culture: *An Evaluation of the Work of Bronislaw Malinowski* ¶ ° △ TB/1133

DAVID LANDY: Tropical Childhood: *Cultural Transmission and Learning in a Puerto Rican Village* ¶ TB/1235

L. S. B. LEAKEY: Adam's Ancestors: *The Evolution of Man and His Culture.* △ *Illus.* TB/1019

EDWARD BURNETT TYLOR: Religion in Primitive Culture. *Part II of "Primitive Culture."* § *Intro. by Paul Radin* TB/34

W. LLOYD WARNER: A Black Civilization: *A Study of an Australian Tribe.* ¶ *Illus.* TB/3056

Art and Art History

WALTER LOWRIE: Art in the Early Church. *Revised Edition. 452 illus.* TB/124

EMILE MÂLE: The Gothic Image: *Religious Art in France of the Thirteenth Century.* § △ *190 illus.* TB/44

MILLARD MEISS: Painting in Florence and Siena after the Black Death: *The Arts, Religion and Society in the Mid-Fourteenth Century. 169 illus.* TB/1148

ERICH NEUMANN: The Archetypal World of Henry Moore. △ *107 illus.* TB/2020

DORA & ERWIN PANOFSKY : Pandora's Box: *The Changing Aspects of a Mythical Symbol. Revised Edition. Illus.* TB/2021

ERWIN PANOFSKY: Studies in Iconology: *Humanistic Themes in the Art of the Renaissance.* △ *180 illustrations* TB/1077

ALEXANDRE PIANKOFF: The Shrines of Tut-Ankh-Amon. *Edited by N. Rambova. 117 illus.* TB/2011

JEAN SEZNEC: The Survival of the Pagan Gods: *The Mythological Tradition and Its Place in Renaissance Humanism and Art. 108 illustrations* TB/2004

OTTO VON SIMSON: The Gothic Cathedral: *Origins of Gothic Architecture and the Medieval Concept of Order.* △ *58 illus.* TB/2018

HEINRICH ZIMMER: Myth and Symbols in Indian Art and Civilization. *70 illustrations* TB/2005

Business, Economics & Economic History

REINHARD BENDIX: Work and Authority in Industry: *Ideologies of Management in the Course of Industrialization* TB/3035

GILBERT BURCK & EDITORS OF FORTUNE: The Computer Age: *And Its Potential for Management* TB/1179

THOMAS C. COCHRAN: The American Business System: *A Historical Perspective, 1900-1955* TB/1080

THOMAS C. COCHRAN: The Inner Revolution: *Essays on the Social Sciences in History* △ TB/1140

THOMAS C. COCHRAN & WILLIAM MILLER: The Age of Enterprise: *A Social History of Industrial America* TB/1054

ROBERT DAHL & CHARLES E. LINDBLOM: Politics, Economics, and Welfare: *Planning and Politico-Economic Systems Resolved into Basic Social Processes* TB/3037

PETER F. DRUCKER: The New Society: *The Anatomy of Industrial Order* △ TB/1082

EDITORS OF FORTUNE: America in the Sixties: *The Economy and the Society* TB/1015

ROBERT L. HEILBRONER: The Great Ascent: *The Struggle for Economic Development in Our Time* TB/3030

ROBERT L. HEILBRONER: The Limits of American Capitalism TB/1305

FRANK H. KNIGHT: The Economic Organization TB/1214

FRANK H. KNIGHT: Risk, Uncertainty and Profit TB/1215

ABBA P. LERNER: Everybody's Business: *Current Assumptions in Economics and Public Policy* TB/3051

ROBERT GREEN MC CLOSKEY: American Conservatism in the Age of Enterprise, 1865-1910 △ TB/1137

PAUL MANTOUX: The Industrial Revolution in the Eighteenth Century: *The Beginnings of the Modern Factory System in England* ○ △ TB/1079

WILLIAM MILLER, Ed.: Men in Business: *Essays on the Historical Role of the Entrepreneur* TB/1081

RICHARD B. MORRIS: Government and Labor in Early America △ TB/1244

HERBERT SIMON: The Shape of Automation: *For Men and Management* TB/1245

PERRIN STRYKER: The Character of the Executive: *Eleven Studies in Managerial Qualities* TB/1041

Education

JACQUES BARZUN: The House of Intellect △ TB/1051

RICHARD M. JONES, Ed.: Contemporary Educational Psychology: *Selected Readings* TB/1292

CLARK KERR: The Uses of the University TB/1264

JOHN U. NEF: Cultural Foundations of Industrial Civilization △ TB/1024

Historiography & Philosophy of History

JACOB BURCKHARDT: On History and Historians. △ *Introduction by H. R. Trevor-Roper* TB/1216

WILHELM DILTHEY: Pattern and Meaning in History: *Thoughts on History and Society.* ○ △ *Edited with an Introduction by H. P. Rickman* TB/1075

J. H. HEXTER: Reappraisals in History: *New Views on History & Society in Early Modern Europe* △ TB/1100

H. STUART HUGHES: History as Art and as Science: *Twin Vistas on the Past* TB/1207

RAYMOND KLIBANSKY & H. J. PATON, Eds.: Philosophy and History: *The Ernst Cassirer Festschrift. Illus.* TB/1115

ARNALDO MOMIGLIANO: Studies in Historiography ○ △ TB/1283

GEORGE H. NADEL, Ed.: Studies in the Philosophy of History: *Selected Essays from History and Theory* TB/1208

JOSE ORTEGA Y GASSET: The Modern Theme. *Introduction by Jose Ferrater Mora* TB/1038

KARL R. POPPER: The Open Society and Its Enemies △
Vol. I: *The Spell of Plato* TB/1101
Vol. II: *The High Tide of Prophecy: Hegel, Marx and the Aftermath* TB/1102

KARL R. POPPER: The Poverty of Historicism ○ △ TB/1126

G. J. RENIER: History: *Its Purpose and Method* △ TB/1209

W. H. WALSH: Philosophy of History: *An Introduction* △ TB/1020

History: General

WOLFGANG FRANKE: China and the West. *Trans by R. A. Wilson* TB/1326

L. CARRINGTON GOODRICH: A Short History of the Chinese People. △ *Illus.* TB/3015

DAN N. JACOBS & HANS H. BAERWALD: Chinese Communism: *Selected Documents* TB/3031

BERNARD LEWIS: The Arabs in History △ TB/1029

BERNARD LEWIS: The Middle East and the West ○ △ TB/1274

History: Ancient

A. ANDREWES: The Greek Tyrants △ TB/1103

ADOLF ERMAN, Ed. The Ancient Egyptians: *A Sourcebook of Their Writings. New material and Introduction by William Kelly Simpson* TB/1233

MICHAEL GRANT: Ancient History ○ △ TB/1190

SAMUEL NOAH KRAMER: Sumerian Mythology TB/1055

NAPHTALI LEWIS & MEYER REINHOLD, Eds.: Roman Civilization. *Sourcebook I: The Republic* TB/1231

NAPHTALI LEWIS & MEYER REINHOLD, Eds.: Roman Civilization. *Sourcebook II: The Empire* TB/1232

History: Medieval

P. BOISSONNADE: Life and Work in Medieval Europe: *The Evolution of the Medieval Economy, the 5th to the 15th Century.* ○ △ *Preface by Lynn White, Jr.* TB/1141

HELEN CAM: England before Elizabeth △ TB/1026

NORMAN COHN: The Pursuit of the Millennium: *Revolutionary Messianism in Medieval and Reformation Europe* △ TB/1037

3

4

VESPASIANO: Renaissance Princes, Popes, and Prelates: *The Vespasiano Memoirs: Lives of Illustrious Men of the XVth Century. Intro. by Myron P. Gilmore* TB/1111

History: Modern European

FREDERICK B. ARTZ: Reaction and Revolution, 1815-1832. * *Illus.* TB/3034

MAX BELOFF: The Age of Absolutism, 1660-1815 △ TB/1062

ROBERT C. BINKLEY: Realism and Nationalism, 1852-1871. * *Illus.* TB/3038

EUGENE C. BLACK, Ed.: European Political History, 1815-1870: *Aspects of Liberalism* TB/1331

ASA BRIGGS: The Making of Modern England, 1784-1867: *The Age of Improvement* ° △ TB/1203

CRANE BRINTON: A Decade of Revolution, 1789-1799. * *Illus.* TB/3018

D. W. BROGAN: The Development of Modern France. ° △ Volume I: *From the Fall of the Empire to the Dreyfus Affair* TB/1184
Volume II: *The Shadow of War, World War I, Between the Two Wars. New Introduction by the Author* TB/1185

J. BRONOWSKI & BRUCE MAZLISH: The Western Intellectual Tradition: *From Leonardo to Hegel* △ TB/3001

GEOFFREY BRUUN: Europe and the French Imperium, 1799-1814. * *Illus.* TB/3033

ALAN BULLOCK: Hitler, A Study in Tyranny. ° △ *Illus.* TB/1123

E. H. CARR: German-Soviet Relations Between the Two World Wars, 1919-1939 TB/1278

E. H. CARR: International Relations Between the Two World Wars, 1919-1939 ° △ TB/1279

E. H. CARR: The Twenty Years' Crisis, 1919-1939: *An Introduction to the Study of International Relations* ° △ TB/1122

GORDON A. CRAIG: From Bismarck to Adenauer: *Aspects of German Statecraft. Revised Edition* TB/1171

DENIS DIDEROT: The Encyclopedia: *Selections. Ed. and trans. by Stephen Gendzier* TB/1299

WALTER L. DORN: Competition for Empire, 1740-1763. * *Illus.* TB/3032

FRANKLIN L. FORD: Robe and Sword: *The Regrouping of the French Aristocracy after Louis XIV* TB/1217

CARL J. FRIEDRICH: The Age of the Baroque, 1610-1660. * *Illus.* TB/3004

RENÉ FUELOEP-MILLER: The Mind and Face of Bolshevism: *An Examination of Cultural Life in Soviet Russia. New Epilogue by the Author* TB/1188

M. DOROTHY GEORGE: London Life in the Eighteenth Century △ TB/1182

LEO GERSHOY: From Despotism to Revolution, 1763-1789. * *Illus.* TB/3017

C. C. GILLISPIE: Genesis and Geology: *The Decades before Darwin* § TB/51

ALBERT GOODWIN, Ed.: The European Nobility in the Eighteenth Century △ TB/1313

ALBERT GOODWIN: The French Revolution △ TB/1064

ALBERT GUÉRARD: France in the Classical Age: *The Life and Death of an Ideal* △ TB/1183

CARLTON J. H. HAYES: A Generation of Materialism, 1871-1900. * *Illus.* TB/3039

J. H. HEXTER: Reappraisals in History: *New Views on History and Society in Early Modern Europe* △ TB/1100

STANLEY HOFFMANN et al.: In Search of France: *The Economy, Society and Political System in the Twentieth Century* TB/1219

A. R. HUMPHREYS: The Augustan World: *Society, Thought, & Letters in 18th Century England* ° △ TB/1105

DAN N. JACOBS, Ed.: The New Communist Manifesto *and Related Documents. Third edition, revised* TB/1078

LIONEL KOCHAN: The Struggle for Germany: *1914-45* TB/1304

HANS KOHN: The Mind of Germany: *The Education of a Nation* △ TB/1204

HANS KOHN, Ed.: The Mind of Modern Russia: *Historical and Political Thought of Russia's Great Age* TB/1065

WALTER LAQUEUR & GEORGE L. MOSSE, Eds.: Education and Social Structure in the 20th Century. ° △ *Vol. 6 of the Journal of Contemporary History* TB/1339

WALTER LAQUEUR & GEORGE L. MOSSE, Eds.: International Fascism, 1920-1945. ° △ *Volume 1 of Journal of Contemporary History* TB/1276

WALTER LAQUEUR & GEORGE L. MOSSE, Eds.: The Left-Wing Intellectuals between the Wars 1919-1939. ° △ *Volume 2 of Journal of Contemporary History* TB/1286

WALTER LAQUEUR & GEORGE L. MOSSE, Eds.: Literature and Politics in the 20th Century. ° △ *Vol. 5 of the Journal of Contemporary History* TB/1328

WALTER LAQUEUR & GEORGE L. MOSSE, Eds.: The New History: *Trends in Historical Research and Writing since World War II.* ° △ *Vol. 4 of the Journal of Contemporary History* TB/1327

WALTER LAQUEUR & GEORGE L. MOSSE, Eds.: 1914: *The Coming of the First World War.* ° △ *Volume 3 of Journal of Contemporary History* TB/1306

FRANK E. MANUEL: The Prophets of Paris: *Turgot, Condorcet, Saint-Simon, Fourier, and Comte* TB/1218

KINGSLEY MARTIN: French Liberal Thought in the Eighteenth Century: *A Study of Political Ideas from Bayle to Condorcet* TB/1114

ROBERT K. MERTON: Science, Technology and Society in Seventeenth Century England ¶ *New Intro. by the Author* TB/1324

L. B. NAMIER: Facing East: *Essays on Germany, the Balkans, and Russia in the 20th Century* △ TB/1280

L. B. NAMIER: Personalities and Powers: *Selected Essays* △ TB/1186

L. B. NAMIER: Vanished Supremacies: *Essays on European History, 1812-1918* ° TB/1088

NAPOLEON III: Napoleonic Ideas: *Des Idées Napoléoniennes, par le Prince Napoléon-Louis Bonaparte. Ed. by Brison D. Gooch* TB/1336

FRANZ NEUMANN: Behemoth: *The Structure and Practice of National Socialism, 1933-1944* TB/1289

FREDERICK L. NUSSBAUM: The Triumph of Science and Reason, 1660-1685. * *Illus.* TB/3009

DAVID OGG: Europe of the Ancien Régime, 1715-1783 ** ° △ TB/1271

JOHN PLAMENATZ: German Marxism and Russian Communism. ° △ *New Preface by the Author* TB/1189

RAYMOND W. POSTGATE, Ed.: Revolution from 1789 to 1906: *Selected Documents* TB/1063

PENFIELD ROBERTS: The Quest for Security, 1715-1740. * *Illus.* TB/3016

PRISCILLA ROBERTSON: Revolutions of 1848: *A Social History* TB/1025

GEORGE RUDÉ: Revolutionary Europe, 1783-1815 ** ° △ TB/1272

LOUIS, DUC DE SAINT-SIMON: Versailles, The Court, and Louis XIV. ° △ *Introductory Note by Peter Gay* TB/1250

HUGH SETON-WATSON: Eastern Europe Between the Wars, 1918-1941 TB/1330

ALBERT SOREL: Europe Under the Old Regime. *Translated by Francis H. Herrick* TB/1121

N. N. SUKHANOV: The Russian Revolution, 1917: *Eyewitness Account.* △ *Edited by Joel Carmichael*
Vol. I TB/1066; Vol. II TB/1067

A. J. P. TAYLOR: From Napoleon to Lenin: *Historical Essays* ° △ TB/1268

A. J. P. TAYLOR: The Habsburg Monarchy, 1809-1918: *A History of the Austrian Empire and Austria-Hungary* ° △ TB/1187

G. M. TREVELYAN: British History in the Nineteenth Century and After: *1782-1919.* ° △ *Second Edition* TB/1251

H. R. TREVOR-ROPER: Historical Essays º △ TB/1269
ELIZABETH WISKEMANN: Europe of the Dictators, 1919-1945 ** º △ TB/1273
JOHN B. WOLF: The Emergence of the Great Powers, 1685-1715. * Illus. TB/3010
JOHN B. WOLF: France: 1814-1919: The Rise of a Liberal-Democratic Society TB/3019

Intellectual History & History of Ideas

HERSCHEL BAKER: The Image of Man: A Study of the Idea of Human Dignity in Classical Antiquity, the Middle Ages, and the Renaissance TB/1047
R. R. BOLGAR: The Classical Heritage and Its Beneficiaries: From the Carolingian Age to the End of the Renaissance △ TB/1125
RANDOLPH S. BOURNE: War and the Intellectuals: Collected Essays, 1915-1919. △ ‡ Edited by Carl Resek TB/3043
J. BRONOWSKI & BRUCE MAZLISH: The Western Intellectual Tradition: From Leonardo to Hegel △ TB/3001
ERNST CASSIRER: The Individual and the Cosmos in Renaissance Philosophy. △ Translated with an Introduction by Mario Domandi TB/1097
NORMAN COHN: The Pursuit of the Millennium: Revolutionary Messianism in Medieval and Reformation Europe △ TB/1037
C. C. GILLISPIE: Genesis and Geology: The Decades before Darwin § TB/51
G. RACHEL LEVY: Religious Conceptions of the Stone Age and Their Influence upon European Thought. △ Illus. Introduction by Henri Frankfort TB/106
ARTHUR O. LOVEJOY: The Great Chain of Being: A Study of the History of an Idea TB/1009
FRANK E. MANUEL: The Prophets of Paris: Turgot, Condorcet, Saint-Simon, Fourier, and Comte △ TB/1218
PERRY MILLER & T. H. JOHNSON, Editors: The Puritans: A Sourcebook of Their Writings
Vol. I TB/1093; Vol. II TB/1094
RALPH BARTON PERRY: The Thought and Character of William James: Briefer Version TB/1156
GEORG SIMMEL et al.: Essays on Sociology, Philosophy, and Aesthetics. ¶ Edited by Kurt H. Wolff TB/1234
BRUNO SNELL: The Discovery of the Mind: The Greek Origins of European Thought △ TB/1018
PAGET TOYNBEE: Dante Alighieri: His Life and Works. Edited with Intro. by Charles S. Singleton △ TB/1206
W. WARREN WAGAR, Ed.: European Intellectual History since Darwin and Marx TB/1297
PHILIP P. WIENER: Evolution and the Founders of Pragmatism. △ Foreword by John Dewey TB/1212
BASIL WILLEY: Nineteenth Century Studies: Coleridge to Matthew Arnold º △ TB/1261
BASIL WILLEY: More Nineteenth Century Studies: A Group of Honest Doubters º △ TB/1262

Law

EDWARD S. CORWIN: American Constitutional History: Essays edited by Alpheus T. Mason & Gerald Garvey TB/1136
ROBERT H. JACKSON: The Supreme Court in the American System of Government TB/1106
LEONARD W. LEVY, Ed.: American Constitutional Law: Historical Essays TB/1285
LEONARD W. LEVY: Freedom of Speech and Press in Early American History: Legacy of Suppression TB/1109
LEONARD W. LEVY, Ed.: Judicial Review and the Supreme Court TB/1296
LEONARD W. LEVY: The Law of the Commonwealth and Chief Justice Shaw TB/1309
RICHARD B. MORRIS: Fair Trial: Fourteen Who Stood Accused, from Anne Hutchinson to Alger Hiss. New Preface by the Author. TB/1335

Literature, Poetry, The Novel & Criticism

JAMES BAIRD: Ishmael: The Art of Melville in the Contexts of International Primitivism TB/1023
JACQUES BARZUN: The House of Intellect △ TB/1051
W. J. BATE: From Classic to Romantic: Premises of Taste in Eighteenth Century England TB/1036
RACHEL BESPALOFF: On the Iliad TB/2006
JAMES BOSWELL: The Life of Dr. Johnson & The Journal of a Tour to the Hebrides with Samuel Johnson LL.D.: Selections. º △ Edited by F. V. Morley. Illus. by Ernest Shepard TB/1254
ERNST R. CURTIUS: European Literature and the Latin Middle Ages △ TB/2015
ADOLF ERMAN, Ed.: The Ancient Egyptians: A Sourcebook of Their Writings. New Material and Introduction by William Kelly Simpson TB/1233
ALFRED HARBAGE: As They Liked It: A Study of Shakespeare's Moral Artistry TB/1035
STANLEY R. HOPPER, Ed : Spiritual Problems in Contemporary Literature § TB/21
A. R. HUMPHREYS: The Augustan World: Society, Thought and Letters in 18th Century England º △ TB/1105
ARNOLD KETTLE: An Introduction to the English Novel. △
Volume I: Defoe to George Eliot TB/1011
Volume II: Henry James to the Present TB/1012
RICHMOND LATTIMORE: The Poetry of Greek Tragedy △ TB/1257
J. B. LEISHMAN: The Monarch of Wit: An Analytical and Comparative Study of the Poetry of John Donne º △ TB/1258
J. B. LEISHMAN: Themes and Variations in Shakespeare's Sonnets º △ TB/1259
ROGER SHERMAN LOOMIS: The Development of Arthurian Romance △ TB/1167
JOHN STUART MILL: On Bentham and Coleridge. △ Introduction by F. R. Leavis TB/1070
KENNETH B. MURDOCK: Literature and Theology in Colonial New England TB/99
SAMUEL PEPYS: The Diary of Samuel Pepys. º Edited by O. F. Morshead. Illus. by Ernest Shepard TB/1007
ST.-JOHN PERSE: Seamarks TB/2002
V. DE S. PINTO: Crisis in English Poetry, 1880-1940 º TB/1260
ROBERT PREYER, Ed.: Victorian Literature TB/1302
GEORGE SANTAYANA: Interpretations of Poetry and Religion § TB/9
C. K. STEAD: The New Poetic: Yeats to Eliot △ TB/1263
HEINRICH STRAUMANN: American Literature in the Twentieth Century. △ Third Edition, Revised TB/1168
PAGET TOYNBEE: Dante Alighieri: His Life and Works. Edited with Intro. by Charles S. Singleton TB/1206
DOROTHY VAN GHENT: The English Novel: Form and Function TB/1050
BASIL WILLEY: Nineteenth Century Studies: Coleridge to Matthew Arnold º △ TB/1261
BASIL WILLEY: More Nineteenth Century Studies: A Group of Honest Doubters º △ TB/1262
RAYMOND WILLIAMS: Culture and Society, 1780-1950 º △ TB/1252
RAYMOND WILLIAMS: The Long Revolution. º △ Revised Edition TB/1253
MORTON DAUWEN ZABEL, Editor: Literary Opinion in America
Vol. I TB/3013; Vol. II TB/3014

Myth, Symbol & Folklore

MIRCEA ELIADE: Cosmos and History: The Myth of the Eternal Return § TB/2050
MIRCEA ELIADE: Rites and Symbols of Initiation: The Mysteries of Birth and Rebirth § △ TB/1236
THEODOR H. GASTER: Thespis: Ritual, Myth and Drama in the Ancient Near East △ TB/1281

C. G. JUNG & C. KERÉNYI: Essays on a Science of Mythology: *The Myths of the Divine Child and the Divine Maiden* TB/2014

DORA & ERWIN PANOFSKY : Pandora's Box: *The Changing Aspects of a Mythical Symbol.* △ *Revised edition. Illus.* TB/2021

ERWIN PANOFSKY: Studies in Iconology: *Humanistic Themes in the Art of the Renaissance.* △ *180 illustrations* TB/1077

JEAN SEZNEC: The Survival of the Pagan Gods: *The Mythological Tradition and its Place in Renaissance Humanism and Art.* △ *108 illustrations* TB/2004

HELLMUT WILHELM: Change: *Eight Lectures on the I Ching* △ TB/2019

HEINRICH ZIMMER: Myths and Symbols in Indian Art and Civilization. △ *70 illustrations* TB/2005

Philosophy

G. E. M. ANSCOMBE: An Introduction to Wittgenstein's Tractatus. ○ △ *Second Edition, Revised* TB/1210

HENRI BERGSON: Time and Free Will: *An Essay on the Immediate Data of Consciousness* ○ △ TB/1021

H. J. BLACKHAM: Six Existentialist Thinkers: *Kierkegaard, Nietzsche, Jaspers, Marcel, Heidegger, Sartre* ○ △ TB/1002

CRANE BRINTON: Nietzsche. *New Preface, Bibliography and Epilogue by the Author* TB/1197

MARTIN BUBER: The Knowledge of Man. △ *Ed. with an Intro. by Maurice Friedman. Trans. by Maurice Friedman and Ronald Gregor Smith* TB/135

ERNST CASSIRER: The Individual and the Cosmos in Renaissance Philosophy. △ *Translated with an Introduction by Mario Domandi* TB/1097

ERNST CASSIRER: Rousseau, Kant and Goethe. *Introduction by Peter Gay* TB/1092

FREDERICK COPLESTON: Medieval Philosophy ○ △ TB/376

F. M. CORNFORD: Principium Sapientiae: *A Study of the Origins of Greek Philosophical Thought. Edited by W. K. C. Guthrie* TB/1213

F. M. CORNFORD: From Religion to Philosophy: *A Study in the Origins of Western Speculation* § TB/20

WILFRID DESAN: The Tragic Finale: *An Essay on the Philosophy of Jean-Paul Sartre* TB/1030

A. P. D'ENTRÈVES: Natural Law: *An Historical Survey* △ TB/1223

MARVIN FARBER: The Aims of Phenomenology: *The Motives, Methods, and Impact of Husserl's Thought* TB/1291

MARVIN FARBER: Phenomenology and Existence: *Towards a Philosophy within Nature* TB/1295

HERBERT FINGARETTE: The Self in Transformation: *Psychoanalysis, Philosophy and the Life of the Spirit* ¶ TB/1177

PAUL FRIEDLÄNDER: Plato: *An Introduction* △ TB/2017

J. GLENN GRAY: The Warriors: *Reflections on Men in Battle. Intro. by Hannah Arendt* TB/1294

WILLIAM CHASE GREENE: Moira: *Fate, Good, and Evil in Greek Thought* TB/1104

W. K. C. GUTHRIE: The Greek Philosophers: *From Thales to Aristotle* ○ △ TB/1008

G. W. F. HEGEL: The Phenomenology of Mind ○ △ TB/1303

F. H. HEINEMANN: Existentialism and the Modern Predicament △ TB/28

ISAAC HUSIK: A History of Medieval Jewish Philosophy JP/3

EDMUND HUSSERL: Phenomenology and the Crisis of Philosophy. *Translated with an Introduction by Quentin Lauer* TB/1170

IMMANUEL KANT: The Doctrine of Virtue, *being Part II of the Metaphysic of Morals. Trans. with Notes & Intro. by Mary J. Gregor. Foreword by H. J. Paton* TB/110

IMMANUEL KANT: Groundwork of the Metaphysic of Morals. *Trans. & analyzed by H. J. Paton* TB/1159

IMMANUEL KANT: Lectures on Ethics. § △ *Introduction by Lewis W. Beck* TB/105

IMMANUEL KANT: Religion Within the Limits of Reason Alone. § *Intro. by T. M. Greene & J. Silber* TB/67

QUENTIN LAUER: Phenomenology: *Its Genesis and Prospect* TB/1169

MAURICE MANDELBAUM: The Problem of Historical Knowledge: *An Answer to Relativism. New Preface by the Author* TB/1338

GABRIEL MARCEL: Being and Having: *An Existential Diary.* △ *Intro. by James Collins* TB/310

GEORGE A. MORGAN: What Nietzsche Means TB/1198

H. J. PATON: The Categorical Imperative: *A Study in Kant's Moral Philosophy* △ TB/1325

PHILO, SAADYA GAON, & JEHUDA HALEVI: Three Jewish Philosophers. *Ed. by Hans Lewy, Alexander Altmann, &Isaak Heinemann* TB/813

MICHAEL POLANYI: Personal Knowledge: *Towards a Post-Critical Philosophy* △ TB/1158

WILLARD VAN ORMAN QUINE: Elementary Logic: *Revised Edition* TB/577

WILLARD VAN ORMAN QUINE: From a Logical Point of View: *Logico-Philosophical Essays* TB/566

BERTRAND RUSSELL et al.: The Philosophy of Bertrand Russell. *Edited by Paul Arthur Schilpp* Vol. I TB/1095; Vol. II TB/1096

L. S. STEBBING: A Modern Introduction to Logic △ TB/538

ALFRED NORTH WHITEHEAD: Process and Reality: *An Essay in Cosmology* △ TB/1033

PHILIP P. WIENER: Evolution and the Founders of Pragmatism. *Foreword by John Dewey* TB/1212

WILHELM WINDELBAND: A History of Philosophy Vol. I: *Greek, Roman, Medieval* TB/38 Vol. II: *Renaissance, Enlightenment, Modern* TB/39

LUDWIG WITTGENSTEIN: The Blue and Brown Books ○ TB/1211

Political Science & Government

JEREMY BENTHAM: The Handbook of Political Fallacies: *Introduction by Crane Brinton* TB/1069

C. E. BLACK: The Dynamics of Modernization: *A Study in Comparative History* TB/1321

KENNETH E. BOULDING: Conflict and Defense: *A General Theory* TB/3024

CRANE BRINTON: English Political Thought in the Nineteenth Century TB/1071

ROBERT CONQUEST: Power and Policy in the USSR: *The Study of Soviet Dynastics* △ TB/1307

EDWARD S. CORWIN: American Constitutional History: *Essays edited by Alpheus T. Mason and Gerald Garvey* TB/1136

ROBERT DAHL & CHARLES E. LINDBLOM: Politics, Economics, and Welfare: *Planning and Politico-Economic Systems Resolved into Basic Social Processes* TB/3037

JOHN NEVILLE FIGGIS: The Divine Right of Kings. *Introduction by G. R. Elton* TB/1191

JOHN NEVILLE FIGGIS: Political Thought from Gerson to Grotius: 1414-1625: *Seven Studies. Introduction by Garrett Mattingly* TB/1032

F. L. GANSHOF: Feudalism △ TB/1058

G. P. GOOCH: English Democratic Ideas in the Seventeenth Century TB/1006

J. H. HEXTER: More's Utopia: *The Biography of an Idea. New Epilogue by the Author* TB/1195

SIDNEY HOOK: Reason, Social Myths and Democracy △ TB/1237

ROBERT H. JACKSON: The Supreme Court in the American System of Government △ TB/1106

DAN N. JACOBS, Ed.: The New Communist Manifesto *and Related Documents. Third Edition, Revised* TB/1078

DAN N. JACOBS & HANS BAERWALD, Eds.: Chinese Communism: *Selected Documents* TB/3031

HANS KOHN: Political Ideologies of the 20th Century
TB/1277
ROY C. MACRIDIS, Ed.: Political Parties: *Contemporary Trends and Ideas* TB/1322
ROBERT GREEN MC CLOSKEY: American Conservatism in the Age of Enterprise, 1865-1910 TB/1137
KINGSLEY MARTIN: French Liberal Thought in the Eighteenth Century: *Political Ideas from Bayle to Condorcet* △ TB/1114
ROBERTO MICHELS: First Lectures in Political Sociology. *Edited by Alfred de Grazia* ¶ ° TB/1224
JOHN STUART MILL: On Bentham and Coleridge. △ *Introduction by F. R. Leavis* TB/1070
BARRINGTON MOORE, JR.: Political Power and Social Theory: *Seven Studies* ¶ TB/1221
BARRINGTON MOORE, JR.: Soviet Politics—The Dilemma of Power: *The Role of Ideas in Social Change* ¶
TB/1222
BARRINGTON MOORE, JR.: Terror and Progress—USSR: *Some Sources of Change and Stability in the Soviet Dictatorship* ¶ TB/1266
JOHN B. MORRALL: Political Thought in Medieval Times △ TB/1076
JOHN PLAMENATZ: German Marxism and Russian Communism. ° △ *New Preface by the Author* TB/1189
KARL R. POPPER: The Open Society and Its Enemies △
Vol. I: *The Spell of Plato* TB/1101
Vol. II: *The High Tide of Prophecy: Hegel, Marx and the Aftermath* TB/1102
JOHN P. ROCHE, Ed.: American Political Thought: *From Jefferson to Progressivism* TB/1332
HENRI DE SAINT-SIMON: Social Organization, The Science of Man, and Other Writings. *Edited and Translated by Felix Markham* TB/1152
CHARLES I. SCHOTTLAND, Ed.: The Welfare State ¶ TB/1323
JOSEPH A. SCHUMPETER: Capitalism, Socialism and Democracy △ TB/3008
BENJAMIN I. SCHWARTZ: Chinese Communism and the Rise of Mao TB/1308
CHARLES H. SHINN: Mining Camps: *A Study in American Frontier Government.* ‡ *Edited by Rodman W. Paul*
TB/3062
PETER WOLL, Ed.: Public Administration and Policy: *Selected Essays* TB/1284

Psychology

ALFRED ADLER: The Individual Psychology of Alfred Adler. △ *Edited by Heinz L. and Rowena R. Ansbacher*
TB/1154
ALFRED ADLER: Problems of Neurosis. *Introduction by Heinz L. Ansbacher* TB/1145
ARTHUR BURTON & ROBERT E. HARRIS, Eds.: Clinical Studies of Personality
Vol. I TB/3075; Vol. II TB/3076
HADLEY CANTRIL: The Invasion from Mars: *A Study in the Psychology of Panic* ¶ TB/1282
HERBERT FINGARETTE: The Self in Transformation: *Psychoanalysis, Philosophy and the Life of the Spirit* ¶
TB/1177
SIGMUND FREUD: On Creativity and the Unconscious: *Papers on the Psychology of Art, Literature, Love, Religion.* § △ *Intro. by Benjamin Nelson* TB/45
C. JUDSON HERRICK: The Evolution of Human Nature
TB/545
WILLIAM JAMES: Psychology: *The Briefer Course. Edited with an Intro. by Gordon Allport* TB/1034
C. G. JUNG: Psychological Reflections △ TB/2001
C. G. JUNG: Symbols of Transformation: *An Analysis of the Prelude to a Case of Schizophrenia.* △ *Illus.*
Vol. I TB/2009; Vol. II TB/2010
C. G. JUNG & C. KERÉNYI: Essays on a Science of Mythology: *The Myths of the Divine Child and the Divine Maiden* TB/2014

KARL MENNINGER: Theory of Psychoanalytic Technique
TB/1144
ERICH NEUMANN: Amor and Psyche: *The Psychic Development of the Feminine* △ TB/2012
ERICH NEUMANN: The Archetypal World of Henry Moore. △ *107 illus.* TB/2020
ERICH NEUMANN: The Origins and History of Consciousness △ Vol. I *Illus.* TB/2007; Vol. II TB/2008
RALPH BARTON PERRY: The Thought and Character of William James: *Briefer Version* TB/1156
JOHN H. SCHAAR: Escape from Authority: *The Perspectives of Erich Fromm* TB/1155
MUZAFER SHERIF: The Psychology of Social Norms
TB/3072

Sociology

JACQUES BARZUN: Race: *A Study in Superstition. Revised Edition* TB/1172
BERNARD BERELSON, Ed.: The Behavioral Sciences Today
TB/1127
ABRAHAM CAHAN: The Rise of David Levinsky: *A documentary novel of social mobility in early twentieth century America. Intro. by John Higham* TB/1028
KENNETH B. CLARK: Dark Ghetto: *Dilemmas of Social Power. Foreword by Gunnar Myrdal* TB/1317
LEWIS A. COSER, Ed.: Political Sociology TB/1293
ALLISON DAVIS & JOHN DOLLARD: Children of Bondage: *The Personality Development of Negro Youth in the Urban South* ¶ TB/3049
ST. CLAIR DRAKE & HORACE R. CAYTON: Black Metropolis: *A Study of Negro Life in a Northern City.* △ *Revised and Enlarged. Intro. by Everett C. Hughes*
Vol. I TB/1086; Vol. II TB/1087
EMILE DURKHEIM et al.: Essays on Sociology and Philosophy: *With Analyses of Durkheim's Life and Work.* ¶ *Edited by Kurt H. Wolff* TB/1151
LEON FESTINGER, HENRY W. RIECKEN & STANLEY SCHACHTER: When Prophecy Fails: *A Social and Psychological Account of a Modern Group that Predicted the Destruction of the World* ¶ TB/1132
ALVIN W. GOULDNER: Wildcat Strike: *A Study in Worker-Management Relationships* ¶ TB/1176
CÉSAR GRAÑA: Modernity and Its Discontents: *French Society and the French Man of Letters in the Nineteenth Century* ¶ TB/1318
FRANCIS J. GRUND: Aristocracy in America: *Social Class in the Formative Years of the New Nation* △ TB/1001
KURT LEWIN: Field Theory in Social Science: *Selected Theoretical Papers.* ¶ △ *Edited with a Foreword by Dorwin Cartwright* TB/1135
R. M. MAC IVER: Social Causation TB/1153
ROBERT K. MERTON, LEONARD BROOM, LEONARD S. COTTRELL, JR., Editors: Sociology Today: *Problems and Prospects* ¶ Vol. I TB/1173; Vol. II TB/1174
ROBERTO MICHELS: First Lectures in Political Sociology. *Edited by Alfred de Grazia* ¶ ° TB/1224
BARRINGTON MOORE, JR.: Political Power and Social Theory: *Seven Studies* ¶ TB/1221
BARRINGTON MOORE, JR.: Soviet Politics—The Dilemma of Power: *The Role of Ideas in Social Change* ¶
TB/1222
TALCOTT PARSONS & EDWARD A. SHILS, Editors: Toward a General Theory of Action: *Theoretical Foundations for the Social Sciences* TB/1083
ARNOLD ROSE: The Negro in America: *The Condensed Version of Gunnar Myrdal's An American Dilemma*
TB/3048
GEORGE ROSEN: Madness in Society: *Chapters in the Historical Sociology of Mental Illness.* ¶ *Preface by Benjamin Nelson* TB/1337
KURT SAMUELSSON: Religion and Economic Action: *A Critique of Max Weber's The Protestant Ethic and the Spirit of Capitalism.* ¶ ° *Trans. by E. G. French. Ed. with Intro. by D. C. Coleman* TB/1131

RELIGION

Ancient & Classical

Biblical Thought & Literature

The Judaic Tradition

Christianity: General

Christianity: Origins & Early Development

Oriental Religions: Far Eastern, Near Eastern

TOR ANDRAE: Mohammed: *The Man and His Faith* △
TB/62
EDWARD CONZE: Buddhism: *Its Essence and Development.* ° △ Foreword by Arthur Waley TB/58
EDWARD CONZE et al., Editors: Buddhist Texts Through the Ages △ TB/113
ANANDA COOMARASWAMY: Buddha and the Gospel of Buddhism. △ *Illus.* TB/119
H. G. CREEL: Confucius and the Chinese Way △ TB/63
FRANKLIN EDGERTON, Trans. & Ed.: The Bhagavad Gita TB/115
SWAMI NIKHILANANDA, Trans. & Ed.: The Upanishads: *A One-Volume Abridgment* △ TB/114
HELLMUT WILHELM: Change: *Eight Lectures on the I Ching* △ TB/2019

Philosophy of Religion

NICOLAS BERDYAEV: The Beginning and the End § △ TB/14
NICOLAS BERDYAEV: Christian Existentialism: *A Berdyaev Synthesis.* △ Ed. by Donald A. Lowrie TB/130
NICOLAS BERDYAEV: The Destiny of Man △ TB/61
RUDOLF BULTMANN: History and Eschatology: *The Presence of Eternity* ° TB/91
RUDOLF BULTMANN AND FIVE CRITICS: Kerygma and Myth: *A Theological Debate* △ TB/80
RUDOLF BULTMANN and KARL KUNDSIN: Form Criticism: *Two Essays on New Testament Research.* △ Translated by Frederick C. Grant TB/96
MIRCEA ELIADE: Myths, Dreams, and Mysteries: *The Encounter between Contemporary Faiths and Archaic Realities* § △ ° TB/1320
MIRCEA ELIADE: The Sacred and the Profane TB/81
LUDWIG FEUERBACH: The Essence of Christianity. § *Introduction by Karl Barth. Foreword by H. Richard Niebuhr* TB/11
ÉTIENNE GILSON: The Spirit of Thomism TB/313
ADOLF HARNACK: What is Christianity? § △ *Introduction by Rudolf Bultmann* TB/17
FRIEDRICH HEGEL: On Christianity: *Early Theological Writings. Ed. by R. Kroner and T. M. Knox* TB/79
KARL HEIM: Christian Faith and Natural Science △ TB/16
IMMANUEL KANT: Religion Within the Limits of Reason Alone. § *Intro. by T. M. Greene & J. Silber* TB/67
K. E. KIRK: The Vision of God: *The Christian Doctrine of the Summum Bonum* § △ TB/137
JOHN MACQUARRIE: An Existentialist Theology: *A Comparison of Heidegger and Bultmann.* ° △ Preface by Rudolf Bultmann TB/125
PAUL RAMSEY, Ed.: Faith and Ethics: *The Theology of H. Richard Niebuhr* TB/129
EUGEN ROSENSTOCK-HUESSY: The Christian Future *or the Modern Mind Outrun. Intro. by Harold Stahmer* TB/143
PIERRE TEILHARD DE CHARDIN: The Divine Milieu ° △ TB/384
PIERRE TEILHARD DE CHARDIN: The Phenomenon of Man ° △ TB/383

Religion, Culture & Society

JOSEPH L. BLAU, Ed.: Cornerstones of Religious Freedom in America: *Selected Basic Documents, Court Decisions and Public Statements. Revised and Enlarged Edition* TB/118
WILLIAM A. CLEBSCH & CHARLES R. JAEKLE: Pastoral Care in Historical Perspective: *An Essay with Exhibits. New Preface by the Authors* TB/148
C. C. GILLISPIE: Genesis and Geology: *The Decades before Darwin* § TB/51
KYLE HASELDEN: The Racial Problem in Christian Perspective TB/116

WALTER KAUFMANN, Ed.: Religion from Tolstoy to Camus: *Basic Writings on Religious Truth and Morals. Enlarged Edition* TB/123
KENNETH B. MURDOCK: Literature and Theology in Colonial New England TB/99
H. RICHARD NIEBUHR: Christ and Culture △ TB/3
H. RICHARD NIEBUHR: The Kingdom of God in America TB/49
R. B. PERRY: Puritanism and Democracy TB/1138
PAUL PFUETZE: Self, Society, Existence: *Human Nature and Dialogue in the Thought of George Herbert Mead and Martin Buber* TB/1059
WALTER RAUSCHENBUSCH: Christianity and the Social Crisis. ‡ Edited by Robert D. Cross TB/3059
KURT SAMUELSSON: Religion and Economic Action: *A Critique of Max Weber's The Protestant Ethic and the Spirit of Capitalism* ¶ ° △ Trans. by E. G. French. Ed. with Intro. by D. C. Coleman TB/1131
TIMOTHY L. SMITH: Revivalism and Social Reform: *American Protestantism on the Eve of the Civil War* △ TB/1229

NATURAL SCIENCES AND MATHEMATICS

Biological Sciences

CHARLOTTE AUERBACH: The Science of Genetics Σ △ TB/568
JOHN TYLER BONNER: The Ideas of Biology. Σ △ *Illus.* TB/570
A. J. CAIN: Animal Species and their Evolution. △ *Illus.* TB/519
W. E. LE GROS CLARK: The Antecedents of Man: *An Introduction to Evolution of the Primates.* ° △ *Illus.* TB/559
W. H. DOWDESWELL: Animal Ecology. △ *Illus.* TB/543
W. H. DOWDESWELL: The Mechanism of Evolution. △ *Illus.* TB/527
R. W. GERARD: Unresting Cells. *Illus.* TB/541
J. E. MORTON: Molluscs: *An Introduction to Their Form and Functions. Illus.* TB/529
P. M. SHEPPARD: Natural Selection and Heredity. △ *Illus.* TB/528
EDMUND W. SINNOTT: Cell and Psyche: *The Biology of Purpose* TB/546
C. H. WADDINGTON: The Nature of Life: *The Main Problems and Trends in Modern Biology* △ TB/580

Chemistry

J. R. PARTINGTON: A Short History of Chemistry. △ *Illus.* TB/522

Communication Theory

J. R. PIERCE: Symbols, Signals and Noise: *The Nature and Process of Communication* △ TB/574

Geography

R. E. COKER: This Great and Wide Sea: *An Introduction to Oceanography and Marine Biology. Illus.* TB/551
F. K. HARE: The Restless Atmosphere △ TB/560

History of Science

MARIE BOAS: The Scientific Renaissance, 1450-1630 ° △ TB/583
W. DAMPIER, Ed.: Readings in the Literature of Science. *Illus.* TB/512
A. HUNTER DUPREE: Science in the Federal Government: *A History of Policies and Activities to 1940* △ TB/573
ALEXANDRE KOYRÉ: From the Closed World to the Infinite Universe: *Copernicus, Kepler, Galileo, Newton, etc.* △ TB/31

11